T H E
Knowledge
FACTORY

Designed and produced by
Aladdin Books Ltd
28 Percy Street
London W1P 0LD

First published in the United States by
Copper Beech Books, an imprint of
The Millbrook Press
2 Old New Milford Road
Brookfield, Connecticut 06804

Editor:
Kate Gillett

Cover design:
David West Children's Book Design

Printed in Italy

Some of the material in this
book was previously published
in other Aladdin Books' series.

Library of Congress Cataloging-in-Publication Data
The Knowledge Factory : a lot of facts about a lot of things/
editors: Alex Edmonds and Kate Gillett.
p. cm.
Summary: A collection of interesting facts
on topics that young people would like to know about
from "Spies for the Revolution" to "What if a bat couldn't hear?"
ISBN (lib. bdg.) 0-7613-0520-3
1. Handbooks, vade-mecums, etc. -- Juvenile literature.
[1. Handbooks, manuals, etc.] I. Edmonds, Alex. II Gillett, Kate.
AG105.K63 1996   96-16148
031.02--dc20   CIP
                                                          AC

THE
Knowledge
FACTORY

Copper Beech Books
Brookfield, Connecticut

CONTENTS

Technology

Geography and the Environment

INTRODUCTION

The *Know*ledge *Fact*ory is no ordinary book – it includes absolutely everything you ever wanted to know. All the information, topics, illustrations, and pictures you could possibly want, right at your fingertips. The *Know*ledge *Fact*ory has a clearly defined contents and an easy-to-use index. It allows you to access various information at the turn of a page. You can pick it up anytime of day, and browse through it at your leisure. Your friends will be astounded and impressed with your great knowledge of almost every subject; from animals, to the latest advances in space technology.

Animals

Animal life is a massive and very complex subject. There are thousands of different amazing species within each animal group. All animals have evolved through time and have adapted to their particular environments in many extraordinary ways! For example, what if giraffes had short necks or if an elephant didn't have a trunk? These questions, and many more, are answered in this book. You can learn everything you need to know about your cat, dog, or bird; even how spiders trap their prey with spun silk and how beetles have survived through the ages.

Art and Music

If you are (or even if you're not!) a budding young artist or musician, you can read up on the various instrument "families" and how each instrument works. You can learn how to paint yourself with the art of self-portraiture; and if you are an avid reader of the comics you can create your own cartoon strips.

Geography and the Environment

The Earth is an amazing and mysterious place. In this day and age, environmental and geographical topics are very important in our society. This book covers many important areas such as saving energy and recycling. After reading these topics you will be able to tell your friends about these subjects, and each of you can play a part in helping the Earth. You will answer questions like, what if the Earth stood still, and what happens when a volcano erupts?

Prehistory

Prehistory is an exciting topic for everyone. There are many things we can learn from studying the past, such as; what are our origins? How did the dinosaurs become extinct, and what did the first primates look like? When looking at prehistoric times we can see how the world today came about, through evolution. We are able to learn about our lives now, compared to the first humans. How they hunted with their primitive, yet very inventive tools – and also used them to fight off the vicious saber-toothed tiger!

Technology

The enormous technological advances of the 20th century have radically changed the way we live. What would people do without cars? Would there be no computer age if the microchip had not been invented? In the last half of this century, humans have been able to exceed the boundaries of the Earth. We have landed on the moon, sent probes to explore the farthest planets in our solar system, and built a reusable spacecraft, which is able to launch valuable satellites into the darkness of space. The technological advances in medicine have saved many lives, and helped rebuild many limbs with artificial implants.

Science

Science covers a broad range of material – from the study of UFOs and aliens to the multiple parts of the brain. We can learn about the effects of sunlight on the Earth and what we would do if the sun went out and left us in complete darkness! Scientific discoveries are the stepping stones for the future, *and* the link to the past.

History

Who was Robin Hood? Was he a real person, or just an infamous character created by some people sitting around a campfire? In this book you can discover the answer for yourself. You will explore medieval castles and ride out west with the North American cowboys and cowgirls. You may even encounter a pirate or two as you sail through the pages!

In the end...The *Know*ledge *Fact*ory has everything you could ever want to know. It will take you on an exciting journey through the world of knowledge. If you wish to find a specific topic check out the concise contents list and use the helpful index at the back of the book. With brilliant pictures and fun-to-read text, it gives you all of those weird and wonderful *facts* you always needed to *know*.

ROBIN HOOD

Who has not heard of Robin Hood? He has acquired such fame that today all kind-hearted bandits are known as "Robin Hoods." And yet no one even knows who the real Robin Hood was, or even if he existed at all.

A document of 1239 mentions a Yorkshireman described as "Robert Hood, outlaw." Tales of Robin the outlaw were circulating by the mid-13th century, and the first written reference appears in the poem *Vision of Piers Plowman* (1378).

In the early poems, printed more than a century later, Robin is more like a real medieval bandit. He kills bloodily and enjoys it. Slaying Guy of Gisborne, he sticks his head on the end of his bow! But with time, as characters and adventures were added (*above*) by writers like Sir Walter Scott (as in the novel *Ivanhoe)*, Robin was transformed into the romantic figure we recognize today.

THE **MERRY MEN.** Robin Hood stories became popular because they satisfy people's needs – ordinary men and women can triumph over privileged and corrupt masters.

Robin's adventures have been turned into dozens of films (*above*), most of which have little to do with the rough life of the medieval bandit!

The People's Champion?

In medieval poems about Robin Hood (below), there is little about robbing the rich and giving to the poor. Robin is far more concerned with fighting the evil sheriff's men and poaching the King's deer.
Medieval bandits might wear woolen breeches and a rough tunic – certainly not the dainty green tights of Hollywood's Merry Men!

SAWNEY BEAN, BANDIT CANNIBAL

By no means did all outlaws become heroes, and certainly not Sawney Bean (1394–1437), who lived in a set of damp caves (*left*) in western Scotland. By robbing travelers on the coastal road near Ballantrae, Sawney and his partner grew rich in everything except what mattered – food. Faced with starvation, they took to eating their victims (*above*)!

When it was finally discovered, the cave was sheltering a clan of cannibal children. The whole family was later executed in Edinburgh.

LONGBOW HOTSHOTS

Today, Robin Hood is famous as a deadly shot with the longbow. In fact, when the Robin Hood legend began, longbows were rarely used. They begin to appear in legal records as a favorite weapon of robbers from the mid- 13th century onward. Later, they played a vital role in England's victories at Crécy (1346) and Agincourt (1415).

The longbow was much cheaper than a crossbow (*left*). It was also quicker and easier to use, too, but needed great skill to be used effectively.

Welsh archers kept their rear foot bare to prevent slipping (right). They could pierce armor at 100 paces with a well-aimed arrow.

WHAT IF GIRAFFES HAD SHORT NECKS?

Some do! The okapi is a type of giraffe found in the tropical rain forests of central Africa. Unlike its taller relative, the giraffe of the African plains, all of its food is within easy reach among the lush jungle vegetation. As a result, it does not need the long neck of the plains giraffe. The tree branches of the African plains are found well above the ground, so the giraffe needs a long neck to stretch up and eat the leaves that can be over 19 ft (6 m) high. The giraffe's unique feature has evolved over years of evolution, so that it is now perfectly suited to its way of life.

Designed by committee

The odd shape of the giraffe, with its big head, long neck, long front legs, and short back legs, has often been described as an animal put together by a committee. However, the peculiar body has evolved naturally over time. The result may look odd, but it works.

Lookout post

Not only does the giraffe's tall neck allow it to reach the highest branches, it lets it see over long distances. High above the grassy plains, the giraffe can spot danger, such as a bush fire or a prowling hunter, or even new trees to eat, from several miles away.

Okapi

All creatures great and small

Just as the neck of the giraffe has developed over millions of years, so nature has created a whole host of different mammals. There are currently over 4,000 species of mammals, ranging from enormous whales to tiny mice, and from peaceful cows to aggressive tigers. Each of these has developed its own method of survival, involving a bizarre array of physical features. These include the hump of a camel, the stripes of a zebra, or the trunk of an elephant. All of these strange-looking features have evolved to help the animal survive in its environment.

The long and short of it
A giraffe, like all other mammals, including the okapi, has only seven vertebrae in its neck. However, these neck bones are greatly elongated (stretched), allowing the giraffe's head to stand way above the ground.

Giraffe

What if dinosaurs were still alive?

Then we would not be here! Mammals and dinosaurs first appeared at the same time, about 200 million years ago. However, it was the dinosaurs who were first to develop and rule the Earth. Mammals could not compete, and they had to be very small to survive. Then, mysteriously, the dinosaurs died out about 65 million years ago, and mammals were able to develop into their many and various forms (see above). If the dinosaurs were still here, then the largest mammal would probably be about the size of a cat.

WARPLANES

In less than a century warplanes have developed beyond recognition. The first dogfight between two aircraft took place in October 1914. Since then, air power has been decisive in almost every major war. Today's warplanes carry a wide variety of armaments, including fast-firing cannons, and sophisticated guided missiles and bombs. Some planes, such as the Stealth fighter and the F-15 Eagle, are developed for one purpose only. "Multi-role" warplanes are designed to be able to carry out different functions by modifying a basic aircraft frame.

Fokker Dr-1 Triplane, maximum speed 103 mph (165 km/h)

World War I pilot dressed in warm clothes against the cold

Early warplanes

World War I planes were maneuverable but had few technological aids. The pilot relied on his own flying skills. The top flying ace was German pilot Manfred von Richthofen, known as the "Red Baron," above. His planes – an Albatros, and later a Fokker Triplane – were painted scarlet. Official war records show that he shot down 80 enemy planes, before being killed in 1918.

World War II

Different planes had different roles during World War II. Fighters were small and fast, but could not carry many armaments or fly long distances. Bombers such as the Boeing B-29 Superfortress shown here were bigger, with enough fuel for long flights. But they were slower, and vulnerable to enemy fighters.

F-117A Stealth Fighter

The coming of Stealth
Ground-based radar systems can detect most enemy planes, unless they are flying very low or between hills. So plane-designers developed so-called stealth technology. The Stealth plane's shape – its curves, edges, and surfaces – are designed to absorb or spread out radar beams, so that they do not reflect back to the receiver. Special paints and surface coatings help this process. Stealth aircraft are designed to be almost invisible on radar, so they can sneak up on the enemy unseen.

The Gulf Conflict of 1991 was won in the air by planes such as the McDonnell Douglas F-15 Eagle (below). It is a large twin-engined air superiority fighter, specialized to destroy enemy planes in flight.

Multi-role or specialist?
In recent years, the distinction between small, fast fighters and big, slow bombers has lessened. But there are still specialist warplanes and multi-role craft. The Mig G-25 Foxbat is specialized as an interceptor, designed to tackle enemy bombers at high altitudes. The Panavia Tornado, below, a multrole aircraft, can carry a variety of weapons at 1,455 mph (2,330 km/h).

Quick escape
If a plane is hit by enemy fire or develops a fault, the pilot has a chance to eject. Pulling a lever opens the cockpit canopy and sets off a small explosive charge, which blasts the seat clear of the plane. A parachute opens, and the pilot sinks to safety.

BLOOD

No matter how frightened the brain is, it never faints at the sight of blood, because blood brings life. Blood carries vital oxygen, energy in the form of blood sugars, nourishing nutrients for growth and repair, the chemical messengers called hormones, and dozens of other essential substances. So smile and be thankful for this red, endlessly flowing river of life.

A heavy ball

BLOOD GROUPS

All blood is not the same. Each body has its own blood group. Doctors found this when they tried transfusing blood (opposite), and often failed. One set of blood groups is A, B, AB, or O. Another is Rh positive or negative, named because it was discovered in rhesus monkeys.

Red blood cell

Platelet

White blood cell

SELF-SEALING SYSTEM

If a blood vessel springs a small leak, it soon seals and mends itself, by forming a sticky scab. Some car radiators do the same (with water).

Injury causes leak

Scab seals leak

BLOOD CELLS

Red cells carry oxygen. White cells fight germs. Platelets help blood to clot.

THREE TUBES FOR BLOOD

Big arteries carry blood from the heart. They divide into capillaries, which are tiny. These join into veins, and return blood to the heart.

Capillary

Main artery

Small artery

Arteriole

O_2 and nutrients out

CO_2 and wastes in

CAROTID ARTERY
This tube brings blood to the face, head and brain.

JUGULAR VEIN
It takes head and brain blood back to the heart.

Subclavian artery and vein

Heart

Aorta (main artery)

Vena cava (main vein)

Iliac artery

Iliac vein

Femoral artery

Femoral vein

Saphenous vein

Tibial artery

Pedal arteries and veins

Venule

Main vein

SPARE-PART SURGERY

Been to the blood bank recently? Most people can safely give, or donate, a small amount of blood. It is treated and put in cold storage. It can be transfused into a person who is injured or ill and needs extra blood.

BODY-WIDE BLOOD

The body's eight or nine pints of blood flow around a network of arteries, capillaries, and veins, called the circulatory system. The regular pumping of the heart keeps blood on the move.

SPIES ON YOUR INSIDES

The angiogram is another type of X ray picture. It displays blood vessels that have been injected with a special chemical, which shows up and reveals any blocks or leaks in the tubes.

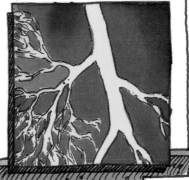

MEASURING EARTHQUAKES

The scientists who study the seismic waves released from the focus of an earthquake are called seismologists. Special measuring instruments, called seismographs, record the pattern of the seismic waves. Seismologists use these patterns to determine the strength and duration of an earthquake, as well as the amount of movement along a fault line. Taking readings at several different points on the earth's surface also helps them to pinpoint the exact location of the earthquake's focus.

Two different scales are used to measure the strength of an earthquake. The most common one is the Richter scale, devised by American seismologist, Charles Richter, in 1935. It calculates the magnitude of an earthquake from seismograph recordings that measure the amount of energy released. An increase of 1 point on the Richter scale means that an earthquake is 10 times stronger than one with the next value below. An earthquake measuring less than 5 on the Richter scale causes minimal damage, while a major earthquake measures 7 or more. The second scale is the Mercalli scale, which calculates the intensity of an earthquake by assessing the damage it causes.

I: Felt by only a very few people. II: Felt by a few, on upper floors.

III: Similar to a passing vehicle.
IV: Felt by many people indoors.

V: Buildings tremble and trees shake.
VI: Felt by all. Plaster cracks.

VII: Bricks loosen. Difficult to stand. VIII: Damage to weak structures.

Jagged tracings (right) are made as the seismograph records the movements of the ground during an earthquake. Scientists can distinguish between the primary, secondary, and surface waves.

IX: Pipes crack. Buildings collapse. X: Huge ground cracks. Landslides.

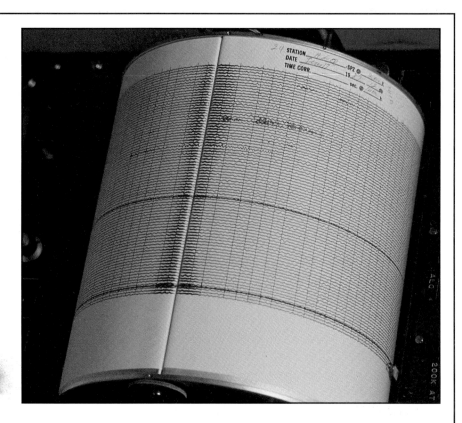

◄ **The Mercalli scale was invented in 1902 by Italian seismologist, Giuseppe Mercalli, and modified during the 1930s by American scientists. The scale describes effects that range from tiny swaying movements (I) to total devastation (XII).**

XI: Most buildings destroyed. *Tsunamis.* XII: Total destruction. Surface waves seen.

Seismographs

One type of seismograph records the horizontal movements of the earth, and the other type vertical movements. A weight is attached to a frame by a sensitive spring. As the ground trembles, the weight remains stationary but the frame moves and a pen records the movement on paper wrapped around a rotating drum. This recording is called a seismogram.

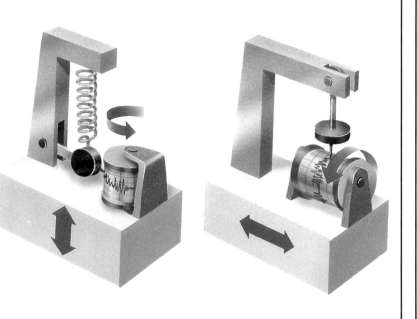

THE PREHISTORIC OCEANS

During the Mesozoic era (which includes the Triassic, the Jurassic, and the Cretaceous periods), the world's oceans were home to many large marine reptiles. Some of these creatures are familiar to us today, like the crocodiles and turtles. Others, like *Ichthyosaurus* (fish lizard), look similar to dolphins, but were reptiles not mammals. Marine reptiles were a very important part of the Mesozoic oceans, but they were not the only creatures to live in them. Some of the most familiar and plentiful fossils, such as the ammonites and "Devil's Toenail," lived in the seas at that time.

Snake stones

Ammonites were molluscs (animals with a shell), distantly related to snails and shellfish. They floated in the water, catching food with their tentacles. When people first found these coiled fossils, they thought that they were snakes that had been turned to stone.

A variety of molluscs including this entolium lived on the seabed.

Entolium

Ammonite

Plesiosaurs had long necks that they used to snatch small fish from the water.

Plesiosaurs

Layers of history

An age can be given to the rocks by looking at the fossils they contain, or by comparing sequences of layers of rock. The layers of rock are called strata. They were originally all more or less level, but movements of the Earth's crust have caused them to move about, sinking and rising.

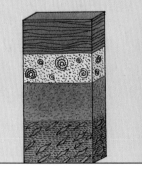
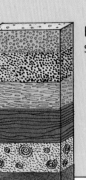

Rock strata

The chalk seas

During the Upper Cretaceous, the world's oceans contained micro-organisms that are now preserved as chalk rock. They lived in the surface of the sea, and when they died, their bodies sank to the seabed, forming chalk.

Ichthyosaur

Ichthyosaurs were dolphinlike reptiles that grew up to 50 feet in length.

Pliosaurs had very short necks, and skulls more adapted to kill larger animals, possibly even ichthyosaurs and plesiosaurs.

Pliosaur

Child scientist

In 1810, Mary Anning found her first whole ichthyosaur fossil at Lyme Regis in England (below). She was only eleven years old at the time. During her life, Mary Anning found many specimens, some of which she sold to British scientists. You may have heard the rhyme "She sells sea shells on the sea shore." which was possibly written about her.

Lyme Regis

Sea dragons

Since the discovery of their fossils, many attempts to produce reconstructions of marine reptiles have been made. Most of the earlier drawings (below) show seas full of fish, ammonites, and reptiles all in dramatic poses, or looking like Scotland's Loch Ness Monster, not at all like the modern, graceful images of them.

THE TELESCOPE AND MICROSCOPE

Do you believe that the Moon is made of green cheese, and that germs don't exist? If you had a telescope and a microscope, you could see for yourself. Telescopes look at outer space, to reveal the mysteries of the universe. Microscopes look into inner space, to show us what our own bodies are made of.

Many inventors and scientists fooled around with curved pieces of glass, called lenses. From the 1200s, lenses of various strengths were used in eyeglasses. Two lenses, specially shaped and put near to each other, make distant things look bigger and nearer. This was probably discovered by Hans Lippershey in Holland, in 1608.

Early spectacles

Within a year, the famous Galileo heard about the new invention, and made his own versions. They magnified up to 30 times. He scanned the dark skies and discovered mountains on the Moon, spots on the Sun, and moons going around Jupiter. He was the first real telescope-user.

Galileo

Types of telescopes
Christian Huygens, who worked on pendulum clocks, also invented better telescopes. In about 1757 a British optician, John Dollond, sandwiched two lenses closely together. These compound lenses gave better, clearer images.

In 1668 the great Isaac Newton designed a telescope with a curved mirror in place of one lens. This was called a reflector. Today, the biggest optical telescopes are reflectors. They look deep into space, to tell us about our Moon and Sun, the planets and stars, and the beginning of the universe.

REFRACTING LENS TELESCOPE

Isaac Newton

Telescope focused by moving extensions

— Extensions

Observatory

Eyepiece lens

GALILEO'S TELESCOPE

REFRACTING LENS TELESCOPE

NEWTONIAN REFLECTOR

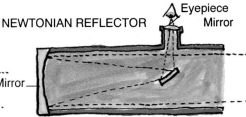

Eyepiece lens

Convex lens

Mirror

Eyepiece Mirror

THE TELESCOPE AND MICROSCOPE

Seeing the invisible

Around 1590, Dutch lens-maker Zacharias Janssen also put two lenses near to each other. He noticed that a tiny thing at one end looked much bigger from the other end – provided the lenses were the right distance apart.

Scientists showed an interest. They realized that a whole tiny world was waiting to be discovered. In 1655, Robert Hooke first used the word "cell" for a microscopic part of a living thing, in his book Micrographia, "Small Drawings." Hooke showed that tiny creatures such as ants had a heart, stomach and other body parts – just like bigger animals, but smaller!

LEEUWENHOEK'S MICROSCOPE

Lens

Object

Draper turned lens-maker

By the 1680s Anton van Leeuwenhoek, in Holland, made fascinating discoveries through the microscope. His homemade microscopes could magnify over 250 times. Through them he saw new wonders such as red blood cells, tiny one-celled creatures like amoebas, the eggs of fleas, insect eyes, and stacks of cells in the thinnest leaf.

Anton van Leeuwenhoek

After Leeuwenhoek, many people looked through microscopes. The science of microbiology began. Soon people were looking at germs, and working out how they invaded the body and caused diseases.

Microscopes became more powerful, with strong lights and changeable lenses that could magnify over one thousand times. Today, medicine and biology would be lost without microscopes.

MODERN MICROSCOPE

Eyepiece

Lens

Variety of lenses

Mirror

Light path

How they work

In a microscope, light waves from the tiny and nearby object are bent inwards by the convex (bulging) lens. They are bent again at the second lens, the eyepiece, so that you see a clear and enlarged view.

In a telescope, much the same happens. But the light waves come from far, far away, so they are parallel when they reach the telescope.

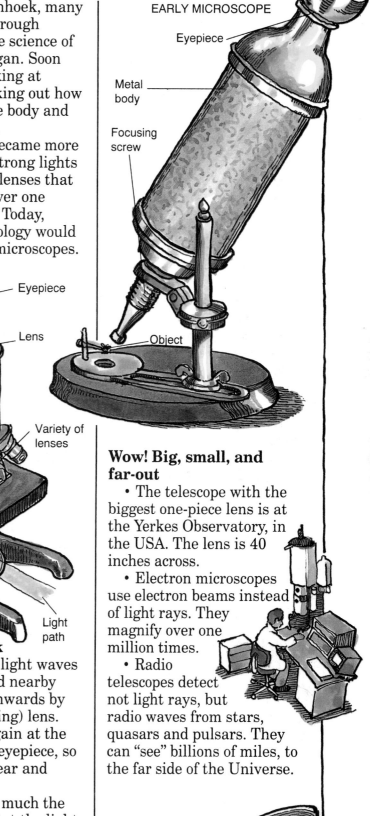

EARLY MICROSCOPE

Eyepiece

Metal body

Focusing screw

Object

Wow! Big, small, and far-out

• The telescope with the biggest one-piece lens is at the Yerkes Observatory, in the USA. The lens is 40 inches across.

• Electron microscopes use electron beams instead of light rays. They magnify over one million times.

• Radio telescopes detect not light rays, but radio waves from stars, quasars and pulsars. They can "see" billions of miles, to the far side of the Universe.

Radio telescopes

WHAT IS DROUGHT?

Drought is a long period with no rain or with much less rainfall than is normal for a particular area. Almost one-third of the land on Earth is prone to drought, which affects more than 600 million people.

During a drought, the soil becomes parched and cracked. The hard-baked surface cannot absorb any water, and so very little moisture is retained in the soil. The dry and dusty topsoil is worn away by wind and rain, leaving behind patches of barren land.

Drought is a natural disaster that can affect any country in the world. However, its effects are made much worse in the developing world by a number of factors. They include overpopulation, overgrazing, and cutting down trees to provide firewood.

Hot, dry winds and very high temperatures, combined with a lack of rainfall and the evaporation of moisture in the ground, produce the conditions of drought. In some areas, periods of drought alternate with periods of flood, continually destroying food crops and farmland.

Hot, dry winds

Eroded topsoil

Dried-up wells

Failed crops

◄ Thousands of people are forced to stand in line for food after the failure of their crops through drought.

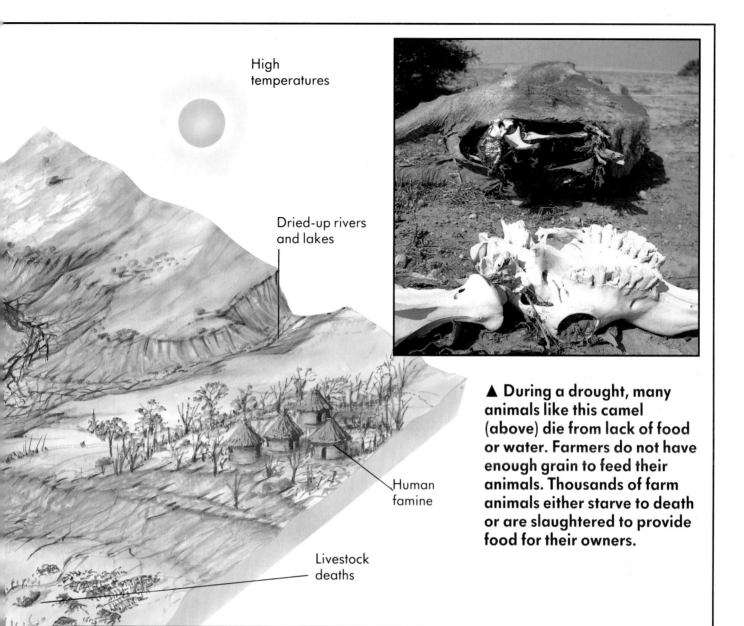

High temperatures

Dried-up rivers and lakes

Human famine

Livestock deaths

▲ During a drought, many animals like this camel (above) die from lack of food or water. Farmers do not have enough grain to feed their animals. Thousands of farm animals either starve to death or are slaughtered to provide food for their owners.

High temperatures
Unusually high temperatures can make water sources evaporate very quickly. Combined with a lack of rain, this can lead to droughts in areas that are not normally prone to water shortages. In 1988, temperatures in the fertile grain-growing regions of the United States soared to record levels. The drought that followed caused a large reduction in the grain harvest.

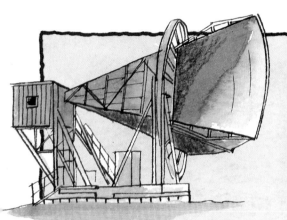

WHAT IF THE UNIVERSE STARTED TO SHRINK?

Echoes in space

Radio telescopes picking up microwaves detect a background "hiss" in space. It shows the temperature of the universe is slightly warmer in some parts than others. These "ripples" are echoes of the Big Bang.

Most experts believe that the universe began as a tiny speck containing all matter, which blew up billions of years ago in a massive explosion, called the Big Bang. It's been getting bigger ever since, as galaxies fly away from one another. This may go on forever, or the universe might reach a certain size, and then maintain a steady state, or it could begin to shrink. All the planets, stars, galaxies, and other matter might squeeze back together to form a tiny speck as the opposite of the Big Bang – the Big Crunch.

What was the Big Bang?

It was the beginning of the universe: the time when all matter began to explode and expand, from a small core full of incredible heat, light, and energy. Was there anything before the Big Bang, like a supreme being? No one knows. There may have been no "before." Space, matter, energy, and even time may have started with the Big Bang.

Strings and clusters

Our galaxy is only one of millions found throughout the universe. Together with a few others, such as the Andromeda galaxy, it forms the *Local Group*, a collection, or cluster of galaxies that circle around space together. The Local Group is, in turn, part of a group of galaxy clusters known as a *supercluster*. These superclusters are linked by massive strings of galaxies that may be up to 300 million light-years long.

How far can we look across our universe?

As telescopes become more powerful, and orbit in space on satellites, they can pick up the faint light and other waves from more distant stars and galaxies. The farthest object currently visible is Quasar (QUASi-stellAR object) 4C41.17. This object is so far away that light reaching us now left the galaxy when the universe was one-fifth its current age.

Happy birthday to you...

The general agreement is that the universe was "born" in the Big Bang about 14 billion years ago. Some believe that it is closer to 17 billion or as low as 10 billion years old. Scientists are still arguing about its exact age. You would need a very big cake for all the birthday candles!

HOW INSECTS FEED

Insects have adapted to make use of every possible food source. Some feed on plants and some on animals. Some suck juices, while some munch on solid food. Many insects consume their prey while it is still alive; many more eat it when it is dead. Some insects are specialized to eat wood or pollen, feathers or blood, even dung. Some eat each other. Many insects feed on humans, causing illness by infecting people with tiny disease organisms. Insects that eat our food can cause famine. Those that eat building materials can cause great damage.

Insect species have different kinds of mouthparts, specialized to cope with their particular diet. All have four main structures. The mandibles are hard jaws for biting, the maxillae are secondary jaws. The labrum and the labium form the upper and lower lips. Caterpillars of butterflies and moths have strong jaws to munch leaves.

Ant

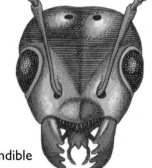

Mandible

Labium

Biting
Ants' saw-shaped mandibles are closed by strong muscles to chomp on solid food. Behind the mandibles, the maxillae taste the food. The labium and labrum chew it and push it into the mouth.

A monarch butterfly caterpillar consumes a leaf.

Food chains
Insects form very important links in food chains, eating plants and in turn being eaten by other insects and larger animals. In temperate climates such as Europe, when the weather warms in spring and the buds on trees begin to burst, thousands of insect eggs hatch into grubs which begin to feed and grow. They provide food for the young of nesting birds such as blackbirds and robins. Swallows return from their warm wintering grounds in South Africa just as the grubs are turning into adult insects. This provides an airborne feast for the swallows (right) to feed to their young as they hatch.

Locust pests

In Africa, the feeding habits of migratory locusts make them one of the most feared of pests. These insects are usually solitary, and dull in color. But when rains come to the parched savannahs and grass begins to grow, they begin to reproduce rapidly, and become brightly colored. They gather in swarms of billions. Such a swarm can strip a field of crops in minutes, leaving the farmer with no food.

Butterfly

Proboscis

Mosquito

Sucking

Butterfly and moth mouthparts have evolved into a long strawlike tube, or proboscis, to enable the insect to suck liquid nectar from flowers. The proboscis is kept rolled up between feeds. The housefly (left) squirts digestive juices down its proboscis onto its food. When the food has gone mushy, the fly sucks it up.

Fly

Piercing

Insects such as shieldbugs and mosquitoes puncture the hard skin of plants or animals to suck out juices. Their mandibles have evolved into needlelike tubes. The insect feels for a suitable place to puncture with the soft labium which surrounds its "needle." Then it stabs its prey, and pumps in digestive fluids before it sucks the victim's juices out.

Mandibles

Wood-boring beetles

The furniture beetle lays its eggs in cracks in old, dead wood. The wood provides a food source for the larvae, whether it is a dead tree or a valuable piece of antique furniture. Undetected, the larvae, or "woodworm," tunnel through the wood, and eventually pupate. Flight holes suddenly appear in the wood as the adult insects leave to mate and lay eggs on a new food source. Flight holes have sometimes been faked in new furniture, to make it appear older, and therefore more valuable.

Insects as food

Although few people from Western countries consider eating insects, they are nutritious, and are eaten as delicacies in many parts of the world. Australian Aborigines eat adult bogong moths, and the fat "witchetty" grubs of the giant wood moth. In Africa mosquito pie is eaten, and in Asia stir-fried locust is popular.

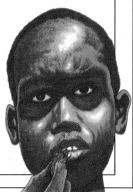

31

ESTIMATING TIME

Hours are artificial units of time, first introduced by the Ancient Egyptians when they observed that shadows follow a similar pattern of movement each day. Shadow clocks and sundials were early time-measurement tools. In the 14th century, the sandglass, or hourglass, was popular, but it could only be used to estimate periods of time, varying from minutes to hours. It could not indicate the time of day. Onboard ship, a four-hour glass timed "watch" for the crew, until John Harrison invented the more accurate chronometer in 1735. This also calculated longitude and latitude. Early sandglasses were filled with powdered eggshell or marble dust.

TIME IS RUNNING OUT

1

1. Wash and dry two small bottles thoroughly. Make an open-ended cylinder of cardboard and slide it over the top of one bottle. Cut out a disc of cardboard to fit inside and make a hole in its center.

2

2. Make sure the other bottle is absolutely dry. Now, carefully pour a measured amount of salt into it.

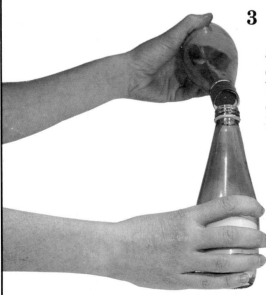

3

3. Position the empty bottle on top of the salt-filled bottle by sliding the cardboard cylinder over the neck of the lower bottle.

4

4. Check that the cardboard "seal" around the middle is secure. Carefully turn your timer over and observe what happens.

5. You can estimate the time taken for the salt to slide into the lower half of the timer by marking the side of the bottle with evenly spaced divisions. Use a stop watch to check exactly how long it takes for all the salt to slide to the bottom.

5

WHY IT WORKS

The upper vessel of the timer holds just enough salt to run through a hole, of a given size, in a given period of time. The force of gravity pulls the salt down through the hole and into the bottom container. The salt grains must be absolutely dry, so they don't stick. The size of the hole between the two vessels will determine the speed at which the grains will flow, but once established, the rate of flow will not vary. The total period of time depends on the quantity of salt.

Salt

BRIGHT IDEAS

Remove the regulator from between the two bottles and replace it with another, in which a hole of a different diameter has been made. Repeat this exercise a number of times, changing the size of the hole each time. What do you discover?

Design a sandglass that will run for exactly 3 minutes - use it as an eggtimer when you boil an egg.

Can you design another kind of sandglass that runs for a much longer period of time? Shape a funnel from cardboard, and insert it into the neck of a measuring container. Fill the funnel with sand and time how long it takes to pour through into the container below. Standardize your method of reading the scale - the top of the mound of sand will be concave.

Funnel

Sand

Scale

SEASHORE LIFE

The seashore is one of the harshest surroundings for living things. Twice a day these creatures are covered by water, then dry out as the tide goes out. They are exposed to heat, cold, and buffeting waves. Conditions keep changing. But each tide brings in a new supply of food in the form of microscopic sea creatures. In spite of the difficulties, many sea animals live on shores. Seaweeds grow among rocks where the water is shallow enough for them to get the light they need. There is a huge number of kinds, but by observation and taking notes you will find you soon get to know the main ones. The seashore is one of the places that is most fun for a naturalist. There is always something to see, and you are never sure what will be in the next pool.

SHORE ZONES
If you map seaweed types on a rocky shore you will find they live at different levels on the beach. The same is true for many of the animals.

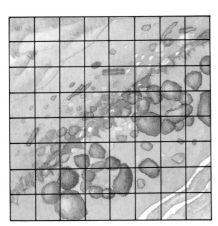

Laver

Limpets

Barnacles

Small periwinkles

Bladder wrack

Starfish

Lobster

Sea wrack

Shore crab

Whelks

SEARCHING THE BEACH

To discover which animals live along a shore, especially at the lower levels, follow the tide out down the beach. Many animals will have hidden in crevices and beneath rock ledges, others may be lurking in rocky tide pools, so you should be able to get close enough to study them.

Gulls are successful scavengers. You will see them swoop down to catch crabs or to gobble up any small fish that may have become tangled in seaweed and stranded by the tide.

Black headed gull

Sea bindweed

Hermit crab

Common dog whelk

VARYING TIDES
The height of the tides varies throughout a month, but parts of the shore are only wetted by the highest spring tides. Some sea creatures can only survive where they are just splashed by spray.

Splash zone

SPRING TIDE
HIGH TIDE
LOW TIDE

LARGER SPECIES

Seals swim near the shore and may climb out to rest if they don't see you. Dolphins and porpoises sometimes play close by the shore. Search the strandline for the remains of these and other dead animals washed up on the beach after storms.

MAKING TRACKS
Seals are graceful swimmers, but are clumsy on land. If they cross sand they may leave tracks like these.

Gray seal and tracks

Bottle-nosed dolphin

Pilot whale

Loggerhead turtle

35

COWGIRLS

Cowboys lived at a time when most women stayed at home looking after children and working around the house. If they went out riding, they usually sat sidesaddle. Their long dresses made it hard to rush around and do the same work as men.

In the West, however, things were sometimes rather different. The women who traveled with the wagon trains often worked alongside the men. When they settled, some managed ranches when their menfolk were away, or after they had died. A few even put on men's clothing and joined the drovers on horseback. This caused confusion among the men, who did not know what to make of such "cowgirls." The women they were used to were either nymphs or the mothers and daughters of the homestead. Cowboys therefore regarded cowgirls with a mixture of fear and scorn. One or two women, such as "Cattle Annie" and "Little Britches" (*below*), even joined outlaw gangs. Later, pioneering women worked in rodeo and "Wild West" shows.

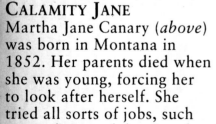

CALAMITY JANE
Martha Jane Canary (*above*) was born in Montana in 1852. Her parents died when she was young, forcing her to look after herself. She tried all sorts of jobs, such as cooking and dancing, but found them all rather boring.

In search of excitement, she took to wearing men's clothes and doing men's work. She was a mule driver, railroad laborer and even joined the army, acting as a scout in the Indian Wars.

After that she drifted west, drawing crowds to the saloons with her swashbuckling behavior. Having lived with Wild Bill Hickok for a time, after his death she joined Buffalo Bill's Wild West Show. Sadly, she was now drinking heavily and was soon fired. She spent the rest of her days in drunken poverty. Dying in 1903, she was buried beside Wild Bill.

BELLE STARR

For sheer excitement, few women could match the career of Belle Starr (*left*), known as the "Bandit Queen." Raised as Myra Belle Shirley in a wealthy middle-class home, Belle soon tired of her respectable life and went to live as a bandit.

She shocked people by having two children by men friends and wearing a revolver on a gun belt over her dress. Yet she still rode her horse, *Venus*, sidesaddle, like a lady (*right*). She was found guilty of many robberies and had several spells in prison. She married the rustler Sam Starr, and after his death continued to run the ranch as a hideout for outlaws. But one evening, while riding alone, she was killed in an ambush by a fellow bandit.

COWGIRLS ON SCREEN. Until the 1960s, women in Westerns were usually portrayed as either flirtatious prairie nymphs or as domestic, pretty, and willing to follow their menfolk.

More recent films, such as *Bad Girls* (*left*), have depicted them as tough fighters, but their true role in settling the West is still to be shown.

Cattle Annie and Little Britches

For a time "Oklahoma's Girl Bandits" – Jennie Stevens and Annie McDougal – were the most famous girls in the West. Meeting some of the Doolin gang at a dance, the girls decided to run away from home and join them. Before long, "Cattle Annie" and "Little Britches," as Jennie was known, were robbing with the Doolin gang. But the law was closing in. The girls were finally cornered by Marshal Tilghman and his assistant. Tracking the girls down was one thing – but capturing them was quite another (left). By the time the girls were handcuffed, both men were nursing painful bruises. After two years in prison, Annie married and settled down. Jennie went to New York, where she died of consumption.

WHAT IS THE WEATHER?

From sunshine and showers to blizzards and hurricanes, the weather is a combination of wind, rain, clouds, and temperature. Believe it or not, all our weather is caused by the air around our planet warming up and cooling down. The average weather in one particular region is called the climate. In some climates, the weather stays much the same all year round. But in many parts of the world, the weather changes at certain times of year. A climate appears to stay the same, but may change quite a lot over thousands of years.

Earth moves around the Sun once a year.

Earth spins once a day.

The Sun and Earth

The Earth moves slowly around the Sun once every year. Because the Earth is tilted, places are closer to the Sun at different times of year. This affects the amount of light and heat these places receive, and produces a pattern of changes in the weather called the seasons. The Earth also spins on its axis once every 24 hours, giving us night and day.

The atmosphere

The Earth is surrounded by a thick blanket of air called the atmosphere, which is made up of five layers. Weather happens only in the layer nearest to the Earth – the troposphere. This stretches up about 7 miles above the surface of the planet, not much higher than the top of Mount Everest. The troposphere is the warmest layer of the atmosphere and contains the most moisture.

Auroras are produced when radiation from the Sun hits the outer layers of the atmosphere.

50 miles

30 miles

Weather occurs in this layer, the troposphere.

7 miles

Sun gods

Many ancient peoples worshiped the Sun as a god. They made sacrifices to the gods to keep the Sun shining. In the Aztec religion, the Sun was the warrior, Huitzilopochtli, who died every evening to be born again the next day, driving away the stars and Moon with a shaft of light.

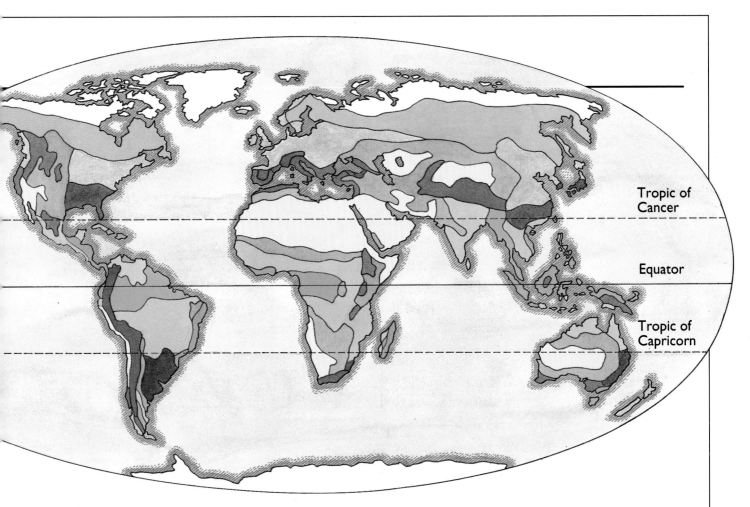

Air pressure

Air pressure is caused by the force of gravity in the Earth's atmosphere pulling air down toward the surface. In 1643, Galileo's pupil, Toricelli, invented the first instrument for measuring air pressure – the mercury barometer. Before weather maps were developed in the early 1800's, the barometer was the most important tool in weather forecasting. High pressure usually indicates fine, settled weather, and low pressure means cloudy, rainy weather. The French physicist, Jean de Borda (1733-1799), was the first to show that changes in air pressure are also related to wind speed. An aneroid (non-liquid) barometer measures the effect of air pressure on a chamber that has part of the air removed.

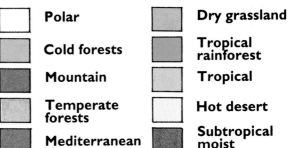

Aneroid barometer

Polar	Dry grassland
Cold forests	Tropical rainforest
Mountain	Tropical
Temperate forests	Hot desert
Mediterranean	Subtropical moist

World climates

Climates depend on how near to the equator a place is, how high it is above sea level, and how far it is from the sea. World climates can be divided into the following categories:

Polar – Cold and snowy, strong winds
Cold forest – Short summers and long, cold winters
Mountain – Cold and snowy high up
Temperate forests – Neither too hot nor too cold, rain all year round
Mediterranean – Long, hot, dry summers and cool, wet winters
Dry grasslands – Hot, dry summers and cold, snowy winters
Tropical rainforest – Hot, rainy, humid, wet
Tropical – Hot all year, wet and dry seasons
Hot desert – Hot and dry, hardly any rain
Subtropical moist – Warm to hot summers, cool winters and moderate rain all year round.

Tropic of Cancer

Equator

Tropic of Capricorn

CATS

The cat family, the Felidae, are all very similar in shape though they come in different sizes. They are all agile hunters that stalk and pounce on their prey. They have excellent stereoscopic vision, they can see in color and in the dark. They have a special layer at the back of the eye, called the tapetum, which reflects light back to the retina, so they can see in low light. All cats have sensitive whiskers for nighttime hunting.

Small Cats

There are 28 species of "small cats." Apart from their size they are very similar to big cats. Small cats can purr, but they cannot roar. Big cats can roar, but cannot purr. The domestic cat (bottom), is descended from the wild cat, which was found in Europe and North Africa. The bobcat, and the lynx (top), are peculiar in having ear tufts and short tails. Many small cats, like the ocelot, have spotted coats for camouflage in the forest.

Cheshire Cat

The grinning Cheshire cat, in *Alice's Adventures in Wonderland*, by Lewis Carroll, caused some difficulty when the Queen of Hearts ordered "Off with its head." The Cheshire cat was able to make its body invisible. The executioner was puzzled as to how he could cut a head off a body that was not there. While the king debated the matter the queen threatened to have all the court executed. Meanwhile the cat had disappeared!

Witch's Cats

Cats have lived alongside people for some 5,000 years, ridding homes of mice and rats. But in the Middle Ages they became associated with witchcraft and the devil. They were cruelly persecuted along with their owners. The Christian Church also tried to rid the world of them because they were symbols of paganism.

Record Breakers

The cheetah is the fastest land animal in the world. It can reach speeds of 60 miles per hour. It can move so fast because it stores energy in its springlike backbone. When it runs its backbone alternately stretches and coils, swinging its long legs forward and backward.

Big Cats

Tigers, cheetahs, leopards, and jaguars are solitary hunters. They usually stalk medium-sized grazers no bigger than themselves. Lions take larger prey, and hunt in prides. Prides consist of a full-grown male and several breeding females and their cubs. Big cats hunt only when they are hungry, gorging on the kill and then dozing for several days.

Tiger

Jaguar

Lion

Agility

Cats are supposed to have "nine lives" – they almost always land on their feet. They do this by a reflex action controlled by the organ of balance in the inner ear. It tells the brain which way up the cat is. The brain matches this information with messages from the eyes. The neck muscles turn the head to the upright position and the body follows – all before the cat hits the ground. Cats are agile climbers, clinging on with their claws. They have powerful legs and can spring straight up into the air, landing on their prey on all fours.

WHAT IF THE SUN WENT OUT?

Who turned off the lights? Why is it suddenly so cold? If the Sun no longer bathed our world in light and warmth, we might last a short time with fires, electric light, and oil or gas heat. But plants could not grow in the dark, and animals would perish from the cold. Soon all life would cease, and our planet would be dark and frozen. In fact this will happen, but not for billions of years. Our Sun is a fairly typical star, and stars do not last forever. They form, grow old, and either fade away or explode in a supernova, a massive explosion.

From the cradle to the grave

Throughout the universe there are massive clouds of gas, called *nebulae*. In some of these, the dust and particles clump together, and over millions of years, these clumps will form stars. Other nebulae are the wispy remains of a *supernova*, a star that has exploded.

What is a red giant?

An enormous human with red clothes? No, it is a star that has been growing and shining for billions of years, and is nearing the end of its life. As it ages, the star swells and its light turns red. Our Sun will do this in millions of years. It will expand to the size of a Red Giant, scorching our planet, before it explodes. Then all that will be left is a tiny white dwarf star that will slowly fade over millions of years.

How can we see a black hole?

When a really big star explodes, its core collapses and leaves behind a remnant whose gravity is so strong that nothing can escape its pull. This remnant is called a black hole. Because light cannot escape, it is impossible to actually see a black hole. However, its presence can be detected by the effect it has on objects around, such as gases, and waves, including light rays and X rays.

Great balls of fire

A typical star is made mainly of hydrogen gas. Huge forces squeeze together its atoms to form helium. This process is called *nuclear fusion*. As the atoms fuse they release energy, which radiates from the core, through the radiation zone. The energy is then carried to the surface by circular convection currents. Finally at the photosphere, the energy is radiated into space as light and other types of rays and waves.

Radiation zone

Convection zone

Photosphere surface

Silent explosion

Sound waves can't pass through the vacuum of space, so we can't hear a star explode. But we can see it, as a glow that appears in the night sky, which then fades. It leaves behind a cloud, called a *nebula*.

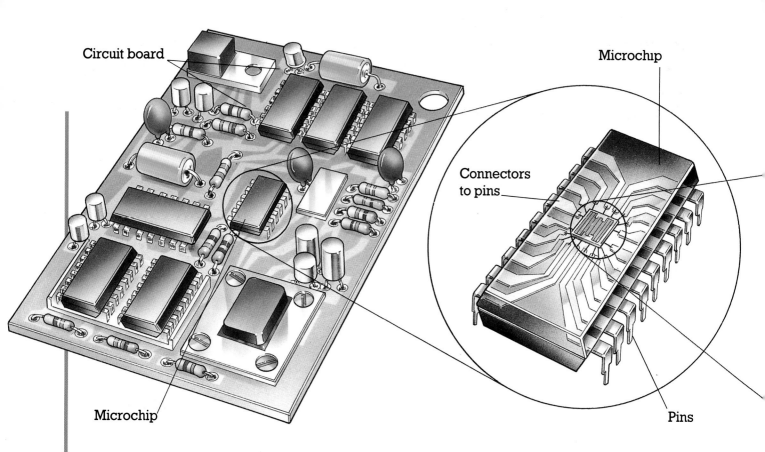

Circuit board

Microchip

Microchip

Connectors to pins

Pins

Inside a computer, electronic circuits are formed from components mounted on circuit boards (see above left), which are linked together by metal tracks on the boards. Many of the components are microchips (see above right). Each of them contains a tiny chip of silicon and this itself contains circuits composed of thousands of microscopically small components (see diagrams opposite).

THE MICROCHIP

Computers process information by first changing it into pulses of electric current that are then directed through complex electrical pathways or circuits. The majority of the electronic components on the computer's circuit boards are microchips. Most of them look like blocks of black or gray plastic with a row of metal pins along each side (see above right). The plastic block is to protect the chip which is buried inside, its metal pins connected to the metal tracks in the circuit board. The chip itself is often no bigger than a fingernail, although some are smaller. It is made from a slice of pure silicon on which intricately shaped layers of chemicals are added to form thousands of individual components. Silicon is one of a group of materials called semiconductors. Its resistance to an electrical current decreases as its temperature rises. This electrical resistance can also be changed by a process called "doping." This involves adding small amounts of different materials to the silicon. Some provide extra charged particles called electrons, forming n-type silicon. Others create a shortage of electrons forming p-type silicon.

Chips are made by adding specially shaped layers of different materials, such as aluminum, to a slice, or very thin wafer, of silicon. Each layer creates pathways for electric currents to flow through the chip. In the transistor illustrated on the bottom right of this page, a positive charge fed to the polysilicon gate attracts electrons from the p-type silicon base. This turns the transistor on as current only flows from the source to the drain when a gate current is applied. A negative charge at the gate repels electrons and turns the current and transistor off. Transistors commonly consist of three layers of silicon, either p-n-p or n-p-n.

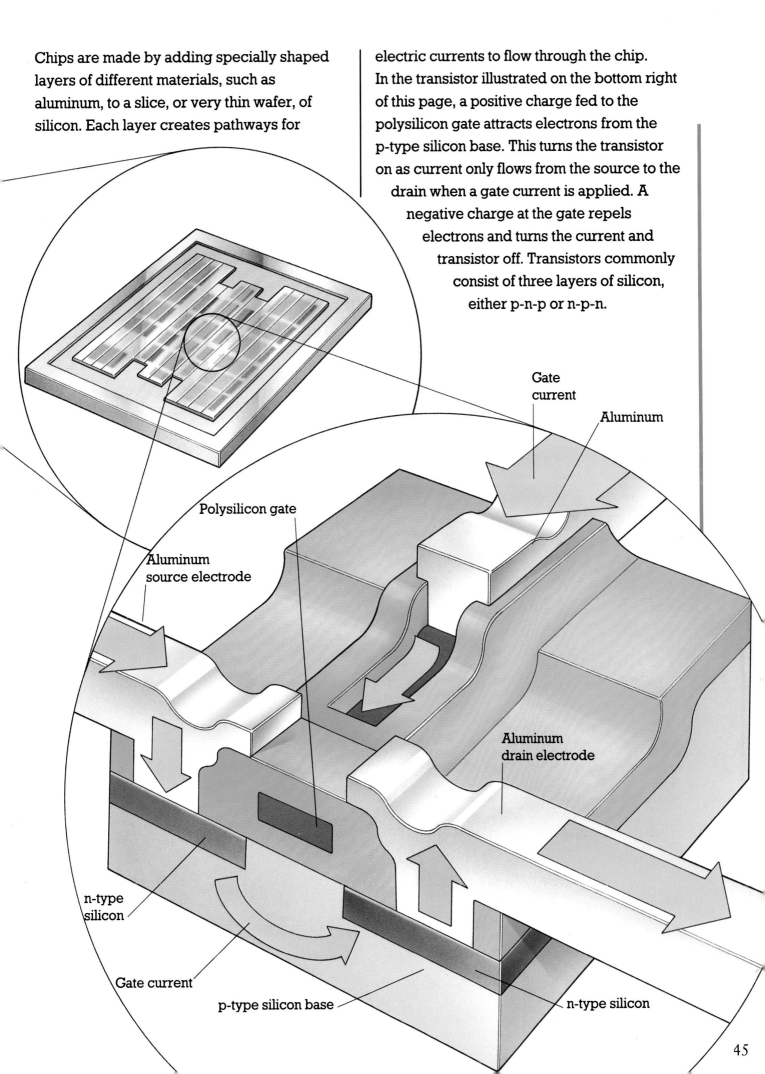

Gate current

Aluminum

Polysilicon gate

Aluminum source electrode

Aluminum drain electrode

n-type silicon

Gate current

p-type silicon base

n-type silicon

THE THINKING BRAIN

The main part of the brain that we use to think, decide and reason is the cortex – the thin gray layer on the wrinkled domes of the two cerebral hemispheres. The cortex looks the same all over. But brain research has "mapped" it to show its different parts are specialized for different jobs. We have maps on the brain!

PERSONALITY
Are you a good, kind person? Of course! The frontal lobes take part in the complex behaviors we call personality.

LEFT BRAIN, RIGHT BRAIN

In most people, the two halves of the cortex seem to have different tendencies. The right side is most involved in creative and artistic abilities such as painting, drawing, writing and playing music.

Artistic brilliance

Scientific excellence

The left side tends to take over in logical and rational thinking, as when solving mathematical sums, doing scientific experiments, playing chess and working out what to say.

SENSOR AND MOTOR

These two drawings show how we would look, if each part of our body was in proportion to the area of cortex dealing with it. One is for skin's touch, the sensory cortex. The other is for muscle movement, the motor cortex.

Motoring man   *Sensitive man*

46

MUSCLE CONTROL
The motor cortex is in overall control of the muscles, ordering them to work so that we can move.

THE INS AND OUTS
Information whizzes around the brain and body along nerves, as tiny electrical blips called nerve signals. Sensory signals come into the brain from the eyes, ears and other senses. Motor signals go out to the muscles.

1 Signals come in from the senses.

TOUCH
The somato-sensory cortex is the "touch center." It receives information from all over our skin, about things we touch, and whether they feel hot or cold, or press hard, or cause pain.

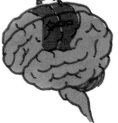

2 The brain decides what to do.

SIGHT
The visual cortex receives and processes information from the eyes. It works out shapes, colors and movements, and identifies what we see. It is the site of the "mind's eye."

3 Signals go out to the muscles.

SMELL AND TASTE
The olfactory cortex sorts out smelly signals from the nose. The gustatory cortex is part of the touch area and receives tastes.

Another scanning method for looking inside the brain is PET (positron emission tomography). The PET scan shows where the brain is busiest and most active.

HEARING
Information from our ears, in the form of nerve signals, travels to the auditory cortex. Here it is sorted out and analyzed. We can identify most sounds by comparing them with sound patterns in our memory banks. For a strange or unusual sound, we may turn the head to see what has made it.

WHAT ARE OUR ORIGINS?

For thousands of years humankind has been preoccupied by the question of its origins. Many cultures have legends explaining how and why humans were created. In the last 200 years these have given way to scientific explanations. Evidence from fossils has convinced most scientists that human beings developed over millions of years. However, we still do not know the whole story, and there are many unanswered questions about the exact pattern of human evolution.

Digging up the bones

Early human fossils are found buried in the ground. Scientists use picks, trowels, and brushes (left) to dig carefully around artifacts on the dig site. The smallest fragments may be very important. The dig site (right) is carefully mapped so that every find can be located. Dozens of people are often needed for the slow, careful work.

Charles Darwin

Charles Darwin (1809-1882) was one of the first scientists to suggest that humans were closely related to apes. His explanation of evolution forms the basis for our understanding of the history of life. Darwin was criticized by religious leaders who believed that his ideas were against God.

Reconstruction

Sometimes a lucky find will be a complete skeleton. One example of this is "Lucy," the fossilized remains of an early human ancestor called *Australopithecus*, found in Ethiopia in 1973. The form of the pelvic bone showed the remains to be female, and the formation of the teeth suggested she was about 20 years old. Only 40% of Lucy's bones were found, but because skeletons are symmetrical we know what the missing bones look like.

Piltdown Man

In 1912, a skull and jaw bone were found near the village of Piltdown in Southern England. Piltdown Man had a large brain and an apelike jaw. English scientists were delighted because they thought it proved that the first intelligent humans had evolved in England. Other scientists were doubtful, and in 1953, it was shown that the specimen was a fake comprising a human skull cap and an ape jaw.

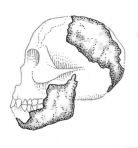

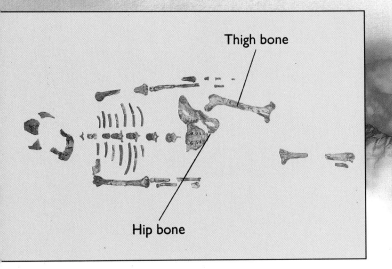

Thigh bone

Hip bone

Famous discoveries

The most important discoveries of early humans have been made in the past 100 years. By 1900, only a few skulls and skeletons had come to light, but many stone tools and pieces of art had been found. During the twentieth century the pace of discovery has quickened, and our understanding of human origins has improved immensely.

Eugène Dubois (1858-1941) found the remains of Java Man, a form of *Homo erectus,* in 1891, the first significant early human fossil. The specimens provoked such fierce debate that Dubois later claimed the bones came from a giant gibbon.

Raymond Dart (1893-1990) was the first to suggest that the earliest human ancestors came from Africa. Here he discovered one of the most important human fossils, the skull of an *Australopithecus.* At first many scientists did not believe that the fossil was human.

Richard Leakey (1944-) has found many human fossils in Africa, notably part of a skull of the oldest known *Homo habilis* fossil dating back 1.9 million years. He also discovered a 1.6 million year old *Homo erectus* skull.

Donald Johanson (1947-) found a series of human fossils in Ethiopia, including Lucy (see left), and he gave *Australopithecus afarensis* its name. He has argued that the first humans could walk upright, but that they had ape sized brains.

CASTLE PEOPLE

A medieval castle housed the lord and his family, his soldiers as well as the servants, who looked after them. In fact, the bailey was a very busy and crowded place.

There was a lot of work involved in running a castle. Blacksmiths or armorers were very important. They had to shoe horses, repair tools and look after the soldiers' armor. The soldiers patrolled the countryside on horses. They had to be looked after in stables. Carpenters made furniture and repaired carts. Other men looked after the buildings and repaired the walls. There was usually a plumber to make new lead roofs and pipes. "Plumber" literally means someone who works with lead.

Life in the Middle Ages was hard. People had to work very hard either growing food or in someone else's service. They did not live as long as they do today – many died of diseases, like the plague, and others died in wars. A 40-year-old was considered old.

COOKING IN A CASTLE

This is the kitchen at Glastonbury Abbey. Sometimes kitchens were built in the bailey. Several men worked in the kitchens preparing food. Food was obtained from the surrounding countryside but in a siege people had to survive on animals living within the bailey or on salted or dried food. Some castles had their own fishponds and dovecots. They provided fresh food throughout the year. Women rarely worked in the kitchen but they did wash the laundry. They had to make their own soap from animal fat and water mixed with vegetable ash. Candles were also made from animal fat.

CROCODILES AND ALLIGATORS

The 22 species of crocodilians are all lurking predators, which also scavenge meat from any dead carcass left by another hunter. They live in tropical regions, in or near water, and spend much of the day basking in the sun to keep warm. The powerful tail and rear limbs are used to propel the animal through the water. The caimans of South America have the shortest, broadest snouts and eat the most varied diet, including frogs, snakes, lizards, birds, and mammals. The gavial of the Indian region has a long, narrow snout and eats mainly fish.

Caiman

Alligator

Crocodile

Gavial

Adapted for water
The alligator is well suited for a watery life. Its broad tail gives powerful swimming propulsion (opposite) and it can hold its breath for minutes at a time.

Strong rear limbs with webbed feet

Front limbs are smaller. Front feet are not webbed.

Crocodilians worldwide
The map shows the distribution of some of the main species of crocodilians. The two main groups are the crocodiles, with 14 species, and alligators, with 7 species, which includes the caimans. The Estuarine crocodile is the only one that lives in salt water.

Key
- Common caiman
- American alligator
- American crocodile
- Nile crocodile
- Estuarine crocodile
- Gavial

The swishing tail

The tail is arched from side to side by powerful muscles running down the animal's body. The main part of the body is relatively stiff and takes little part in swimming.

With a crocodile's help

The crocodile features in many stories. In *The Just So Stories* by Rudyard Kipling (1902) a crocodile seizes a young elephant by its nose, which is "no bigger than a boot." The elephant tries to get away, and its nose stretches – which is how, supposedly, the elephant got its trunk!

From rare to common

American alligators live in the southeastern United States. They were hunted so much for their skins and because they threatened people and livestock, that they became in danger of extinction (dying out completely). Wildlife laws were introduced in 1969 to protect them. In 1987 the species was declared to be out of danger of extinction. Today they are more common and a few are hunted (below).

Crocodile swimming

The main swimming power for crocodilians comes from the deep tail, which swishes from side to side like a fish's tail. This pushes the animal forward. The front legs are usually held up against the underside of the body, for better streamlining. The rear legs can be used for steering, and for paddling at slow speeds. By thrusting its rear feet forward and up, with its webbed toes spread, a crocodile can suddenly stop moving forward and sink down under the water.

Crocodile songs

Crocodilians feature in various plays and also in popular songs. These include *See You Later Alligator* (1956), the early rock'n'roll jive-talking hit by Bill Haley and the Comets, and *Crocodile Rock* (1973) by Elton John.

Bill Haley

FREEDOM
BUILDING IN SPACE

The United States is preparing to spend nearly $30 billion building a space station to orbit the Earth. If it is built, it will be the most ambitious construction project ever attempted in space, and will provide a laboratory for experiments in a weightless environment. Since it was first proposed in 1984, the *Freedom* space station has been repeatedly redesigned to save money. The latest designs are far less ambitious than the earlier ones, but stick to the basic idea of a long spine, to which a variety of different modules can be attached. By 2001, the U.S. space agency, NASA, hopes astronauts will be based permanently on the station.

The space station could pave the way for a manned base on the moon sometime in the next century.

Research on the Freedom *space station would include studies of the effect of prolonged weightlessness on humans, and attempts to produce new materials and drugs in zero gravity. But powerful critics question the whole project, and* Freedom *may never fly.*

The first stage in building the station would be to create the basic structure and attach the solar panels. The space shuttle would be used to carry the U.S.-built modules to the station and attach them, with the international modules following.

The ultimate prize could be a base on Mars, the only planet in the solar system, apart from earth, which appears remotely habitable. The first manned visit to Mars is planned sometime in the next century.

Latest designs for Freedom, are a greatly simplified version of the original. One major change is the removal of costly windows.

COLORS OF THE RAINBOW

Sunlight appears colorless but really it is made up of different colors. Sometimes you can see these colors — on the surfaces of bubbles or if there is oil on water. You may also see the colors across the sky in the form of a rainbow. In each case "white" light is being separated into different colors called the spectrum.

HOW A RAINBOW IS MADE

When the Sun comes out during a shower you may see a rainbow. The sunlight shines on the droplets of rain and gets separated into the colors of the spectrum. From a distance the light appears as a colored arc across the sky. People divide the rainbow into seven bands of color — red, orange, yellow, green, blue, indigo and violet. The colors always appear in the same order, with red on the outside and violet on the inside of the arc. The diagram shows how light which enters each raindrop is reflected, bent and separated into all the colors of the spectrum, which together form a rainbow in the sky.

△ It is impossible to reach the end of a rainbow — you can only see it shining in the sky at a distance.

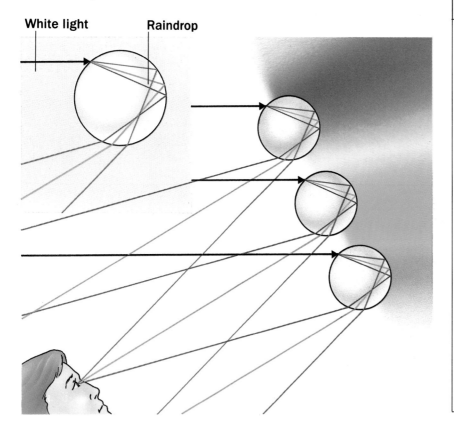

White light   Raindrop

MAKE A RAINBOW

You can see the colors of the spectrum by making your own rainbow. On a sunny day fill a pan of water and rest a mirror at an angle inside it. Stand the pan in front of a window so that sunlight falls onto the mirror. Then hold a piece of white cardboard in front of the mirror and move it around until you see a rainbow appear on it. You may have to move the mirror to get this right. The mirror and the water act as a "prism" — they separate white light into the colors of the spectrum.

THE NORTHERN LIGHTS

Sometimes dazzling displays of colored lights appear in the sky at night in parts of the world which are far from the equator. These lights are caused by huge explosions on the surface of the Sun known as "flares." During a flare, millions of tiny particles are sent out from the Sun. They travel very fast and some eventually reach the Earth's atmosphere. The Earth's magnetism bends the paths of the particles so they only reach the Earth's atmosphere near the poles. As they travel through the air they bump into other particles. These collisions produce light. In the North they can be seen best in parts of Canada, but they can also be seen in northern Scotland and Scandinavia. They are called the Northern Lights or "Aurora borealis." Similar lights can be seen in the South where they are called "Aurora australis."

△ The Northern Lights make an impressive display of color which looks like a constantly moving curtain in the sky.

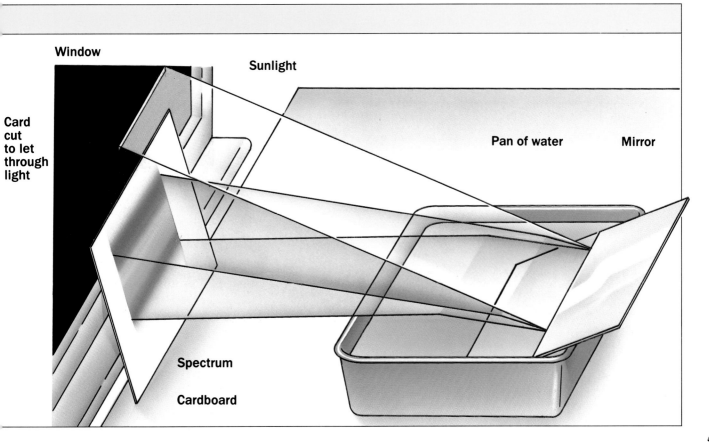

Window

Sunlight

Card cut to let through light

Pan of water   Mirror

Spectrum

Cardboard

MAKING A POND ENVIRONMENT

If you have a yard you can construct a real pond, but failing this, a coldwater aquarium can be stocked with plants and animals to make a "natural" habitat. One secret of success is to make sure that the animals have enough oxygen. Choose an aquarium with a big surface, not one that is tall and narrow. Do not overcrowd it, and above all do not put in fierce hunters such as diving beetles and dragonfly larvae that will eat other insects and small fish.

FISH
Goldfish make good pond fish, as they can survive in stagnant water. Sticklebacks are found in all kinds of water. Minnows can live in ponds, but prefer clear, moving water.

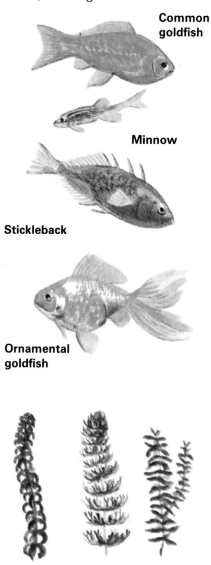

Common goldfish

Minnow

Stickleback

Ornamental goldfish

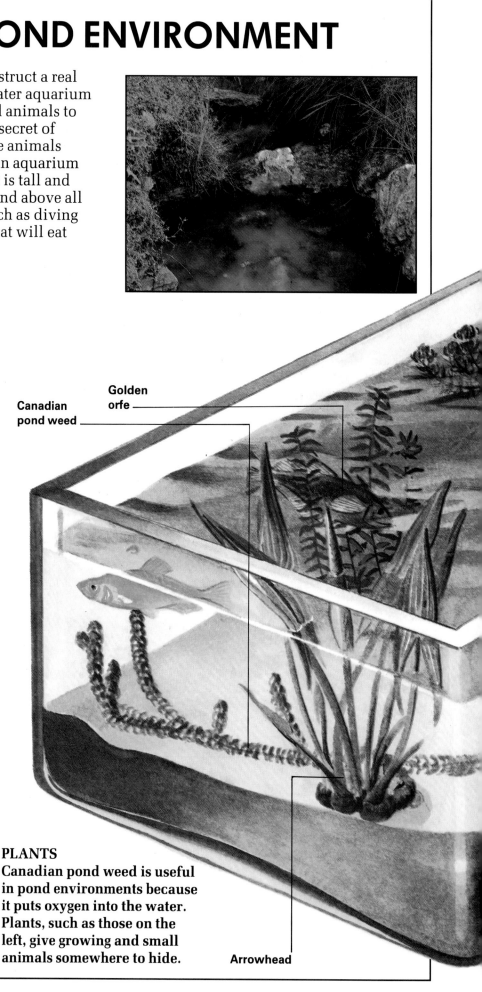

Canadian pond weed

Golden orfe

PLANTS
Canadian pond weed is useful in pond environments because it puts oxygen into the water. Plants, such as those on the left, give growing and small animals somewhere to hide.

Arrowhead

FROG SPAWN
You can follow a frog's growth from spawn (eggs) to tadpoles and then tiny frogs over about 12 weeks.

Frog spawn

MOLLUSKS
Snails climb on the plants and over the sides of a pond. They eat the green algae that would otherwise cover these surfaces.

Great diving beetle

Common snail

Stonefly nymph

Hornwort

INSECTS
Water insects include plant and meat eaters among the many kinds of beetles and bugs. They often arrive attached to new plants.

Great diving beetle

Water scorpion

Water-stick insect

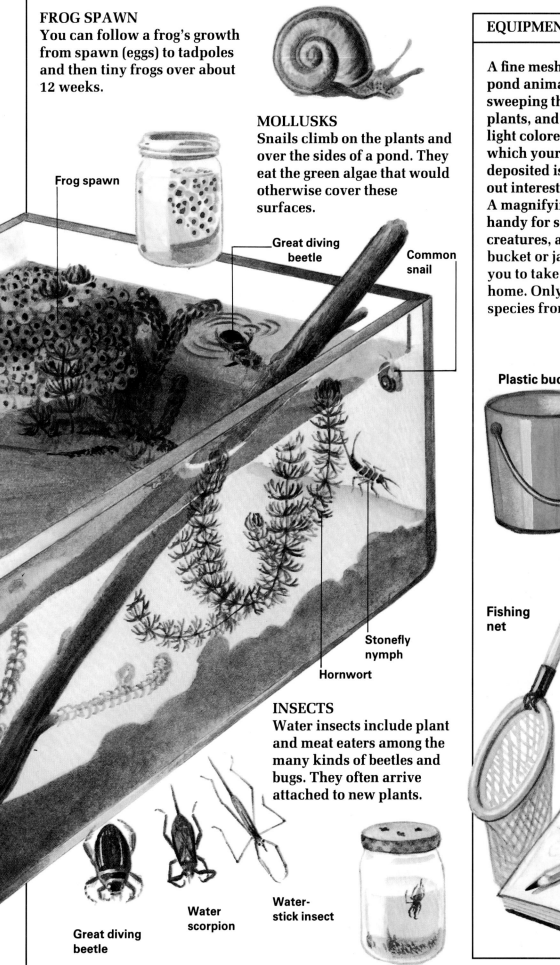

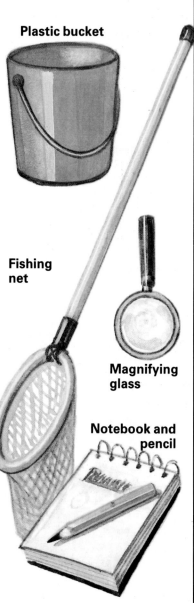

THE THUNDER OF GUNS

When guns were first introduced in the early 14th century, they had more influence on siege warfare than battle tactics. By 1425, there was not a castle that could not be battered into swift submission by cannon fire.

Armored knights hung on longer. The final proof that they were no longer needed came at the Battle of Ravenna (1512), when French cannons destroyed a large Spanish army. By the 17th century, the wide use of handguns meant that armor was all but stripped away (*left*).

Chivalric ideals survived, however. Knightly honors were given for feats of bravery and other services, and chivalric orders, such as the Burgundian Order of the Golden Fleece, were still admired.

HAIL THE MIGHTY CANNON

The first cannons were cast from bronze, brass, or iron bars. Gunpowder, a mixture of charcoal, potassium nitrate, and sulfur was made on the spot because of the danger of transporting it.

The gun was loaded by pouring powder down the barrel and holding it in place with wadding. A cannon ball was then rolled down the barrel and secured with more wadding.

To fire the gun (above) *the gunpowder was lit through a small hole in the rear. The explosion blasted the ball out of the barrel toward its target. Gunners were protected from arrows by a wooden screen.*

Watch Out for the Big Bang!
Gunners cover their ears from the blast (above). In the early days, cannons frequently exploded upon firing. Also, the ignition of the slow-burning powder was so random that accuracy was almost impossible.

A TUDOR SUMMIT

Though knights were no longer a powerful force on the battlefield, many of the traditions and customs survived.

In 1520, King Henry VIII led the elite of English chivalry to meet the elite of Francis I's French knights on the Field of the Cloth of Gold *(left)*.

By now the jousting and feasting were supposed to demonstrate Anglo-French friendship, rather than a show of military force.

Fantasy Land
Scholars believe the original Camelot was in the English counties of Cornwall, Hampshire, or Somerset.

None of this is relevant to the musical Camelot, *which places the court of King Arthur in a singing and dancing medieval fantasy land* (right)!

DON QUIXOTE. Miguel de Cervantes Saavedra mirrored the decline of Spanish chivalry in his two-part novel *Don Quixote de la Mancha* (1605-1615). It is a story about a Spanish landowner who adores tales of the knights of old. Wishing to live like the knights, he takes the name Don Quixote and sets out to perform great deeds of chivalry, accompanied by his loyal friend Sancho Panza (*left*).

Don Quixote *attacks windmills he thinks are giants and flocks of sheep he mistakes for armies! When all his adventures prove romantic follies, he returns home to die.*

Arise, Sir Francis!
No longer was the honor of knight reserved for mounted warriors. When Francis Drake returned from sailing around the world, *on April 4, 1581 Queen Elizabeth knighted him on board his ship* (right). *He hadn't been near a horse for almost three years!*

WHERE BIRDS LIVE

With their adaptations for flight and feeding, birds are able to live all over the world. They range from the freezing Poles to the baking deserts, and from rushing rivers to steamy jungles. Flight has given them the mobility to exploit a wide variety of food supplies and habitats. Being warm-blooded, they also have the advantage of maintaining a constant body temperature and staying active whatever the weather.

Antarctica

The 16 species of penguin all live in the Southern Hemisphere. Six species, including these emperor penguins, are even found in Antarctica itself, despite the extremely cold temperatures and wind. Emperors are the largest of all penguin species. They grow to about three feet (1 m) tall.

The tropics

About two-thirds of all species of birds live in the world's tropical rain forests. They include trogons and parrots. Rain forest birds are often brightly colored. The bright green feathers of this rainbow lorikeet blend in with the foliage. Even its colorful markings could be mistaken for flowers or fruits in the lush forest.

Bird-watching

The best places to observe birds are parks, gardens, or wooded areas. Sit very quietly and try to keep out of sight. In a forest you will see that different species prefer a particular part of the woods. Some birds will feed on the ground, others might nest among shrubs, and some will sing from tree branches. Watch patiently and note down the colors, shape, and behavior of different types of birds, and where and when you saw them.

Desert

Roadrunners live in the North and Central American deserts. They rarely fly, but can race at great speeds after their prey – insects, lizards, and snakes. They survive the scorching heat of the desert by staying in the shade until dusk, when the air and ground cool off.

Mountains

Some birds of prey, like this golden eagle, soar above high mountains. They glide on rising currents of air, keeping a lookout for prey below. They nest on cliff faces where they can rear their eaglets, protected from predators.

Never disturb nests or harm birds or eggs.

Keep a scrapbook to record the birds you see. Later you can compare it with a bird identification book.

National birds

Birds can be found virtually all over the world. Many nations have adopted as symbols birds that are native to the country or which migrate through the region. Often they are chosen for their beauty, rarity, or some other special feature. Some birds have even been incorporated onto national flags or emblems. Try to think of other ways in which birds have been used as symbols.

Australia

The black swan of Australia is revered as it is one of only three swan species in the Southern Hemisphere. It is all black with white wing feathers and a red bill.

Papua New Guinea

The flag of this country carries the silhouette of a bird of paradise, which is native to New Guinea. These birds are famed for their dazzling plumage and courtship displays.

The United States

The bald eagle was adopted as the national emblem of the United States in 1782. It was chosen because it is such a powerful, noble-looking bird.

Egypt

Egypt's national flag shows a bird of prey, which symbolizes strength. Kestrels were held sacred in Ancient Egypt, and were often mummified.

Uganda

The national flag of Uganda in East Africa shows an African balearic crane, also known as a crowned crane. They are residents of this region and are held in special regard because of their striking appearance and amazing dance.

MAKING AN ASTRONAUT'S HELMET

This mask, a must for all space games, is based on a shell made of papier mâché. It is a vital piece of equipment when visiting alien worlds.

You could cut zigzag shapes from paper and glue them on to decorate the visor.

You could add a stars and stripes flag, painted on or made with pieces of straw.

Measure and pierce two small eyeholes in the mask with scissors. Alternatively, you could make the visor from transparent plastic so that you can see out more easily.

1 To make papier mâché, mix flour and a little water in a bowl, until you have a thick paste. Tear a newspaper into strips. Blow up a balloon and stand it in another bowl. Dip a strip in the paste, run it through your fingers to remove excess paste, and lay it on the balloon. Repeat this until the top half of the balloon is covered with at least three layers of newspaper. Leave it to dry overnight. Burst the balloon. **2** Trim the bottom of the papier mâché shape flat with scissors. Draw on the shape of the visor, and cut it out with scissors. **3** Cut two segments from an egg carton to make earpieces, and tape them on the sides of the helmet. **4** Cut out a circular piece of trash can liner to make the visor, and tape it inside the helmet. **5** The astronauts's eyes are two Ping Pong balls, and the nose is a cork. Cut eyebrows from an egg carton and tape all these features to the visor. Splay one end of a drinking straw, and tape it to the top of the helmet to make a radio receiver. Pierce a hole through the straw, cut another straw in half and push it through the hole, to form a crosspiece.

drinking straws

balloon

egg carton

Ping Pong balls

flour

STEP BY STEP

1

2

3

4

5

PLANTS AND AIR

Air is just as vital to the survival of plants as it is to animals. Plants need carbon dioxide from the air to make food during the process of photosynthesis. But they also take in oxygen from the air and give out carbon dioxide, just as animals do. The waste product of photosynthesis is oxygen, which plants release into the air. During the history of the earth, plants gradually built up the oxygen in the atmosphere. Only after there was enough oxygen in the air, could animals develop.

oxygen

Dispersal record
You could make your own nature diary to keep a record of seeds which are spread by the wind, such as sycamore or dandelion seeds. Stick the seeds into your scrapbook and write down the date and where you found them. In spring and summer, look out for plants that use the wind to spread their pollen, such as tree catkins.

poppy seeds

Using the wind
Pollen and seeds that float on the wind are usually very light, but some use other floating devices such as little "wings," parachutes or air sacs. Seeds move away from the parent plant to reduce the competition for light, water and food nutrients.

water and minerals

A giant puffball can produce 7,000 billion spores in a lifetime. The spores (simple seeds) puff out in clouds every time the wind blows against them. Even an ordinary field mushroom can release 100 million spores in an hour.

dandelion spores

Land plant roots obtain the oxygen they need from water in the soil

The epidermis is covered in a waxy layer called the cuticle. Though this prevents the leaf losing water, it also prevents carbon dioxide from entering. So there are stomata (usually on the shady side) to let carbon dioxide in.

water

carbon dioxide

hairs

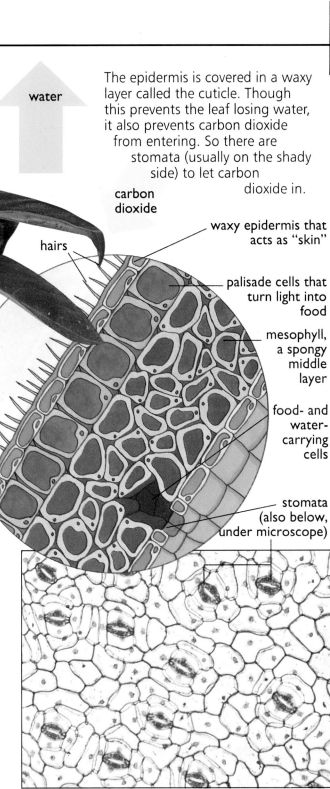

waxy epidermis that acts as "skin"

palisade cells that turn light into food

mesophyll, a spongy middle layer

food- and water-carrying cells

stomata (also below, under microscope)

Hay fever

Many people suffer from an allergic reaction to plant pollen called hay fever. Symptoms include a runny nose, sneezing, and watery eyes, but they are seasonal since plants only release pollen in spring and summer. Pollen counts are often given as part of weather forecasts to warn sufferers when to expect problems.

Plant "breathing"

Water plants take in gases from the water all over their surface. Land plants breathe through little holes called stomata in the leaves or stem. Woody stems have small raised pores called lenticels instead of stomata. The stomata or lenticels open and close to control the flow of gases and water vapor in and out of the leaf or stem. On a leaf, the stomata are mostly on the underside. There may be from 20 to over 1,000 stomata per square inch, depending on the species. The stomata usually open during daylight hours when the plant is busy taking in and giving out gases during photosynthesis.

Plants on mountains

At high altitudes, there is less oxygen for plants to breathe and less carbon dioxide for them to make their food. So mountain plants tend to grow slowly and function at a slow rate. The thin mountain air also fails to protect the mountain slopes from strong sunlight during the day and cold at night. Mountain plants tend to be short to hug the ground for warmth and to trap moisture, often growing in closely packed cushions for mutual protection.

Food from air

Plants make their own food from carbon dioxide and water, using the energy in sunlight. This process is called photosynthesis. The food that plants make is a sort of sugar called a carbohydrate. Some food is broken down during respiration to release energy.

WHAT IF THE CONTINENTS DIDN'T MOVE?

The land under your feet may seem solid and still. But each main landmass, or continent, is drifting very slowly across the face of the Earth, by less than 2 inches (5 cm) each year. The Earth's outer "skin," or crust, is made up of 12 giant, curved plates, like a vast, ball-shaped puzzle. They are called *lithospheric* (curved-rock) *plates*. As the plates rub against each other, their edges crack or get pushed deeper. Some plates enlarge, while others shrink. This has been going on since the Earth began, 4.5 billion years ago.

We would see some strange animal meetings!

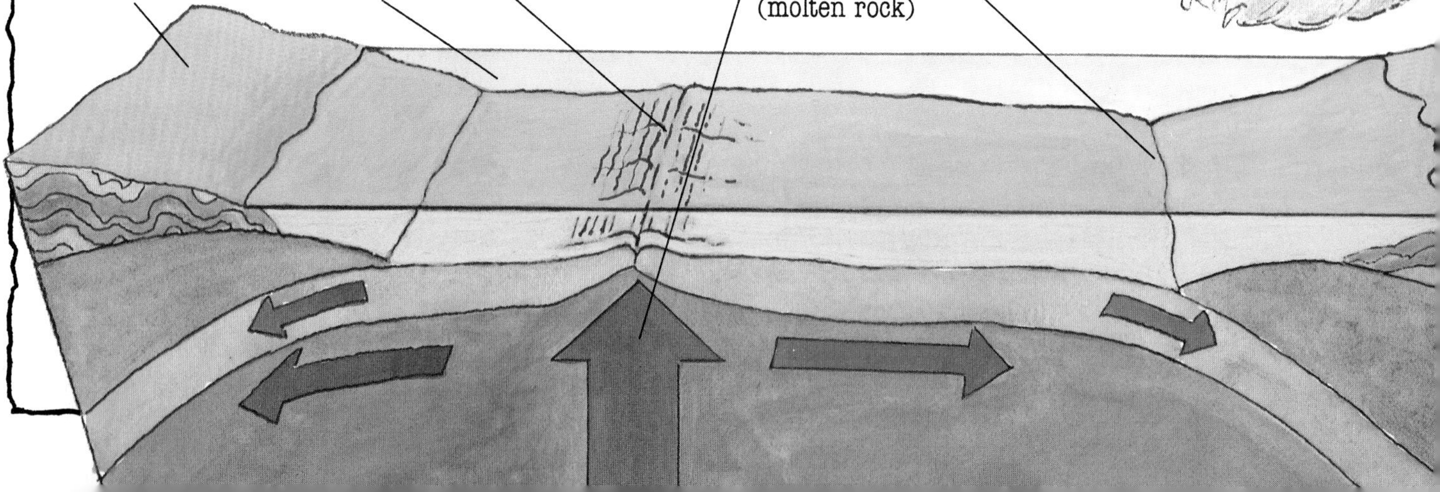

The plates under the ocean are thinner. Molten rock from deep below becomes solid, adds to the plate, pushing it sideways.

An oceanic plate pushes into a continental plate. The oceanic plate is forced down and an ocean trench forms.

Continent

Ocean

Magma (molten rock)

Rock steady

Without continental drift, there could be no metamorphic rocks, like marble. These form when other rocks are squeezed incredibly hard in the roots of new mountains. Igneous rocks, like granite, form when melted rock, such as the lava from volcanoes, cools and solidifies. Sedimentary rocks, such as chalk, form when tiny particles settle in a lake or sea, and get pressed and cemented together.

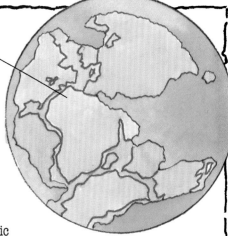

Pangaea

Metamorphic rock

Igneous rock

Sedimentary rock

Mapping out the world

About 250 million years ago all the continents were joined into one vast land mass, the super-continent of Pangaea. The continuous ocean around it was the Tethys Sea. If continental drift had stopped, the map would still look like this. A journey from North America to Europe, or South America to Africa, could be by car!

The layers of rock in the continental plate are crumpled by movements. This creates huge folds – mountains.

Highs and lows!

The world would be much flatter and less exciting without continental drift. The deepest part of the oceans, the Marianas Trench in the Pacific, and the highest mountain, Mount Everest in the Himalayas, wouldn't exist.

Fold mountains

DINOSAURS

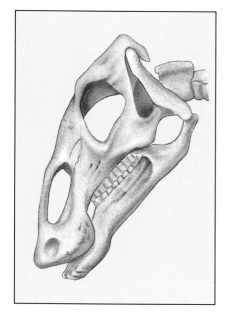

Dinosaurs, the word means "terrible lizards," were reptiles which became extinct about 65 million years ago. They lived on the earth for over 140 million years, but the last ones suddenly died out. This was possibly due to a rapid cooling of the planet's climate. Before that time most of the earth was warm and damp so that even in the Arctic Circle there were tropical plants and dinosaurs that ate them. Dinosaurs vanished from the earth millions of years before people evolved. We have to reconstruct what they might have looked like from their fossils. Today the animals that are related most closely to them are crocodiles and birds. Up to now scientists have discovered many hundreds of species of dinosaur.

The Protoceratops, when fully grown to six feet in length, had horns. The discovery of complete nests of fossil eggs (below) told scientists how dinosaurs looked after their young. The baby Protoceratops was about one foot long. The size of dinosaurs varied a lot.

The Brachiosaurus, for example, was 75 feet long and weighed 80 tons. The Cynognathus, from which the tooth (below right) came, was only five feet long. This reptile lived 200 million years ago.

Eggs

Cynognathus

Not all creatures that lived during the "Age of the Dinosaurs" were dinosaurs. Dinosaurs lived on the land. In the air were flying reptiles called pterosaurs, and in the sea were various types of swimming reptiles including plesiosaurs and ichthyosaurs.

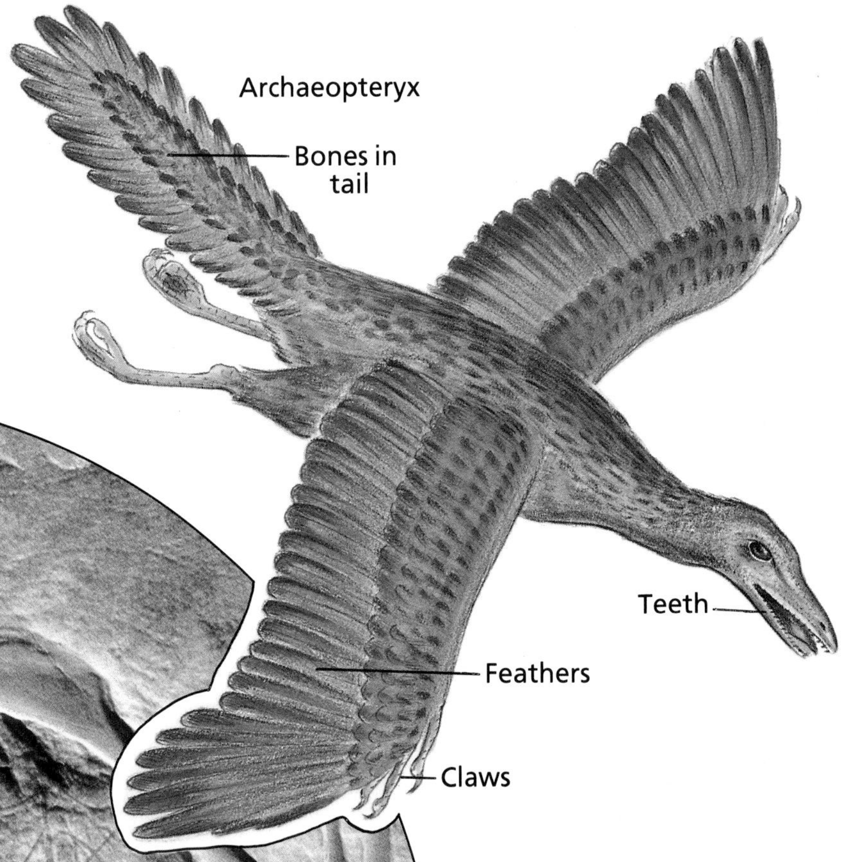

Archaeopteryx

Bones in tail

Teeth

Feathers

Claws

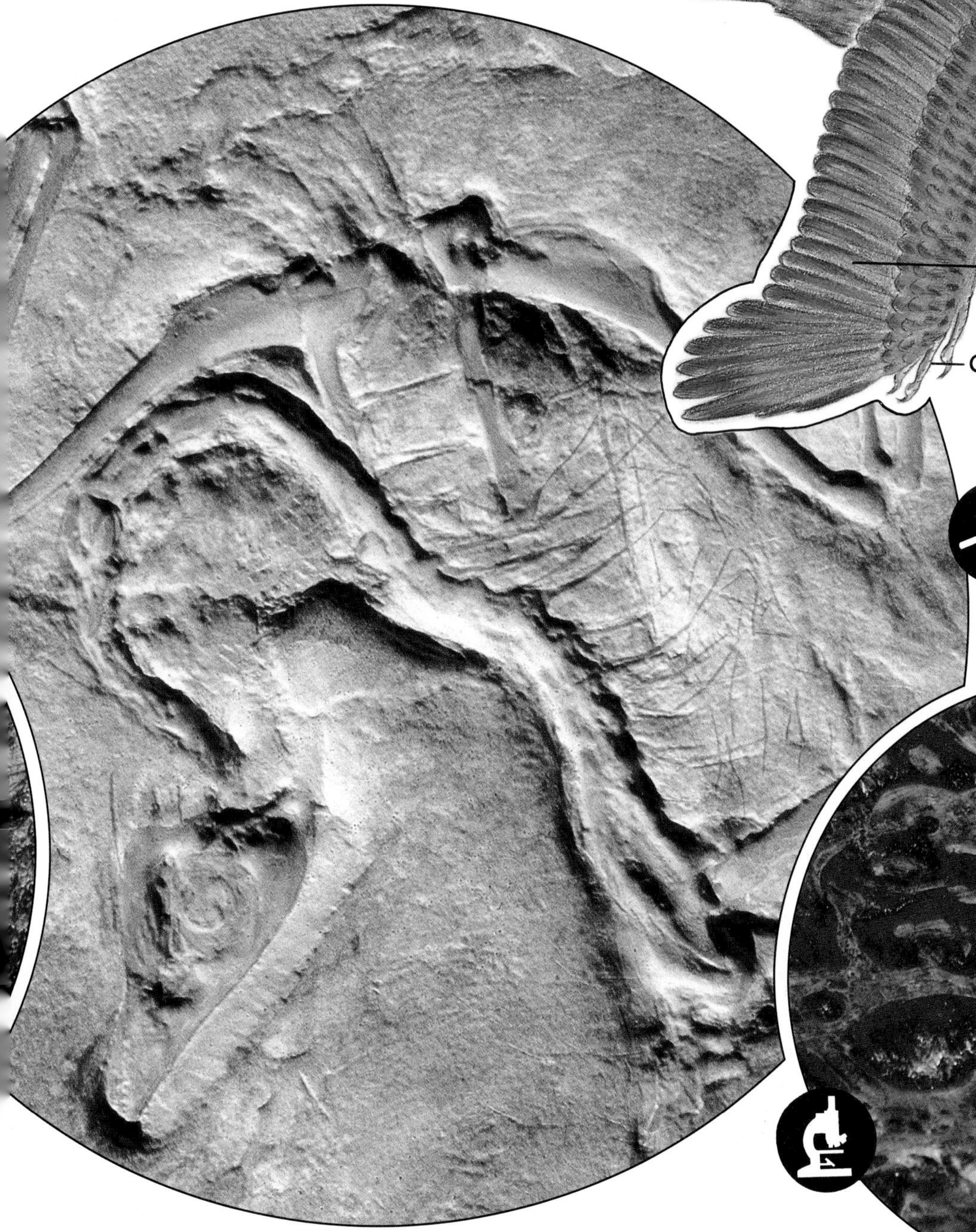

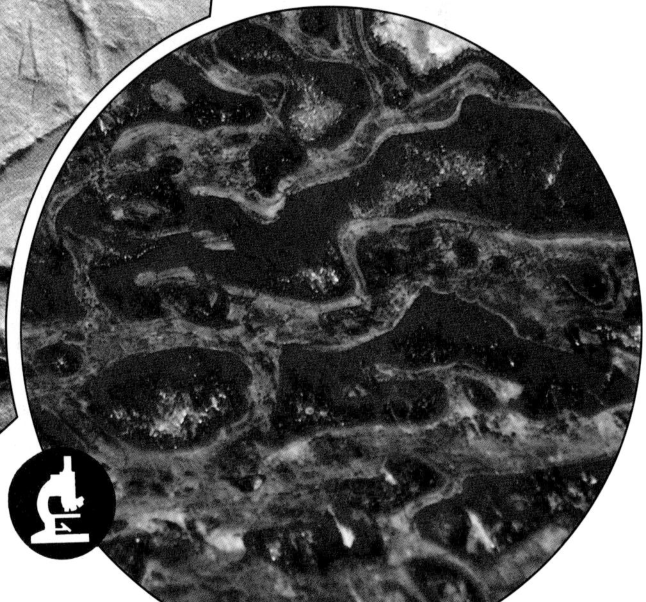

Some people claim that Archaeopteryx, see illustration top right and fossil above, is the missing link between extinct dinosaurs and the birds which we all know today. It was about the same size as a modern crow and ate insects and small reptiles. These strange flying animals had feathers, jaws with sharp teeth, wing claws for climbing trees, and a long bony tail.

Sometimes geologists, investigating rock layers, come across a cluster of fossilized bones. Under a microscope (see above) these can appear to be very beautiful. Paleontologists, scientists who specialize in fossils, will often have to study these finds in detail.

71

THE LEGACY OF ANCIENT GREECE

Many of the ideas of Ancient Greece were so intelligent or entertaining that they have attracted people from many times. During the Middle Ages, the long centuries in which Christianity dominated Europe, most Greek literature was lost forever. But from the fifteenth century people rediscovered how interesting the Greeks had been.

From that time until the present day, some schools have taught ancient Greek. Greek writings on politics and religion are still read with respect by many people. And modern scientists, when they want new words for new notions, often make them up — like "catalyst" and "electron" — from the language of the Greeks.

The Olympic Games
Today's Olympic Games are not very old. They began in 1896. They are modeled on the ancient Greek games, which were held every four years at Olympia. Like the modern Olympics (right), the ancient games were the supreme contest for athletes. Ancient Greek states, like nations today, used athletes for propaganda. They fixed races and bribed umpires!

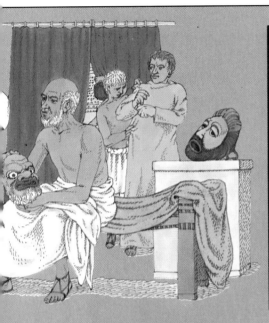

The theater
Drama seems to have originally grown from a simple chorus, which sang in honor of the god Dionysus. The illustration shows a famous playwright of Ancient Greece — Aeschylus — with his players. Plays were presented in theaters specially built into a hillside so that as many people as possible could see. Some of these theaters are still used today (above), and their design has been copied in many modern theaters.

Doric   Ionic   Corinthian

Architecture
Greek architecture is famous for its tall columns. They decorated important buildings, such as the Parthenon (above) in ancient times. Today, many towns have buildings in the Greek style, especially buildings where people go to think, like libraries and museums.

WHAT ARE MAMMALS?

Mammals are the most successful animals with backbones on Earth today. There are about 4,500 species, and they live in all habitats, from the coldest to the hottest, on land, in the sea, and in the air. Each one looks different, but in certain ways they are all alike. Mammals have large brains and keen senses. They communicate by sounds, smells, and visual means. They are warm-blooded, have an efficient circulation system and they care for their young. Human beings can even change their environment.

Mother's Milk

One of the reasons for the success of mammals is the care that they give to their young. Mothers provide instant food until the babies are big enough to feed themselves. This food, a liquid secretion called *milk*, contains nutrients and immunity to some diseases. It is made by mammary glands under the mother's skin, and the baby sucks it from nipples during nursing.

First Mammals

The last 65 million years, since the dinosaurs died out, has been the "Age of Mammals." But the first mammals appeared long before this, about 200 million years ago. They evolved from a group of mammal-like reptiles that were successful even before the reign of the dinosaurs. *Megazostrodon* and *Purgatorius* were among the first true mammals. These tiny animals hid in trees and undergrowth, hunting insects at night.

Taeniolabis (An early plant eater)

Purgatorius

Megazostrodon

Warm Blood

Mammals can live in any climate because they are warm-blooded, or *endothermic*. This means they can keep their bodies at the same temperature no matter how cold or hot the weather is. Endotherms generate heat by chemical reactions that go on inside the body tissues. They keep this heat in with layers of insulating fat and fur. If they get too hot, most mammals can produce sweat. Sweat is a liquid secreted onto the skin surface which evaporates and cools the body.

Food, Clothes, and Shelter

When people migrated from the warmth of Africa, where they first evolved, to colder northern latitudes, they began to use the skins of other mammals to keep themselves warm. In the far north, where there were no caves and no trees to build huts, they used colossal mammoth bones and tusks for the framework of shelters. This may have led to the first man-made extinctions, about 10,000 years ago, when the mammoths died out.

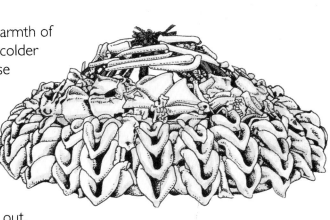

Vertebrates

Mammals belong to the group of animals known as *vertebrates*. They all have backbones as part of their internal skeletons. Skeletons provide support and protection for internal organs and enable movement. A gorilla's skeleton (left) is similar to that of an orang-utan (above).

Aesop's Fables

Aesop was a Greek storyteller who lived in the 6th century B.C. He used animal stories to show people how to deal with life's little problems, and to teach right from wrong. One story (below) tells of a race between a slow tortoise (a reptile) and a swift hare (a mammal). The hare is so far ahead, and so confident of victory, he takes a nap. The tortoise plods along steadily, passing the hare, who wakes up to see his opponent crossing the finishing line. The tale teaches that persistence can be more important than speed.

Adaptable Mammals

After the demise of the dinosaurs, mammals soon adapted to fill every habitat. Some mammals are perfectly adapted to a particular habitat. Dolphins are so well adjusted to life in the water they can no longer live on land. Others survive by being adaptable. The wolf lives by its wits, eating almost anything it can find, and taking advantage of any situation.

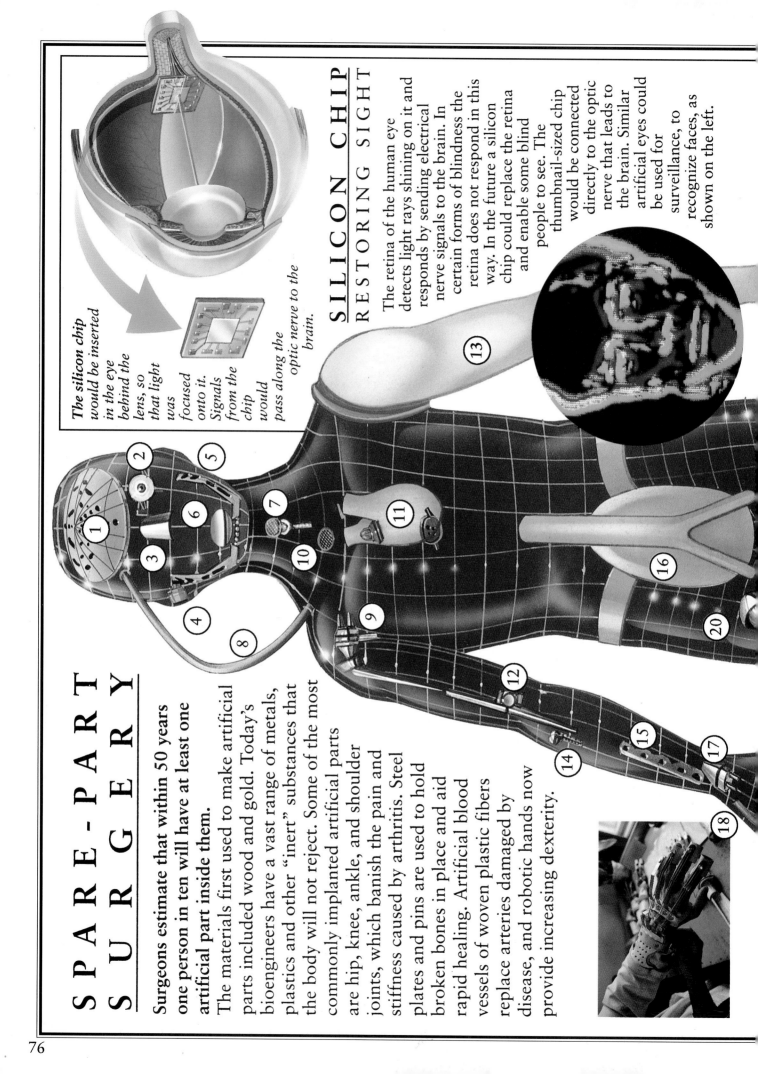

S P A R E - P A R T S U R G E R Y

Surgeons estimate that within 50 years one person in ten will have at least one artificial part inside them.

The materials first used to make artificial parts included wood and gold. Today's bioengineers have a vast range of metals, plastics and other "inert" substances that the body will not reject. Some of the most commonly implanted artificial parts are hip, knee, ankle, and shoulder joints, which banish the pain and stiffness caused by arthritis. Steel plates and pins are used to hold broken bones in place and aid rapid healing. Artificial blood vessels of woven plastic fibers replace arteries damaged by disease, and robotic hands now provide increasing dexterity.

The silicon chip would be inserted in the eye behind the lens, so that light was focused onto it. Signals from the chip would pass along the optic nerve to the brain.

SILICON CHIP
RESTORING SIGHT

The retina of the human eye detects light rays shining on it and responds by sending electrical nerve signals to the brain. In certain forms of blindness the retina does not respond in this way. In the future a silicon chip could replace the retina and enable some blind people to see. The thumbnail-sized chip would be connected directly to the optic nerve that leads to the brain. Similar artificial eyes could be used for surveillance, to recognize faces, as shown on the left.

The chip contains hundreds of light-sensitive cells. All the cells operate at once, processing data very fast.

The latest artificial limbs are a huge improvement on previous versions. Here a champion at the Paralympic Games shows how the revolutionary "flex foot" enables him to run. The foot has a joint that bends (flexes) and then springs back. The latest artificial hands can be connected to nerves in the arm. Tiny electrical signals from the nerves control motors and levers, to reproduce some of the movements of real hands.

Above, a victim of the siege of Sarajevo is fitted with a new artificial hand.

Real hands can both grip and feel. The pincer movement between fingers and thumb is especially important for picking things up. Advances in the robot industry have produced artificial hands with touch-feedback that can grip items lightly or firmly. Some patients prefer simpler devices.

Artificial implants
1. Skull plate 2. Eye 3. Nose bridge
4. Hearing aid 5. Jaw plate
6. Chin implant 7. Electronic larynx
8. Valve to control water on the brain
9. Shoulder joint 10. Filter to prevent blood clotting in the lungs 11. Artificial heart
12. Elbow hinge 13. Artificial arm
14. Radial bone-head 15. Metal forearm plate
16. Stoma appliance 17. Wristbones
18. Tendon 19. Thumb/wristbone connection
20. Hip joint 21. Femoral bone
22. Knee hinge 23. Artificial leg
24. Big toe

The String Family

The violin is the smallest member of the string family, and the highest in pitch. It was also the first to be invented. The violin's immediate relatives — the viola, cello, and double bass — can also be either bowed or plucked. As the body of the instrument gets bigger, so its range of notes becomes lower.

VIOLA, CELLO, AND DOUBLE BASS

The viola (below) is slightly bigger than the violin, and is held in the same way. The cello (right) is even bigger, and is played sitting down. The instrument is held between the player's knees, and rests on an endpin or spike. Largest and deepest is the double bass (far right), which has the same strings as the violin, but in the reverse order. Bass players play sitting on a high stool, or standing up.

THE CONCERT HARP

The other member of the string family with a regular place in the symphony orchestra is the concert harp. Each string of the harp produces one note when plucked; each of these notes can be lowered or raised half a tone by means of pedals. The characteristic sound of the harp makes it instantly recognizable, even when the whole orchestra is playing. Also related are the guitar and the zither, which is a folk instrument.

THE STRINGS IN THE ORCHESTRA

The stringed instuments form the mainstay of the modern Western symphony or chamber orchestra. Together the strings cover a range of over seven octaves. It is even possible to have an orchestra made solely of string players – a string orchestra. The variety of effects possible with stringed instruments, such as *pizzicato* makes them very popular with composers.

GEOGRAPHY OF THE ORCHESTRA

The diagram below shows how a symphony orchestra is usually laid out. The stringed instruments are spread across the front of the platform in a semicircle, ranging from the violins on the left to the double basses on the far right. The conductor stands at the front, surrounded by string players. If the piece is a concerto, the soloist stands or sits next to the conductor.

POSITIONS OF THE STRINGS

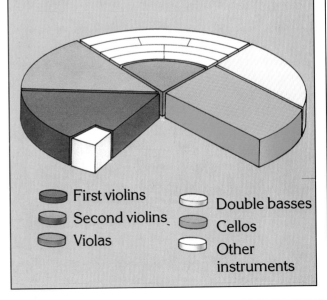

- First violins
- Second violins
- Violas
- Double basses
- Cellos
- Other instruments

ALTO AND BASS CLEFS

The lower stringed instruments read music written in different clefs, although both the viola and the cello sometimes use the treble clef. The viola usually plays music written in the alto clef (below left) and the cello uses the bass clef (right). So does the double bass, but its notes sound an octave lower than written.

PLOTTING THE STARS

Astronomy is the study of the stars, planets and other objects in the universe. For centuries, astronomers have striven to learn more about our Universe. Through observation and careful measurement, using scientific tools like the telescope, we now know that the Sun is the center of our solar system. Accurate measurement of star distance is a science developed over the centuries by astronomers like Tycho Brahe (1546-1601). Centuries ago, sailors calculated time at night by observing the movements of star clusters near the fixed Pole Star. Watches aboard ship were timed from the position of these constellations in the sky.

STAR TIME

1

1. Use the star chart opposite to trace the positions of the stars in the northern hemisphere and the related months.

2. Mount the tracing of the star chart on stiff cardboard.

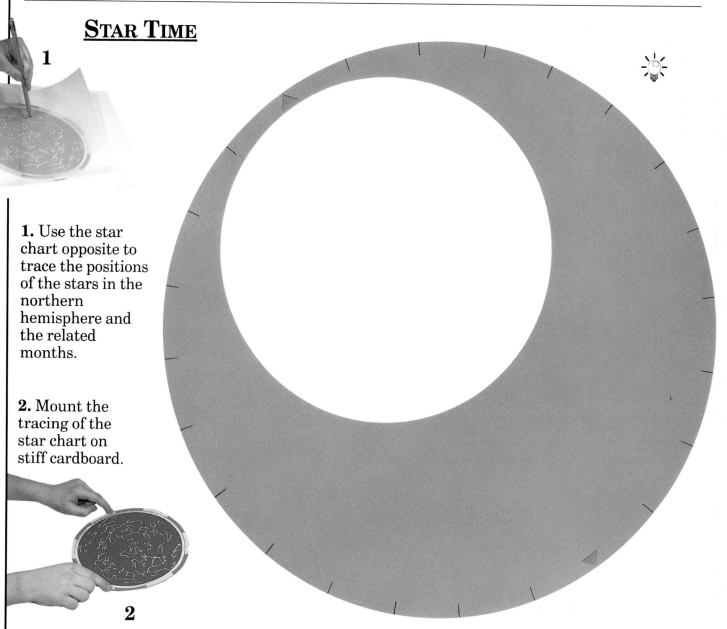

2

3. Trace the shape on the opposite page onto cardboard. Mark the 24 hours of the day, starting with Noon at the bottom.

4. Proceed counterclockwise covering the "window" of the planisphere with transparent plastic. Pin it to the starchart through the center.

3

4

5. On a starry night, rotate the planisphere until the time of day, marked on the edge, is lined up with the appropriate month at the bottom of the star chart. Compare what you see with the stars in the sky.

WHY IT WORKS

As the Earth revolves around the Sun, different constellations of stars appear and disappear in a continous cycle that can be observed. This planisphere shows where these groups of stars can be seen at any given time of the year, in the northern hemisphere. By matching up the time of day with the date, you can view the stars that should be visible in the night sky through the cut out "window." The planisphere should be held up and viewed from underneath. The stars visible through the window should match those in the sky. The Sun is a star. It is the only star close enough to look like a ball. The other billions of stars are so far away, they appear to be pinpoints of light.

AIR POLLUTION

The Earth's atmosphere is polluted naturally by sandstorms and the dust and gases from volcanoes. But the most serious kind of air pollution comes from people. Factories, power stations, and vehicle exhausts pump harmful gases into the air, contributing to global warming, causing acid rain, and destroying the ozone layer. On a much smaller scale, air pollution causes all sorts of breathing problems. There are no simple solutions to air pollution, but people could reduce air pollution by saving energy and reducing harmful emissions from vehicle exhausts and power stations.

Noise pollution
Loud noises not only annoy people but can damage hearing. Noise is measured in decibels, with 0 decibels being the lowest sound audible to human ears. A level of 160 decibels, such as the noise of a jet airplane taking off at close range, will cause damage to hearing.

Air pollution is at its worst over big cities where millions of people live, work, and travel about in cars, buses, and trucks. Factory chimneys can be fitted with devices to cut down air pollution, but this is expensive. If better public transport and cycle lanes were available in towns and cities, people would be less likely to use their cars, reducing the overall amount of pollution.

Smoking
Smoking cigarettes adds to the general levels of air pollution as well as damaging our health. Cigarette smoke contains chemicals that can cause cancer, a gas which stops oxygen being taken into the blood and a substance called nicotine which raises blood pressure and makes the heart beat faster. No-smoking areas cut down on this pollution and save non-smokers breathing in other people's cigarette smoke.

Volcanic pollution

When a volcano erupts, dust is blasted high above the troposphere and may take weeks to be carried around the world. It is above the weather zone, so cannot be washed out of the air by rain. It will eventually fall to Earth after a few years.

Radioactive pollution

In 1986, part of a nuclear reactor at Chernobyl in the Ukraine exploded, releasing dangerous radioactive pollution into the atmosphere. This was carried around the world by winds and rain, polluting countries many thousands of miles away. The radioactivity was passed on from plants, which took it from the air, to animals eating plants. People were also affected (such as young children) and health and farming problems persist today.

Detecting pollution

To find out more about the air pollution in your local area, try putting out squares of card covered in grease or vaseline. Put them in different places and leave them for a week or so. Which card collects the most dirt? How does the weather affect the amount of dirt in the air?

Plants called lichens are very sensitive to air pollution. If there are no lichens in your area, the air is very dirty. Leafy or bushy lichens indicate clean air, while the presence of flat, crusty lichens – like the orange circles on rooftops and walls – mean the air is very dirty.

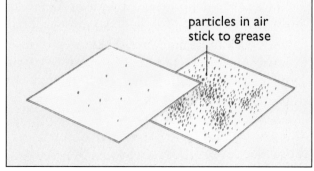

particles in air stick to grease

GOING WEST

European settlers arrived in North America in the early 17th century. For over a hundred years they remained largely on the Atlantic seaboard, but by the beginning of the 19th century, the United States was on the move, heading west. By 1820 the frontier was across the Mississippi. Texas was annexed twenty-five years later and by 1853, apart from Alaska, the frontiers of the United States were as they stand today.

Two events followed this expansion. One was the migration of thousands of Americans to start new lives on the Great Plains and beyond. The other was the Civil War (1861–65). The era of the cowboy was about to begin.

STEER ROPERS. One of the biggest differences between screen cowboys and real ones is racial. The movie cowboys are generally white and English-speaking. Many real cowboys were non-white, and the working language of nearly all cowboys was Spanish.

One in seven cowboys was an African American, including two of the most skilled and famous, Nat Love (*above left*) and John Ware. There were also many Native Americans and Mexican cowboys. But the movie makers had different ideas. When cowboys passed through the filter of Hollywood, only the white ones were left (*above right*), thus creating one of the most powerful myths of modern culture.

Wagon trains were the final phase of westward expansion. First came the explorers and trappers, then the cattlemen, and finally farmers and their families in the long trains of wagons. The three great trail routes ran west from St. Louis and Natchez on the Mississippi, and Fort Smith on the Arkansas River.

ABRAHAM LINCOLN

Born of pioneer parents in 1809, Lincoln (*left*) trained as a lawyer and became President of the United States in 1860.

He guided the North (also known as the Union) through the Civil War, firmly believing that slavery was a moral evil. He abolished slavery in 1863. He was assassinated in 1865.

HANDS FOR HIRE

Men – and a few women – became cowboys for all kinds of reasons. The Civil War, fought between the Northern and Southern states over the issue of slavery, had put almost three million men in arms. When the North won in 1865, many returned home to find there was no work.

These included some of the 200,000 ex-slaves who had fought for their freedom with the North. A number of discharged troops, black and white, signed up as cowboys (*below*). They were joined by a few young men leaving prosperous homes in the northeast in search of adventure. But the life of the cowboy was anything but romantic. It was dirty, often dull, and always hard.

Discharge
After the Civil War, many ex-soldiers became cowboys.

85

BEETLES

In terms of numbers, the group of beetles, or Coleoptera, has been more successful than any other kind of animal. There are at least 370,000 known species in the world, and new ones are being discovered all the time. Beetles are armor-plated insects. The head and thorax are covered in tough cuticle, formed into strange, threatening shapes in many species. Despite their heavy appearance, most beetles fly very well. Beetle grubs undergo complete metamorphosis to become adult.

Some species of beetles are herbivores (plant-eaters), others are carnivores (meat-eaters). Some kill prey and eat it. Many perform the important function of consuming the dead bodies of animals, some eating the flesh, others eating fur or feathers. Some feed on animal dung. Some beetle pests consume grains or vegetables. Colorado beetles attack potato crops. Others attack vegetation, such as elm bark beetles that spread Dutch elm disease.

Weevil

Burying beetle

Most beetles have biting jaws to seize their prey. In weevils the jaws are located on the end of a long nose or rostrum.

Light show

Glowworms, or fireflies, are neither worms nor flies. They are beetles that produce light to attract mates. During dark evenings, males and females flash signals to each other, like morse code signals from a lantern. The code is different for each species. In South-East Asia, whole trees pulse with thousands of these tiny lights. The light is made by a chemical reaction involving an enzyme which releases energy in the form of light.

Holy beetle

The female scarab beetle rolls a ball of dung to her burrow. She lays her eggs in the dung, and the larvae feed on it. The scarab beetle was sacred to the ancient Egyptians. They compared the insect's behavior with the action of their god Ra, who, they believed, rolled the sun across the sky each day. Egyptian craftsmen made scarab jewelry, using gold, lapis lazuli, and semi-precious stones.

Rove beetle

Chafer beetle

Many kinds of beetles have fierce-looking jaws and horns. These are often for show, to frighten off predators, or for fighting between males. Stag beetles (left) are so named because the male has fearsome, antlerlike jaws. Sparring stag beetles wrestle, each trying to turn his opponent over. In beetles, the front pair of wings form tough, often colorful wing cases, called elytra. These fold back when the insect is not flying, to protect the delicate wings beneath. In flight, the wing cases are raised.

Elytron

Insect machines

Some engineers have used insects as inspiration in the design and manufacture of machines. In the late 1940's the vehicle manufacturer Volkswagen pioneered a family car with a rounded beetle shape. Its success was phenomenal, and over 19 million Volkswagen Beetles were produced and exported to nearly 150 countries worldwide.

Heralds of death

Deathwatch beetles are wood borers. The larvae live in the dead wood of trees or in cut timber such as the roof timbers of a house. At mating time the males and females call to each other from the tunnels they have bored, tapping their jaws on the wood, and making an ominous ticking noise. In the days before pest control and when illnesses were difficult to treat, this sound in old houses was thought to foretell a death in the family, ticking away the last minutes of someone's life.

HOT-AIR FLIGHT

Have you seen a hot-air balloon? More than 200 years ago, two French brothers, Joseph and Jacques Montgolfier, discovered that rising hot air could be captured and used for flight. They made a huge balloon from linen and paper and built a fire underneath it. The balloon trapped the hot air and smoke rising from the fire and lifted the two men into the air. As the air cooled, the balloon floated back down to the ground. Since that first flight, people have used hot-air balloons for pleasure, for racing, and even for warfare. You can make your own hot-air balloon.

BALLOON LIFT-OFF

1

1 To make a balloon that traps hot air to fly, you need four large sheets of tissue paper. Fold each sheet in half and lightly copy this shape on to one using a pencil. When you are happy with the outline cut out your first "panel."

2

2 Use the first panel to help you mark out the next three. Cut them out and trim them carefully to make sure they are all the same size.

3

3 Unfold your first panel and spread glue on the edge of one half. Stick the second panel on top and press down. Repeat with the next panel until all four panels are joined into a balloon.

4

4 Make a small "passenger basket" from a piece of folded oak tag. Attach the basket to the open end of the balloon with four lengths of thread.

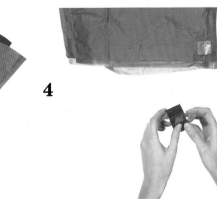

5 Take the balloon outside for your first flight. Blow up the balloon with hot air from a hair dryer and watch it lift off.

5

Lift

Balloon

WHY IT WORKS

Your hot-air balloon rises because it contains air that is warmer – and therefore lighter – than the surrounding air. (Air, indeed all gases, expand when heated. They become lighter because the same amount of gas takes up more space.) Hot air from the dryer enters the bottom of the balloon and rises inside to the top, causing the balloon to lift off. The colder the air around it, the faster the hot air will rise. A hot-air balloon has no power to move along – it needs a wind to help it.

Heated air

Gravity

BRIGHT IDEAS

See if your hot-air balloon works better in a hot room or a cold room. (See why it works, above.)

Make some modeling clay passengers for your basket. Notice whether the balloon needs more hot air for lifting power.

Will a larger hot-air balloon rise even better? Build one and find out.

Watch the smoke rising above a campfire. Do you see how the hot air carries it up? As the air cools the smoke stops rising as fast. Notice what happens then. Does the smoke scatter in the wind?

CREATING A SUPERHERO

A comic strip is a series of pictures that tell a story, from the adventures of mischievous school friends to the exploits of fantasy superheroes. The next two pages are about creating your own comic strip, and the first step is to invent the characters.

What do Superman, the Incredible Hulk, and the Teenage Mutant Ninja Turtles have in common? Most superheroes are concocted from a recipe of certain ingredients. Looking at these ingredients can help you build your own characters.

Factor X

Some superheroes come from other planets but most are from Earth; they are ordinary people or (animals) who have acquired a special ability, often as a result of some extraordinary event. This is sometimes linked to radiation, but not always; Popeye gets his great strength from an ordinary can of spinach.

A superhero has his or her own territory, a particular location to patrol. Cities are popular, and, of course, the far reaches of outer space.

Missions and superskills

All superheroes have a cause - to fight villains like the one shown above left, or to right a particular injustice in the world. Your superhero will need a mission and a special ability - think about the superpower you would most like to have for yourself!

A superpower can be extra strength, vision, or hearing, or it can be something new, from X-ray vision to the ability to change shape. A superhero associated with an animal takes on the creature's powers - so the owl girl above might be able to see in the dark. Other favorite crime fighters are themselves animals.

Developing a script

Your superhero can be developed by thinking about costume, weaknesses, likes and dislikes, sidekicks and friends. But the best way of learning about your superhero is to set out on an adventure and see how he performs!

What makes a good storyline? Cartoon scripts often contain certain key ingredients. The strip begins with a problem: a crime or mystery which is often the the work of the villain. It may be almost too late before the hero learns of the trouble and decides to step in.

Meanwhile problems may mount up, and friends may be captured or wounded. In the nick of time comes a moment of inspiration, and the tide turns. Triumph! There is often a celebration before the hero heads home. Develop your plot along these lines and your superhero is ready to go!

▷ *"My superhero. Cartoonman, is a cool customer; here you can see him studying his script, unconcerned by the battle raging around him. To find out what problems lie in store for him, see the script in the box above.*

Cartoonman's first adventure
Rocketwoman is guiding her spaceship across the galaxy when the engine develops a fault. Forced to crash land on an unknown planet, she is besieged by alien lifeforms. Using his superhearing, Cartoonman learns of the danger. He speeds to the planet and soon has things sorted out. Returning Rocketwoman to her own planet, he receives a hero's send off and returns to base.

91

SUNLIGHT

The Sun is a star that gives us light and heat energy. The Sun is about 93 million miles from the Earth. All plants grow toward the sun. If you see a field of sunflowers, like the one pictured here, you will notice that they all face the same way, toward the Sun. Plants use the Sun's energy to make their own food. This energy is trapped by the green chlorophyll in a plant's leaves. During a process called photosynthesis, oxygen is released into the air as the sunlight is used to convert nutrients from the soil into food. The Greek word "photo" means light. Bioethanol is a fuel made by fermenting the food produced by plants like wheat. One day it could replace gasoline.

LEAVES

1. Half fill a shallow container with soil and scatter watercress seeds on the top. Keep the soil moist and place the tray in a sunny position. Leave it until the seeds sprout.

2. Cut out your initials from some cardboard, and place it over the seedlings. Make sure the sunlight cannot reach the plants beneath.

3. Leave the tray in its sunny position. You may have to wait as long as two weeks. Keep the soil moist while the cress is growing.

4. During this growing time do not remove the cardboard. You may want to turn the tray occasionally to allow an equal amount of light to reach every part of the tray.

5. When you observe that the watercress is fully grown, remove the cardboard. You should be able to see your initials in the seedlings. They will be a much darker green than the rest of the cress, where the light could not reach.

1

2

3

4

WHY IT WORKS

Sunlight is used by plants to convert nutrients from the soil into chemical energy for growth. When the leaves are covered, sunlight cannot be absorbed. No food can be manufactured inside the plant. Plants absorb carbon dioxide and water. These are converted by the green chlorophyll in the leaves into oxygen and simple sugars. The sugars are converted into food for the plant while the remaining oxygen and water is released into the air through small holes called stomata. These are located on the underside of the leaves. This process is called photosynthesis.

Sunlight

Carbon dioxide absorbed

Water absorbed

Oxygen and water released

5

BRIGHT IDEAS

Starch is produced when leaves photosynthesize. You can test for starch. Ask an adult to help you. Remove some cress from different parts of the tray and soak them in rubbing alcohol to remove any green chlorophyll. Then place them on a clean surface and put drops of dilute iodine on the surface of each. Where starch is present, the leaves will turn blue, where there is no starch they will turn brown.

Plants always grow toward the sun. This is called phototropism. Plant a seedling in a pot and place it in a shoe box. Place a hole at one end of the box for the light to enter. The shoot will appear through the hole.

One of the greatest problems with cars is finding somewhere to put them. Renault's concept car, the Matra Zoom, gets around this problem by making itself smaller, tucking its rear wheels under itself for parking, and stretching them out again for the open road. Other manufacturers have turned to electronics. Volkswagen's concept car, the Futura, is fitted with lasers and

Matra Zoom

ultrasound sensors to measure the space, and to park the car.

Driving position

Parking position

Route-planners linked to a central computer will guide the driver. In a strange area, the planners will suggest the best route. At home, where routes are familiar, they will warn of road works, congestion, and accidents. Systems like these are already being tested and could be common within about five years. The dashboard of the future will be designed to provide lots of clear information. Speed, fuel level, and warnings of dangers ahead may be shown as "head-up displays" on the screen, close to the driver's line of sight.

SMART CARS
DRIVING MADE EASIER

The car of the future will make driving easier and safer.

Onboard computers will control many parts of the car, including the suspension and anti-lock brakes. Communication links will provide driver information.

Once on a highway, cars will be driven automatically a few feet apart, using sensors to prevent crashes. This technique, called "platooning" and already tested in California, is safer and makes much better use of roads. If someone pulls out unexpectedly, all the cars will automatically slow to prevent a crash. Onboard route maps will show the way, or direct the driver by voice control. Each car will be centrally monitored, with systems that can override the driver.

Driving in the future is unlikely to be free. Some of today's road and fuel taxes will be replaced by "road pricing" systems, which will charge for the use of busy city streets or highways. The ADEPT plan, being developed by 16 European countries, would use beacons on the roadside and meters in the cars to deduct payments from the user's "Smart card." Charges could be based on the distance traveled, limited to a city center, or levied only when the roads are congested. The congestion meter would be activated by microwave beacons located on the outskirts of the charging area.

THE AIR BAG
HOW LIVES ARE SAVED

Air bags are triggered by the rapid deceleration in a crash. Instantly, a small explosive charge fires, inflating the bag with gas. In a 30-mph crash into a solid barrier, the charge fires in under ten milliseconds – blinking the eye takes fifteen times as long. By 20 milliseconds, the driver is moving forward and the bag is expanding fast. At 80 milliseconds, the car has stopped dead and the driver's head has hit the air bag, which vents gas to absorb the energy. The driver bounces back unhurt. Air bags were developed in the United States where many people are reluctant to wear seat belts. It was important to develop a restraint that was automatic, and did not rely on the drivers remembering to use it. Combining the air bag and seat belt will virtually eliminate serious head and facial injuries, even in faster crashes.

Seat belts have cut road deaths dramatically, but not everybody wears them. Even when they are worn, they do not offer complete protection. In frontal crashes at 20-30 mph, almost a third of the drivers hit their heads on the steering wheel even if they are belted up. The airbag prevents this, inflating in a fraction of a second to provide a soft cushion absorbing the impact of the crash. Air bags are a masterpiece of engineering, although there have been a few problems. Some materials burn due to the friction caused by the inflating bag.

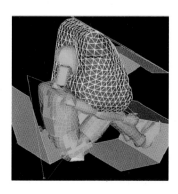

THE BODY SYSTEMS

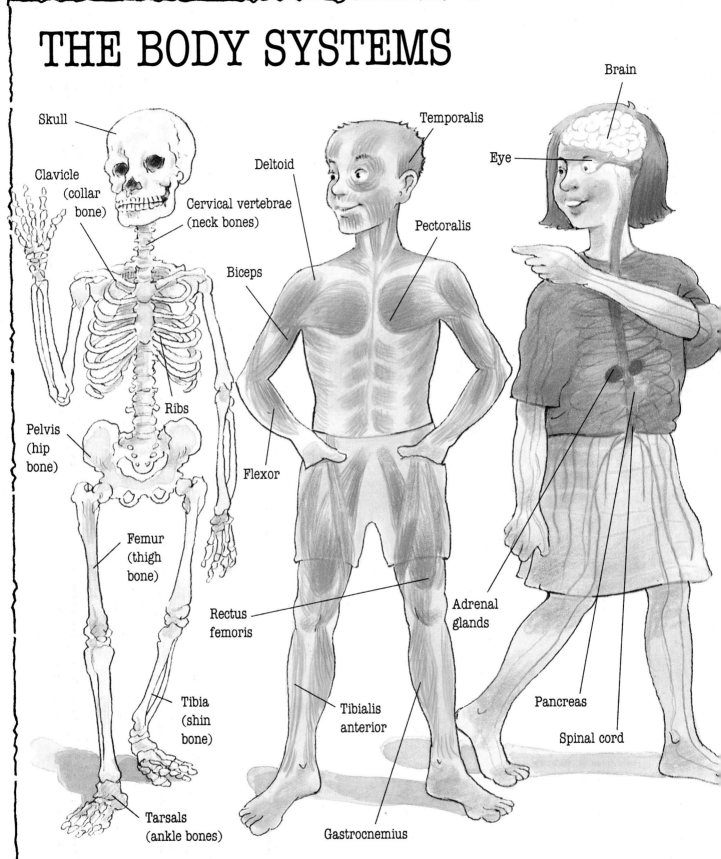

Skull

Clavicle (collar bone)

Cervical vertebrae (neck bones)

Ribs

Pelvis (hip bone)

Femur (thigh bone)

Tibia (shin bone)

Tarsals (ankle bones)

Temporalis

Deltoid

Pectoralis

Biceps

Flexor

Rectus femoris

Tibialis anterior

Gastrocnemius

Adrenal glands

Brain

Eye

Pancreas

Spinal cord

The Skeleton
206 bones provide a rigid frame-work moved by muscles and protect soft parts like the brain.

Muscles
Over 640 muscles pull bones, so you can move. Muscles are two-fifths of our total body weight.

Nerves, Senses, and Glands
The nerves and glands control the body's systems, using either chemical or electrical messages.

Jugular vein

Aorta (main artery)

Heart

Windpipe (trachea)

Saliva gland

Liver

Gullet

Lungs

Kidneys

Stomach

Ureter

Large intestine

Femoral artery and vein

Bladder

Anus

Small intestine

Circulation

The body's cardiovascular system circulates blood through the blood vessels pumped by the heart. The blood spreads oxygen and nutrients, and collects any of the body's waste products.

Respiration and excretion

In respiration, the lungs absorb oxygen from the air, and excrete, or get rid of, carbon dioxide. The kidneys excrete wastes by filtering them from the blood, to form urine.

Digestion

The mouth, gullet, stomach, and intestines break down food and absorb nutrients into the body. The pancreas makes digestive juices, and the liver processes and stores nutrients.

WHAT IS A VOLCANO?

Volcanoes are openings in the surface of the earth, from which molten rock, called magma, and gases can escape.

The earth is made up of three layers – the crust, the mantle and the core. The crust is the outermost layer of rock and can be quite thin. The continental crust is between 20 and 30 miles thick, but the oceanic crust is only about 3 miles thick.

The crust feels solid but it consists of giant plates (see illustration, right)

which float on the upper mantle. The upper mantle is made of hot, molten rock called magma which is always moving. Pressure in the mantle forces magma to the surface.

Volcanic eruptions occur where the rising magma finds a way through a crack or weakness in the earth's crust, usually at the edges of plates. These are called plate margins.

Central vent
Pressure causes gases to build up and force the magma up the central pipe and out through the vent. A deep, steep-walled crater forms around the vent.

Lava stream
Bubbles of gas force the rising magma to the surface. At the surface, magma is called lava. As lava cools, it solidifies into rock.

Layers

The steep slopes are built up of alternate layers of ash, and hardened lava. Sometimes lava bursts through in other places and forms other cones on the sides of the central cone.

Ash

The clouds of ash and gas that pour from the volcano help to form the cone shape around its vent. The ash consists of tiny pieces of lava, which harden into rock called tuff.

Magma

Magma collects in a chamber in the upper mantle. It is formed when two plates collide. The edge of one plate is dragged down under the other and melts into magma.

Plate movements

200 million years ago, all the land was joined together in one big continent called Pangaea. Gradually the pieces drifted apart and formed the seven continents we have today. Active volcanoes are usually found in definite zones, near plate margins. They are mostly caused by plate movement.

Active volcanoes marked in red

200 million years ago — 100 — 50 — Present day

Types of volcano

Thick, slow moving andesite lava builds up high, cone-shaped volcanoes. Andesite volcanoes are very violent.

Shield volcanoes form when runny lava escapes through a fissure and flows a long way. The volcano has broad sloping sides like a shield.

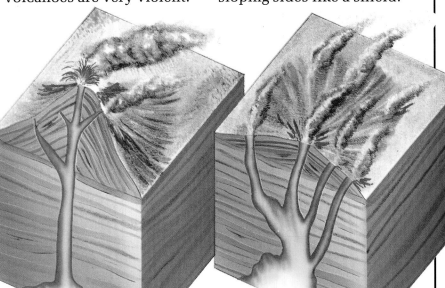

99

HOOFED ANIMALS

Ungulates walk on the tips of their toes which are protected by hard hooves. Hooves are made from keratin, the same horny material as claws and nails. Solid hooves are an adaptation for running away from predators. Ungulates are divided into three groups: the elephants and their relatives (such as hyraxes); the perissodactyls or odd-toed ungulates, such as horses and zebras; and the artiodactyls or even-toed ungulates, such as cattle.

Odds and Evens

The skeletons of ungulate feet show how they walk on the tips of their toes.
Originally all mammals had five digits or toes. But as ungulates evolved they lost toes to improve their speed. Some ungulates, like elephants, still have five toes. Pig trotters have two large hooves and two small hooves which do not touch the ground. Rhinos (upper left) walk on three toes, deer have four (lower left) but walk upon two, and horses have only one.

Mythical Horses

In Ancient Greek mythology, the winged Pegasus flew up to heaven and was tamed by the goddess Athena with a magical golden bridle. The Unicorn is a white horse with a spiral horn growing from its forehead. It is said that whoever drinks from its horn is protected from poisoning.

Diseases

Foot-and-mouth disease affects animals with cloven (split) hooves, such as cattle and sheep. It spreads rapidly through the herds and can bankrupt farmers. Some animal diseases spread to humans. Sleeping sickness is transferred from cattle to humans via the blood-sucking tsetse fly (below).

Migration

Many animals make seasonal migrations to new habitats, to find better living conditions. Huge herds of wildebeest walk hundreds of miles across the African plains in search of grass and water. The urge to move is so strong they will tackle any obstacle. Many die on the way, drowning in rivers, falling down gorges, or caught by predators.

Ungulate Relatives

Camels (left) and llamas are even-toed ungulates. But they do not walk on the tips of their toes like other cloven-hoofed animals. The weight is carried by soft pads behind their hooves. Camels are ideally suited for desert life. Their wide feet do not sink in the sand, their humps store food for long-distance travel, and their stomachs can hold 22 gallons of water. Rhinos are primitive relatives of horses. They have stumpy feet with three hoofed toes, and thick, hairless skin folded into armorlike plates.

Horsemanship

Man's first association with horses was to hunt them for meat. Horses were domesticated in Asia about 6,000 years ago. Until the horse collar was invented, horses were not used to pull heavy loads, but for pulling warriors in chariots. In the Middle Ages horses were bred to be strong enough to carry knights in full armor. These thoroughbreds are among the 150 breeds known today.

Zebras (left) are closely related to horses and donkeys. They live in sociable groups, grazing on the African plains.

101

WHAT IF THERE WERE NO PILOT?

Sometimes there isn't. At least, not a human pilot actually operating the controls. Many modern planes have an automatic pilot. It's not a robot sitting in the pilot's seat, but a set of controls incorporated into the main controls. The real pilot sets the plane's speed, height and direction, then switches to automatic, for a break. Of course, if something happens, alarms activate, and the real pilot takes the controls. In very modern planes, the computer-based auto-pilot can even take off and land the aircraft.

How do pilots "fly by wire?"

Computer screens are wired up to show speed, direction, engine conditions, and other information. Small levers and switches activate the flaps, rudder, and other control surfaces. This happens by sending electrical signals along wires to motors. This system is all controlled by the avionics system.

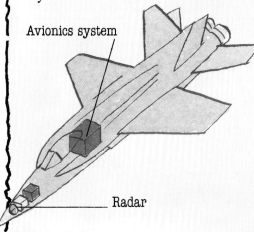

Avionics system

Radar

What is a "black box?"

It's not usually black or box-shaped. It may be bright orange and cylindrical. But it's the usual name for an aircraft's flight data recorder. This device continually records the plane's speed, height, direction, and other information from the instruments, as well as radio signals and voice communications. It is specially made to be fireproof, shockproof, and waterproof. In the event of emergency or disaster, it can be recovered, and its recordings give valuable information about what happened.

Tires, skis, skids, and floats

Airplanes can be equipped with a variety of landing gear, depending on their size and the conditions. Jet liners require wheels to withstand the pressure. Seaplanes need floats to keep them above water. Gliders and early rocket planes use skids, while planes that have to land on snow and ice use skis!

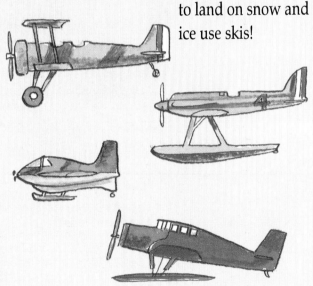

Do you have to be strong to fly a plane?

Not really. Some controls are simple electrical switches and knobs. Others are levers, like the control column and rudder pedals, but they are well-balanced with counterweights and cables, so they aren't too heavy to move. But to fly a plane well, you do have to be alert and physically fit, with good coordination and quick reactions.

When can you see two sets of controls and instruments?

In the "head-up display." There are not really two sets. Part of the main display is reflected or projected upward onto the front windshield or canopy, or into the pilot's special helmet visor. The pilot can look ahead and see outside, and the controls at the same time.

FLOWERS

The main function of a tree's flowers is to produce seeds that will grow into new trees. Flowers contain the tree's reproductive parts. They can be male or female or contain both male and female parts. Willows and poplars have male flowers on one tree and female on another. Most conifers have separate clusters of male and female flowers on the same tree. The wind carries pollen from the male flowers to fertilize the female flowers.

A flower's shape, color, and smell are designed to transfer male pollen grains to the female parts efficiently. Pollen is mainly transferred by insects or wind. Plants that rely on insect carriers have evolved brightly-colored, sweetly-scented flowers that have a landing platform for insects. In warm climates, birds and bats transfer pollen when they fly from flower to flower sipping nectar.

APPLE BLOSSOMS

Looking into flowers

Flowers vary from species to species in their shape, color, and size. Many trees in temperate (moderate, seasonal) climates are wind-pollinated, so they have unspectacular flowers because they do not rely on attracting insects.

Nikau palm flowers

Palms have small flowers which grow in large clusters. The pollinated flowers later develop into dates, coconuts, or other fruits, depending on the species.

Walnut trees grow male hanging catkin flowers 2-4 inches (5-10 cm) long. The female flowers are rounded and stand upright.

Cones of Norway spruce

Pine flowers are very inconspicuous. The red or yellow clustered flowers develop into cones about a year after being fertilized.

Walnut catkin and flowers

There are many different kinds of magnolia trees, but all are known for their beautiful flowers which lure insects.

Magnolia flowers

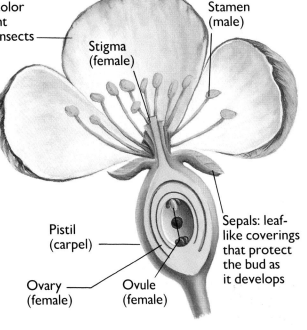

HONEYBEE

Pollination

For a new seed to grow, male pollen grains must reach the female ovules, which are contained in the ovary. This is called pollination. Even if a flower contains both male and female parts, it very rarely pollinates itself. Pollen usually travels from the male parts of a flower to the female parts of a different flower – this is called cross-pollination. The design of a tree's flowers shows how they are pollinated. Willow catkins use the wind to carry their pollen. Their dangling shape allows the wind to scatter the pollen grains. Flowers pollinated by insects, such as bees and butterflies, attract them with their color, smell, and a store of sweet nectar to eat. Pollen sticks to the insects' legs and hairy backs, and is carried to the next flower they visit, where it may join with an ovule.

Petals: color and scent attract insects

Stamen (male)

Stigma (female)

Pistil (carpel)

Sepals: leaf-like coverings that protect the bud as it develops

Ovary (female)

Ovule (female)

This flower has both male and female parts. Stamens produce millions of pollen grains at a time, each grain is only .008 inches across.

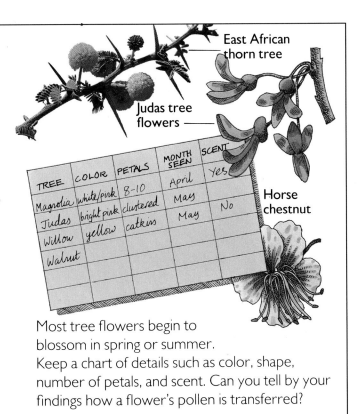

East African thorn tree

Judas tree flowers

Horse chestnut

TREE	COLOR	PETALS	MONTH SEEN	SCENT
Magnolia	white/pink	8-10	April	Yes
Judas	bright pink	clustered	May	No
Willow	yellow	catkins	May	
Walnut				

Most tree flowers begin to blossom in spring or summer.
Keep a chart of details such as color, shape, number of petals, and scent. Can you tell by your findings how a flower's pollen is transferred?

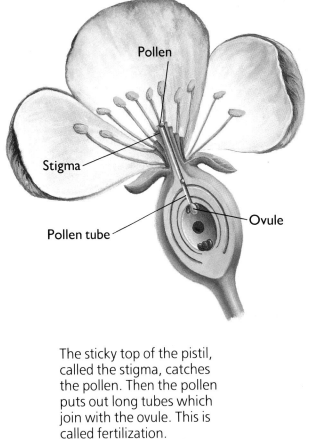

Pollen

Stigma

Pollen tube

Ovule

The sticky top of the pistil, called the stigma, catches the pollen. Then the pollen puts out long tubes which join with the ovule. This is called fertilization.

RECYCLING
REUSING MATERIALS

Many materials can be recycled and used again. Energy can be saved provided recycling uses less energy than the original production process.

Recycling aluminum drink cans uses only a twentieth as much energy as making new ones from bauxite ore. Steel has always been recycled and scrap iron is often added to the process. About a quarter of the materials in every new car are recycled from an old car. Cars contain many different materials that are expensive to separate when the product is scrapped. Some car manufacturers have come up with better designs to make recycling easier, saving a lot of energy and making expensive raw materials go farther. The average family in a developed country throws away about two tons of waste material each year. Much of this waste could be used again. Fuel pellets made of garbage, comprising mainly paper, will burn well to generate heat. Plants for sorting garbage are expensive to build but they start paying for themselves in a few years.

Using fewer different materials in cars would make recycling easier. Plastics are difficult to recycle, but BMW has come up with a car that is made from a large proportion of recycled or recyclable plastic (below). The parts shown in green are recyclable plastics, those shown in blue are made from recycled plastics.

T I R E   P O W E R
ENERGY FROM RUBBER

The main reason for burning garbage is to dispose of it efficiently. But waste also has an energy content and the easiest way to recover energy is by burning. Old car tires are among the hardest things to dispose of because they contain rubber, steel, and fabrics that cannot easily be separated. Often, old tires are piled in huge heaps, that can easily catch fire and burn for weeks on end. A use has now been found for old tires. A British power station (left) has been built that generates electricity, by burning tires, leaving only ash behind. This solves the problem of piles of old tires and also generates useful amounts of energy.

The French car company PSA, is moving toward the fully recyclable car. At present, about 70 percent of the average scrapped car is recycled, either as second-hand parts or as scrap metal. The remaining 30 percent is crushed into blocks as inert compacted waste. Much of this is plastic, which is hard to recycle. In the new cars, plastics used will be ground and made into a fuel with properties similar to coal.

The past is divided into two main eras: the prehistoric and the historic. History began between 4,500 and 5,000 years ago, when writing was first used to record events. Little information was recorded at first, but in time the historical records became more detailed. Information about prehistoric times is more difficult to obtain – the main evidence is what we can dig up out of the ground. Even in studies of historic times, a lot of useful information can come from such archaeological digs.

The earliest human ancestors were ape-like animals, and the only remains they left behind were their teeth and bones, which sometimes turned to fossils. The study of fossils – animal or human – is known as paleontology.

In time, our ancestors began to make tools out of sticks, and then out of pebbles. Stone tools were very durable and they have survived more often than bones. Other human activities, such as building huts and making fires, also left evidence behind.

Over the centuries, human activities became more and more complicated, and with each stage there is more evidence to find – complex stone tools appear, then stone carvings and cave paintings, then buildings, pottery and metal tools. The study of such man-made objects is called archaeology.

Teeth

Teeth are harder than bones and they are often the only part of the body to be preserved. An electron microscope can reveal how fragments of bone leave a particular type of scratch mark, showing that meat was on the menu. Soil particles from tubers and roots leave a deeper type of scratch mark.

Footprints

Very occasionally footprints are preserved in mud or volcanic ash, if it dries to a hard surface and is then covered by more sediment.

Bones

Bones eventually rot, but where they are preserved by sediment, they may turn into fossils. In this process, minerals from the rock gradually replace the bone itself, creating a stone 'replica' of the bone.

Plants

Plants produce pollen grains which have a characteristic shape and pattern for each species of plant. They are also very tough and are often preserved. They can be seen in rocks using a microscope, and can reveal what the climate was like at the time, and what sort of food plants our ancestors ate.

Dating a site

Finding out the age of a site is very important. One method of dating is based on radioactive materials, which occur naturally and "decay" at a fixed rate. A radioactive form of carbon, carbon-14, is found in the carbon dioxide gas in the atmosphere, and therefore in all living plants and animals. Once they die, no more carbon is taken into the body, and the carbon-14 already present slowly decays.

By measuring the amount remaining, scientists can work out how long ago organisms died. Carbon dating works well, but only for objects less than 70,000 years old.

Older archaeological sites are more difficult, but the ages of some can be worked out using potassium-argon dating, which measures the radiation from a radioactive form of potassium found in volcanic ash.

2 mya
River lays down sediments

1.9 mya
Volcano erupts and lays down ash in the sediments

1.3 mya
More sediments accumulate

Present day
Erosion exposes sediments

mya=million years ago

Wood and hide

Although wooden tools and animal hides are not preserved on prehistoric sites such as this, they would survive on more recent sites.

Fire

Fire leaves burned stones and baked clay, although it is not always easy to tell if the fire was a natural one or a man-made campfire. In later sites the signs are clearer, because people built hearths and used them often.

Tools

In prehistoric sites, any wooden tools have long since rotted away, but stone tools are often preserved. The way in which the tool is used leaves a particular "polish" on its surface. By looking at this tool under a microscope scientists would know that it had been used to scrape animal skins – which shows that skins were used for making bags, tents or clothing.

Studying our past requires a lot of detective work – especially on prehistoric sites such as this one, dating from half a million years ago. Archaeologists must be able to piece together fragments of evidence to build up a picture of how our ancestors lived.

As well as human bones, the remains of animals which were eaten are often found at campsites. They show if the people hunted big game or small. Cut marks on the bones from stone tools reveal how the animal was butchered.

Once people began burying their dead, far more human bones were preserved.

THE SPACE AGE BEGINS

World War II ended in 1945, but the Cold War, an era of confrontation between the United States and the Soviet Union, began soon after. Both countries developed rockets to display their military might and national pride. Under a brilliant leader, Sergei Korolyev, the Soviets had by 1956 built a giant rocket, the SS-6, capable of carrying a two-ton bomb 4,000 miles. To demonstrate the rocket, Korolyev was ordered to launch a satellite, a small object that would stay in space, and circle around the Earth. On October 4 1957, the satellite Sputnik 1 was launched. The Space Age had begun.

Launchers

Sputnik's SS-6 launcher was big and simple, but very effective. It consisted of a central core, with four strap-on boosters to increase lift off power.

Compared to the Soviet design, the American rockets (below) were lighter and more delicate in construction. They used high-technology fuel tanks instead of the thick-walled steel tanks of the SS-6. Less power meant that American satellites had to be light. This gave a boost to the development of min-iaturized electronic devices such as new transistors, which were soon used in portable radios and other everyday objects.

A-1 Sputnik

Vanguard

Juno 1

◀ Explorer 1

◀ Sputnik 1

The response to Sputnik

By late 1957, the United States was ready to match Sputnik with a satellite of its own. But the first launch, of a Vanguard rocket with a tiny 3.4 pound satellite, was a dismal failure. It rose only a few feet before crashing back to the launch pad and exploding in a ball of flame. In desperation, the United States turned to Wernher von Braun, whose satellite project had been in need of money.

American success

Von Braun put together a Jupiter C rocket and a satellite called Explorer. This was launched successfully on January 31, 1958 (see the photo on the opposite page). Explorer 1 was a much smaller satellite than either of the first two Sputniks which preceded it into space. Other early American launches met with less success: a Mercury rocket suffered premature engine cut-off during its launch in 1960 (above left).

In April 1958, the National Aeronautics and Space Administration (NASA) was created, to survey the Moon and put a man into space. It has been a force in world science and politics ever since.

▲ NASA's first office building in Washington D.C.

Sputnik

Sputnik 1 (left) was a simple metal sphere that weighed 184 pounds. Its transmitter emitted a series of beeps. In November 1957, the much larger Sputnik 2 carried a passenger: the dog Laika, who became the first space traveler.

The van Allen belts

One of the instruments on Explorer 1 was designed to count and measure electrically charged particles in space. This instrument led to the first space discovery. James van Allen, the scientist responsible, noticed that at certain heights the counter seemed to stop working, and he realized it had been overloaded. The reason was a region in space dense with charged particles - now known as the van Allen belts. These sometimes disrupt radio communications.

Voices from the sky

A satellite is an object that goes around another. Scientists realized that artificial radio satellites could relay radio, TV, and telephone signals around the Earth. The first was Telstar, (below right) launched by the U.S. in 1962. In 1965, Early Bird became the first geostationary satellite. People could watch the Beatles (below) live on TV beamed from another continent.

THE BITS OF THE BRAIN

The top half of your head is filled with a large lump of pinkish-gray, wrinkled looking substance, that feels like a mixture of pudding and jelly. But don't worry. All brains are like this. The human brain is the most amazing bio-computer. It can think, remember, predict, solve, create, invent, control, and coordinate.

BRAIN POWER

Are you smarter than a rabbit? Almost certainly. Your brain is much bigger than the rabbit's brain. Are you smarter than a sperm whale? Again, almost certainly, even though this huge beast's brain is five times bigger than your own. Intelligence is not just a matter of brain size. It depends on the relative sizes of the brain parts, and how they are connected. The cortex, the wrinkly gray part, is huge in the human brain. This is where intelligence, thinking, and complicated behavior are based.

SPIES ON YOUR INSIDES

The CAT (computerized axial tomography) scanner pictures a "slice" of the brain, with no discomfort or risk. It beams weak X rays through the head and displays the results on a computer TV screen.

Computer

CORTEX
The outer gray part, where thinking takes place.

X rays beamed from all angles as camera goes around head.

CEREBRAL HEMISPHERES
These are the bulging, wrinkled parts. They have gray cortex on the outside, and white nerves inside.

CORPUS CALLOSUM
This long bundle of nerves links the two halves of the brain, so the right hand knows what the left hand is doing.

THALAMUS
An egg-shaped area that helps to process and recognize information about touch, pain, temperature, and pressure on the skin.

LIMBIC SYSTEM
Sometimes called the "emotional brain," the wishbone-shaped limbic system is involved in anger, fear, pleasure, and sorrow.

HIPPOCAMPUS
Supposedly shaped like a seahorse, hence its name, the hippocampus is part of the memory system.

CEREBELLUM
This is like a mini-brain within the whole brain. It is vital for carrying out skilled, complicated movements, like doing a brain operation.

Stalk of cerebellum

ELECTRICAL BRAINS
In 1800, Alessandro Volta of Italy invented the battery. He spent many years arguing with Luigi Galvani, who had discovered electricity while experimenting on animal nerves and brains.

PONS
This name means "bridge." The pons is a crossroads for nerves going up to the cortex, back to the cerebellum, and down to the spinal cord.

Medulla

Spinal cord

Marsupials

Marsupials, or pouched mammals, differ from humans in that they carry their underdeveloped newborns in a pouch outside the mother's stomach. They feed on grass and other plant life, and mostly inhabit grasslands and forests. There are several types of marsupials, such as kangaroos, wombats, opossums, wallabies, and Koala bears.

The Red Kangaroo is the largest of the marsupials. It can grow as large as 6½ feet long and 200 pounds in weight. However, at birth they are only ¾ inch long and ⅓₀ oz. The baby is born after only five weeks in its mother's womb, and spends the next six months inside her pouch feeding on her milk.

The babies of most mammals grow and develop inside their mother's body until they are fully formed. They get all their nutrients from a sack inside the womb called a placenta. But female marsupials do not have placentas; their babies come out of the womb at a very early stage and suckle milk constantly until they can look after themselves.

marsupial mouse

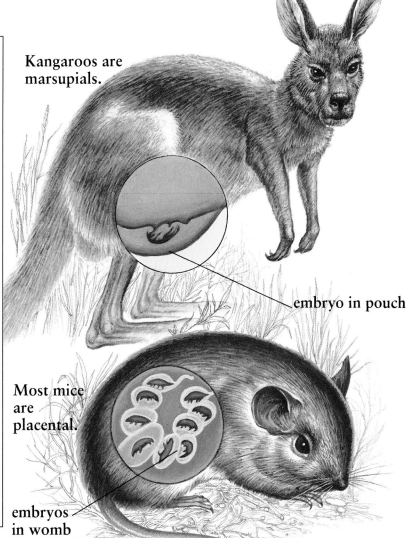

Kangaroos are marsupials.

embryo in pouch

Most mice are placental.

embryos in womb

◁ **A mother Gray Kangaroo with her young in her pouch**

SPEED AND ACCELERATION

Speed is how fast something is moving. Velocity describes both speed and direction. When a car turns a corner, speed may stay the same, but velocity changes. Speed describes how far an object travels in a period of time. For example, a snail moves at about 0.03 miles per hour, while Concorde travels about 1,300 miles per hour. A speedometer, like the one pictured here, indicates how fast a car is moving. Acceleration is how much the speed increases in a period of time. A decrease in speed is called deceleration.

AT FULL SPEED

1. Cut the road from stiff cardboard as wide as a shoe box, but twice as long. Secure a small peice of cardboard in the middle of one side with a paper fastener.

2. Tape one end of the road to the narrow end of a shoe box. It can be lifted to different heights.

3. Cut out one quarter of a circle. Divide it into angles of 10 degrees, and cut slits along the edge. Attach to the side of the box.

4. Check that the piece of cardboard on the road is in the correct position to slide into a notch. Pierce a hole in the lid of the plastic bottle. Cut off the bottom section. Tape over the hole, invert and fill with paint. Mount on top of the car.

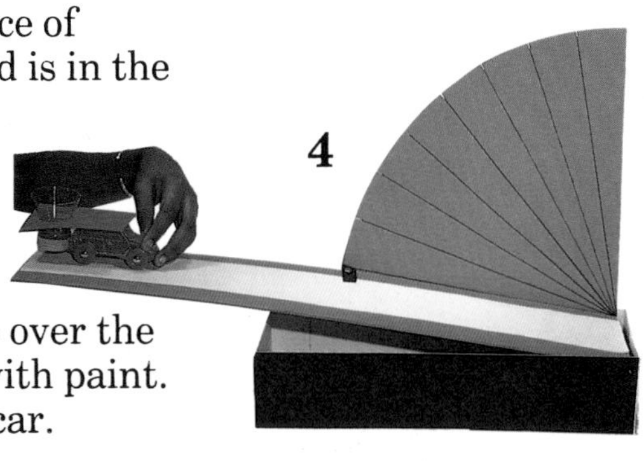

WHY IT WORKS

By observing the distance between the drops of paint on the inclined ramps you can estimate the speed of the vehicle. When they are close together, the speed is slowest. If the spaces are uniform, the vehicle must be traveling at a constant speed. If the spaces widen, the vehicle has accelerated, if they narrow it has decelerated. The bigger the mass of an object, the greater the force needed to make it move. When the slope is steeper, the truck accelerates faster. The spaces between the drops are wider apart toward the bottom of the slope. The speed can be calculated by dividing the distance by the time taken.

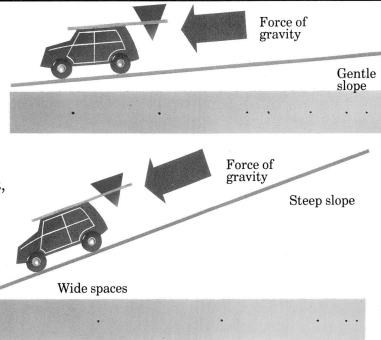

Force of gravity

Gentle slope

Force of gravity

Steep slope

Wide spaces

BRIGHT IDEAS

☀ Use a variety of toy cars on a sloping ramp and experiment with differing angles. Which car travels furthest? Did you use the same "push" each time to ensure a controlled experiment?

☀ Run the same car down a variety of angles, and allow it to run into a shoe box each time. Measure the distance that the box has moved. The distance that it moves depends on the speed.

☀ Try running on a beach at various speeds. Use a stop-watch to time yourself and measure the spaces between the footprints. Your footprints will be further apart, the faster you run.

5

5. Set the angle of the road. Place a long piece of paper over the road to record your results each time. Position the car at the top of the slope. Remove the tape just before it is released. Time each run accurately. Be careful not to push the car.

WATER AT WORK

From industry to agriculture to generating power for factories and homes, we make water work for us. To make the paper for this book, about 4 gallons of water were used, and other industrial processes, such as making cars, use vast amounts of water. Some power stations use water to generate electricity, while others need large quantities of water to cool machinery – you can often see water vapor escaping into the atmosphere through huge cooling towers (shown above).

Water power

Water generates power when it flows from a higher to a lower place. Waterwheels were originally used to capture the energy of flowing water and use it to turn millstones that ground corn or wheat into flour. Today, turbines use moving water to generate electricity. Modern turbines are huge machines weighing thousands of tons. They are usually placed at the bottom of a dam to make the best use of the energy made by falling water.

Waterwheel

The Itaipú Dam (shown above), on the Paraná River in Brazil, is one of the world's largest hydro-electric dams. Its 18 turbines can produce 13 million kilowatts of electricity.

Industry

In the United States, industry uses around 320 million gallons of water each day. Water is used for washing, cleaning, cooling, dissolving substances and even for transporting materials, such as logs for the timber industry (above). About 7,100 gallons of water are needed to make a car and eight quarts of water are used to produce just one quart of lemonade. The largest industrial users of water are paper, petroleum, chemicals, and the iron and steel-making industries.

Dam problems

Dams can cause problems for people and for the environment. Before a dam is built, people and animals have to be cleared from the area. If trees or plants are left to rot under the water, they make the water acidic and the acid may corrode (eat away) the machinery inside the dam. Reservoirs may become clogged by mud and silt which cannot be washed away downstream.

Irrigation

Crop plants, such as wheat or rice, need large quantities of water to grow properly. In places where there is not enough water, or the supply varies with the seasons, farmers irrigate the land. Most irrigation systems involve a network of canals and ditches to carry water to the crops. The sprinkler irrigation system (below) has an engine and wheels and moves across a field spraying crops with a fine mist of water.

Flood irrigation is used to grow rice. The fields of young rice plants are flooded, covering them in water. These fields are called paddy fields (above). It takes about 9,900 pounds of water to grow just one pound of rice.

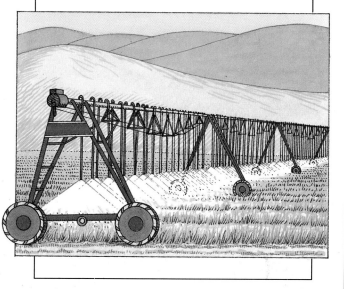

An Archimedes screw lifts water up a spiral screw to a higher level. The device was invented by the Greek scientist Archimedes over 2,000 years ago. It is still used in some parts of the world today.

Hydroponics

Plants can be grown without soil using a watering technique called hydroponics. A carefully controlled mixture of nutrients are dissolved in water and passed over the roots of plants which are suspended in a tank of water. Hydroponics does not produce better or larger crops, but it is important in the study of plants and can be used in areas where soil is not easily available, such as on board a ship or in Arctic areas.

Solar salt

For centuries, salt has been a vital part in people's diets and has even been used instead of money. In countries such as China, India and France, salt is harvested from seawater and used for food flavoring or to make industrial chemicals. Seawater is left in shallow pools in the hot sun so the water evaporates, or disappears, into the air. Salt crystals are left behind and can be raked by hand or collected by machines. The salt is then taken to a refinery where it is crushed, ground and sorted before being packaged and sold. Evaporating seawater is the oldest method of obtaining salt. This kind of salt is called solar salt.

DINOSAUR EXTINCTION

The most intriguing question about dinosaurs has always been "why did they die out?" There is no simple answer to this question, even though many hundreds of scientists are studying the problem. They are not studying the extinction of the dinosaurs alone, but the whole question of extinction. Many other plants and animals have died out in the past, and it is important to understand how and why this happened. Having this information could help save many species that are under threat in the modern world. Humans are causing extinctions now, because of pollution and other damage to the environment. Maybe the dinosaurs can tell us how to save the earth today, because of their extinction 65 million years ago!

Early ideas
Some of the early dinosaur scientists, 100 years ago, thought the dinosaurs died out because the air changed, and they could not breathe. Others thought that the dinosaurs disappeared simply because they became too big. They were too heavy to move without falling over, and could not find enough food to survive.

One theory is that a huge killer meteorite hit the earth. Smaller meteorites have fallen since then, making craters like this one in Arizona.

Survivors
Whatever happened 65 million years ago, most plants and animals were not wiped out. Among the reptiles, the crocodiles, turtles, tortoises, lizards, and snakes survived. So too did the mammals, birds, amphibians, fish, and most plants and sea creatures.

Tortoise

Crocodile

Perhaps huge amounts of lava poured out of volcanoes in India. This sent up vast clouds of dust that blacked out the sun, and made the earth icy cold.

Dinosaurs and people in films

A lot of dinosaur films in the past have shown people and dinosaurs living at the same time. There are often epic battles between spear-waving cavemen and dinosaurs. No human being, however, could have wrestled with a dinosaur, since the dinosaurs died out 60 million years before the first humans lived!

Measuring rates of extinction

You've probably heard the expression "dead as a Dodo." The Dodo is just one of millions of species of plants and animals that have died out. Extinction is quite normal. However, sometimes so many species die out all at the same time that something unusual must have been going on.

Dodo

One of these mass extinctions happened when the dinosaurs died out.

Evidence from fossil leaves (above) shows that climates became colder. Perhaps that was enough to kill off the dinosaurs?

The final curtain

Dinosaurs were not the only animals to die out 65 million years ago. The flying pterosaurs also disappeared, as did the swimming plesiosaurs and some other reptile groups and shellfish in the sea. Many other plants and animals, however, did survive, and life on earth had returned to "normal" about 10 million years later. "Normality," of course, also meant a world without the dinosaurs. 160 million years of domination by these beasts had ended.

MOTORCYCLES
FASTER AND SAFER

The quickest way through the traffic is on a motorcycle. But while cars have been getting safer and more economical, motorcycles have gone the other way. Better and better performances from bigger and bigger engines may be exciting, but fuel economy has suffered. A typical, modern "superbike" has an engine as powerful as most cars, and gets no more than 40 miles per gallon. Meanwhile, little progress has been made toward creating a safer bike, or one that protects the rider from the cold and wet. "A rider simply gets colder, and wetter, and uses more fuel on a bike than in a car," says British motorcycle enthusiast Royce Creasey, who designed his own improved machine, the *Voyager.*

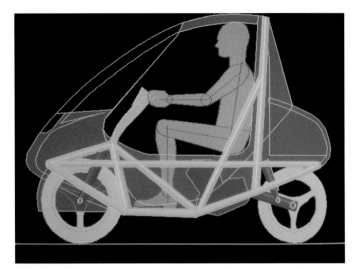

The BMW C1, a prototype machine, protects the rider from the weather with a full roof and the option of fitting side panels for long journeys. Anti-lock brakes and an air-bag can be fitted, and there is space for luggage. Most car journeys are short (an average of just four miles) and are made alone; perfect for a motorcycle.

The safety of the C1 is provided by a strong, aluminum space frame, made of tubes welded together. In a crash, this would distort in a controlled fashion, providing a motorcycle for the first time with "crumple zones" just like those of a modern car. Computer simulation shows that the C1, in fact, provides the same protection in a head-on collision as a small car. The frame would also protect the rider from glancing blows and from being thrown over the handlebars, a major cause of serious injury.

Rear wheel

Now the big manufacturers are beginning to take the hint, with a new generation of machines that provide protection, greater safety, and fresh thinking about steering and bodywork. Steering is the key to improving a motorcycle's handling. Traditional front forks are designed to absorb bumps and to steer. Separating suspension from steering could be the answer, many engineers believe.

The rotor draws the fuel through the inlet port, and into the cavity.

As the rotor continues to turn, the fuel is compressed into a smaller space. The spark plug fires.

The burning fuel expands into the larger space beyond the plugs, driving the rotor around. As the rotor turns, it exposes the exhaust ports, and the burned fuel escapes.

THE WANKEL ENGINE
HOW ROTARY ENGINES WORK

The ultimate engine for a motorcycle is one that does not vibrate as pistons and connecting rods hurl themselves to and fro thousands of times a minute. Such an engine was designed in 1956 by German engineer Felix Wankel, and fitted in the late 1980s to the *Norton Commander*, claimed to be "the smoothest motorcycle in the world." The Wankel engine has a triangular rotor, geared to the drive shaft, and rotating in the combustion chamber. As it turns, the rotor draws in fuel, compresses it, ignites it, and finally exhausts it like a normal four-stroke. It works: but wear on the rotors, poor fuel consumption, and high emission levels count against it.

Swing arm

Yamaha's GTS1000 makes a break with traditional front forks. The wheel is mounted on a swing arm with a single shock-absorber. The steering column does not have to absorb shocks at the same time as steering.

Fairing

Rider's seat

Front wheel

Popular PYRAMIDS

Central and South America saw the rise and fall of many civilizations, such as the Olmecs, Toltecs, Maya, Incas, and Aztecs, before the arrival of European settlers in the sixteenth century. These peoples first built great mounds of earth, then developed flat-topped pyramids by casing the mounds in stone with steep steps. These were places where gods and people could meet. The pyramids had temples on top, but some had burials underneath. The Europeans destroyed hundreds of ancient cities, and many treasures and artifacts were lost.

SACRIFICE AND CEREMONY
To please their gods, the Maya offered their own blood at special rites. Sometimes they also offered human lives. The Aztecs believed that their many gods needed human hearts to stay strong, and sacrificed thousands of people to them. Aztec and Mayan sacrifices were made before shrines on flat-topped pyramids, like that at Tikal in Guatemala (right). Mysterious picture writing has been found on some Mayan pyramids, and is now being translated.

INCA PYRAMID MOUNDS
The Incas ruled a vast area of South America in the fifteenth century. In the city of Cuzco in Peru they built a great temple called the Coricancha (right) for their sun-god, Inti. There they offered food and beer and sacrificed animals to their god.

THE MODERN MONUMENT
A glass pyramid (right) is the entrance to the Louvre Museum in Paris.

Did other peoples mummify their dead?
Mummification is a very old practice in South America. Mummies of the Nazca people in Peru date from about 200 B.C. to A.D. 500. Human sacrifices were sometimes buried in the Andean mountains, where they were naturally preserved in the snow and ice.

REMEMBERING THE DEAD
Stone or ceramic funeral masks were used in the traditional funeral rites of several Native American cultures, similar to those of the Egyptians.

NORTH AMERICA

Some Native North American peoples also built pyramids. The Mississippians built towns in A.D. 700-1500. The important buildings were set on great mounds of earth (above). Many peoples buried their dead in earth mounds with gifts and treasure.

A lasting impression

In modern times, many architects have used pyramid shapes and Egyptian decorations as part of their designs. For example, the casino based on the Great Pyramid which was built in Las Vegas. It is the same size as Khufu's tomb, and is guarded by a giant Sphinx! Decorations, such as those on the Empire State Building in New York or these apartments in San Francisco, (below), are directly influenced by Egyptian pyramid paintings, while tiles and wallpaper often show decorative lotus or papyrus-leaf designs.

BIBLICAL BUILDINGS

The early peoples of Mesopotamia built mud-brick temples on platforms on the ruins of older temples. The platforms got taller over the years and became huge, stepped mounds similar to early pyramids.

We call them ziggurats. The great ziggurat Etemenanki was built by King Nebuchadnezzar (604-561 B.C.) in Babylon, home of the famous Hanging Gardens. It might have igiven rise to the story of the Tower of Babel (right).

BABY MAMMALS

Young mammals do not have to fend for themselves until they are almost fully grown. Some, like mice, are born with their eyes closed, have no fur and are cared for in a cosy nest. Others, like zebra foals, are able to run with their mothers very soon after birth. All mammal babies, however, are fed on milk. Mothers, and sometimes fathers, keep their babies clean and warm, teach them the skills they will need in adult life, and protect them from predators. Baby mammals spend a lot of time playing, which strengthens their bodies and improves their co-ordination.

Multi-birth

Wolves grow up in large families. This mother wolf suckles four cubs. She provides shelter in a den and the rest of the adult pack protect them. Babies brought up in dens or nests are happy to be left alone while the mother goes out to search for food. She cannot take them with her until they are much bigger and stronger.

Number of Babies

Having lots of babies at a time is an insurance policy. Parents divide their energy between all the babies in the hope that at least one of them will survive attacks from predators (below). Having only one baby at a time is too risky; if the baby dies the parents have wasted all their energy.

Only Child

The mother sloth hangs upside down and carries her single infant on her stomach. This way she does not need to leave it alone in a den and can protect it all the time. The baby suckles for about one month, but stays put for another five months, reaching out to grab leaves as its mother slowly creeps along the branches. Eventually, it slowly wanders off on its own.

Baby Face

All parents find their babies attractive. This ensures that they will care for their young. The features of all baby mammals are similar – huge eyes set in round faces. These features often appeal to cartoonists and animators. The film *Watership Down*, about a rabbit warren endangered by human destruction, stars young rabbits who have appealing features and individual personalities.

Growth Rates

The rate at which a baby animal grows depends partly on its size. A harvest mouse is independent at 16 days – a giraffe grows for ten years. A gorilla baby also takes ten years to grow. It is much smaller than a giraffe, but it has a much bigger brain. The fastest growth rate of any baby mammal is that of the baby blue whale. During the last two months of pregnancy it puts on 220 pounds of weight daily.

The simplest family is a mother and her babies. In some cases a father is present. Elephants form stable families where babies are looked after by sisters and aunts. The leader is an old female called the *matriarch*.

Meet the family...

1. Sire Bull

2. Matriarch

3. Sisters and Aunts

4. Infant

WHAT IF ROCKETS HADN'T BEEN INVENTED?

We would still be wondering about the empty space above us, instead of launching astronauts into space and sending probes on space missions. A rocket can fly fast enough to get into space. To do this, it must reach the speed called *escape velocity*, 17,700 mph (28,500 km/h), to escape from the pull of Earth's gravity. A rocket engine can work in airless space, unlike jets and other engines, as explained below. The other way to get into space might be a gigantic gun that fires spacecraft and satellites into space. However, any astronaut would be crushed by the g-forces of acceleration!

Dawn of the rocket age

The first rockets used a type of gunpowder and flew in warfare in China, in A.D. 1232. The first modern rocket to use the liquid fuel that today's rockets use was launched by American scientist Robert Goddard in 1926.

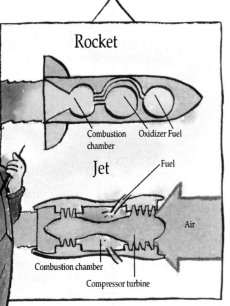

Rocket

Combustion chamber Oxidizer Fuel

Jet

Fuel

Air

Combustion chamber

Compressor turbine

Rockets and jets
Rockets carry their own oxidizer substance. Jets, however, need oxygen from the air to burn their fuel.

Why can't jets fly in space?

Like a jet engine, a rocket burns fuel in a type of continuous explosion. Hot gases blast out of the back, and thrust the engine forward. Space has no air, which is needed for the burning that takes place inside the jet engine. A rocket must carry its own supply of oxygen.

Up, up, and away in my beautiful balloon

Special weather balloons go higher than 31 miles (50 km). They carry radiosondes that measure temperature, air pressure, and humidity, and send back the results by radio. The balloon is quite small and floppy when it takes off, but it gradually expands as it rises, as the air pressure decreases. However, no weather balloon could carry a heavy satellite high enough, or give it the required speed to put it in orbit.

Would we have fabulous firework displays?

Perhaps, but we would have to power the rockets by other types of engines, maybe a mini jet engine. Firework rockets use solid fuel such as gunpowder or other fuel-oxidizer mixtures to launch into the air. Many space rockets use liquid fuel, and have the propellant and oxidizer in liquid form.

Multi-staged rockets

A staged rocket may have two, three, or more rockets, placed on top of each other in decreasing size. The biggest one launches the entire rocket, then stops firing and falls away. The rocket's weight is now less and so is the effect of the Earth's gravity, so the second-stage rocket is much smaller, and so on with the remaining stages. Extra rockets, called boosters, may assist the main rocket engine at launch and then fall away, as in the space shuttle.

THE WORLD OF WOODWIND

The woodwind family includes the clarinet, oboe, English horn, bassoon, and saxophone, which use a single or double reed to make the air vibrate inside the instrument. Many different kinds of musicians play woodwind instruments, from the musician on the street corner to the folk or jazz player, and the professional in the concert hall.

Woodwind instruments are important in the orchestra, and are also used in chamber music, played by a small group of musicians. The wind quintet is a popular combination for chamber music, but almost any group of instruments can play. The position of woodwind in the orchestra is shown below right.

Flutes and other woodwind instruments are used as solo concert instruments or are accompanied by the piano, harp, or guitar. Baroque music now performed by the flute and piano was probably written for another keyboard instrument, the harpsichord. A good performer will communicate with both the accompanist and the audience.

If you get the chance, join a chamber group or an orchestra. Look for these orchestral pieces with famous woodwind passages:
Debussy, *L'après-midi d'un faune*
Stravinsky, *Petrouchka* and *Firebird*
Saint-Saëns, *Carnival of the Animals*
Prokofiev, *Peter and the Wolf*
Rossini, *William Tell Overture*

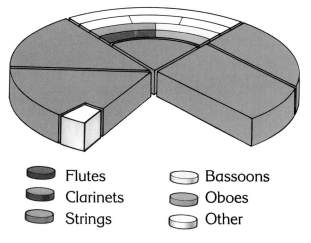

▬ Flutes	▭ Bassoons
▬ Clarinets	▭ Oboes
▬ Strings	▭ Other

JAMES GALWAY

James Galway is one of the best known flutists performing today. He is famous for his golden flute and the recordings he has made of concertos by Khachaturian and Rodrigo — the second of these was actually written for Galway. These pieces show off his bright, brilliant sound, and his superb tongue and finger technique.

Flute   Oboe   French Horn   Clarinet   Bassoon

The standard woodwind instruments are the flute, clarinet, oboe, and bassoon. Each instrument has larger or smaller relatives which produce a lower or higher sound. The little cousin of the flute is the piccolo, which is pitched an octave higher.

The clarinet, oboe, and bassoon all have vibrating reeds. The oboe has a double reed and a conical shape, opening out at the bottom. It produces a mellow sound. Richard Strauss and Vaughan Williams have written concertos for the oboe.

The clarinet has a single reed which vibrates against the mouthpiece. It has a beautiful, flowing sound and a range of three and a half octaves. Clarinets emerged in the 18th century, and were improved by Boehm. The bass clarinet is pitched an octave lower.

The bassoon has a distinct tone, which can sound comic or sorrowful. It, too, has a double reed. Its relative, the contrabassoon, plays an octave lower. The wind quintet (above) is completed by the horn, a member of the family of brass instruments.

WHAT IS ELECTRICITY?

Electricity is an invisible form of energy which is stored in electrons and protons. These are the tiny particles in atoms (below) which make up all matter. Electricity is created when there is an imbalance of negatively charged electrons and positively charged protons. Current electricity is made up of moving electrons which travel through wires. In static electricity the electrons remain still. Electricity is a powerful and useful source of energy, but it can also be very dangerous.

Discovering electricity

Electricity was first discovered by the ancient Greeks, about 2,000 years ago. A Greek scientist called Thales noticed that a piece of amber (the hard fossilized sap from trees) attracted straw or feathers when he rubbed it with a cloth. The word "electricity" comes from the Greek word for amber – "elektron."

In 1600, William Gilbert (left), a doctor to Queen Elizabeth I of England, was the first person to use the word "electric." He carried out experiments and discovered that materials such as diamond, glass and wax behaved in a similar way to amber.

the atom's nucleus – made up of protons (green) and neutrons (black)

From the stars

The Sun and other stars send out radio waves through space. They are a form of electrical and magnetic energy which travel through space at the speed of light. They are picked up by huge dishes called radio telescopes. The radio waves are changed into electrical signals that give astronomers information about distant galaxies.

Investigating static electricity

Static electricity, used inside photocopiers and paint-spraying machines, can be generated by rubbing different materials together.

You can test materials for static charges, which are either positive or negative. Opposite charges attract things and like charges repel things. Experiment by rubbing different materials such as paper, plastic, metal, wood, and rubber with a cloth. Do they attract or repel things? Make a chart of your results.

negatively
charged
electron

Electrons everywhere

A particle accelerator (above) is used for research into atoms. By smashing atoms together, scientists have discovered over 200 particles, even smaller than atoms. A beam of electrons in an electron microscope (above left) enlarges objects millions of times.

Switch on the light

In fluorescent lights, an electric current makes gas glow. Neon gas makes red light, sodium gas yellow light, and mercury gas makes blue light.

Electricity for life

Most animals rely on electrical signals which provide them with information about their environment and control the way their body works. A network of nerve cells collects the information and sends out instructions. Invertebrates such as an octopus (right) have simple nerve nets.

Humans have more complex systems. The brain has an intricate network of nervous tissue (below). Our brain buzzes with tiny electrical signals, which trigger our heartbeats, to make our muscles move and sustain our body processes.

SEASONS

A season is a time of year with a particular kind of weather.
Each season has a different effect on plant and animal life.
Areas around the poles have only two seasons – six months of
summer, when it is light nearly all the time, and six months of
winter, when it is dark most of the time. Places near the equator
have less defined seasons. Often there are only two, one wet and one dry. It is hot
all year round, and the length of the day stays the same all year. Temperate regions
between the equator and the poles, have four seasons – spring, summer, fall,
and winter. The days are longer in summer and shorter in winter.

Life in the fall and winter

During these seasons, the weather
may turn cooler, wetter, and more
windy. There is little food for animals
to eat. Some gather stores of food in
the fall to help them survive the
winter. Plants also rest over the winter
when it is too cold for them to grow
and water in the
soil is frozen.
Areas closer to
the equator
remain warm.

People in the
north-east of
Brazil (above)
can still spend
time on the
beach, even in
the winter.

Winter in Canada (above)
often brings snow.

Seasonal festivals

In the northern hemisphere, the
Christian festival of Easter happens
in springtime. Easter symbols, such as spring
flowers and eggs, represent new life and the
resurrection (or rising from the dead) of Jesus
Christ. Some Hindu festivals are connected
with the annual cycle of the seasons. Pongal,
or Sankranti, marks the end of the south-east
monsoon and the reaping of the harvest.
Beautiful kilars (decorative designs) are traced
on floors with moistened rice flour.

Life in spring and summer

Spring in temperate climates brings warmer weather and the days get longer. Day and night are almost the same length. The warmth and spring showers encourage plants and trees to grow and buds to burst open. Many animals have their young in spring so that they will have time to grow strong enough to survive the cold autumn and winter seasons. Summer in the Mediterranean climate of Spain is very hot and dry. Olive trees (top left) are suited to this environment, and olive groves flourish.

Summer in Southeast Asia (above) and parts of eastern Africa can be very wet when the monsoon rains arrive between April and July.

Spring bud

Hibernation and migration

To survive cold, hot, or dry seasons, animals may move away or migrate to warmer, cooler, or wetter places. The arctic tern migrates from one end of the world to the other and back again, covering about 25,000 miles a year. But other migrations, such as that of the wildebeest on the African grasslands, are over much shorter distances. Instead of moving away, other animals, such as dormice, stay put and go into a deep sleep in a safe place. This behavior is called hibernation in a cold climate and aestivation in a hot climate.

Dormouse

Arctic tern

The four seasons

The Italian composer, violinist, and conductor Antonio Vivaldi (1678-1741) wrote four famous violin concertos called "The Four Seasons" in about 1725. Each one consists of three pieces which convey the characteristics of each season. It is one of Vivaldi's best known compositions. Vivaldi wrote nearly 50 operas, church music, and hundreds of concertos for almost every instrument known at the time.

Tricks and IMAGINATION

In the 20th century, UFOs and aliens have become a familiar part of our culture. Many science fiction books are bestsellers, films like *E.T.*, *Close Encounters of the Third Kind*, *Alien*, and *Star Trek* attract enormous audiences, and organizations have been set up around the world to record and investigate UFO sightings. This fascination has led to some clever hoaxes. Many fake photographs of UFOs have been made by photographing miniature models in close-up, or by tampering with photographic negatives. Some people have faked UFO sightings and evidence of landings by spacecraft. There have even been suggestions that extraterrestrials are living in secret on Earth...and a few people have claimed to be aliens!

THE REAL UFOS
During World War II, U.S. pilots reported seeing fiery balls in the sky, which they nicknamed "foo fighters." They were thought to be natural phenomena or UFOs. In fact, the Germans had invented disk-shaped anti-radar craft whose fuel caused a fiery "halo." Since then, Russia and the U.S. may have created a disk-shaped supersonic craft, using UFO reports as a cover-up.

STRANGE SIGHTS IN OUTER SPACE
Many reports of moving lights in the sky are often found later to be sightings of falling meteors or comets. Venus, the brightest planet in the night sky, is clearly visible with the naked eye and has frequently been mistaken for a UFO.

SKY LIGHTS
Ball lightning has scared people for centuries. It appears as a red, yellow, orange, or green fiery ball and is seen during storms, usually after ordinary lightning. No one knows why it occurs.

Fake photographs

A photograph of a UFO, apparently taken by an airline pilot over Venezuela in 1965, was believed to be genuine until 1971. A U.S. photographic expert pointed out that the UFO was too sharply outlined to be a distant object and could not have created the shadow underneath it. The "UFO" was a button, placed over a picture of the sky and re-photographed. The shadow had been chemically burned in during the processing of the film. This is one of the most convincing UFO fakes ever, but there have been many more since then!

NATURAL UFOs

Horizontal formations of cloud can look saucer-like, especially when light shines on them. Unusual weather conditions can cause strange signals on radar screens, which may be mistaken for UFOs.

THE CROWDED SKIES

All kinds of flying objects have been mistaken for UFOs over the years, including planes, airships, weather balloons, satellites, kites, and even flocks of birds.

NEW THEORIES

A report has suggested a link between alien stories and the drama of birth. Aliens are often described as having big heads and short limbs, like unborn babies. Do tales of bright tunnels resemble a baby's experience of being born?

How are movie UFOs created? For many years, special effects teams have used small models to create UFO effects. The models are photographed in a series of pictures which, when played back at speed, give the illusion of movement. Recently, hi-tech computer programs have made it possible to achieve even more spectacular extraterrestrial action, allowing animators to move and manipulate all sorts of images.

THE FIRST FISHES

Fossil fishes are first recorded in rocks of Cambrian era, but preservation is quite poor. By the Ordovician, however, the fossils show enough detail for scientists to give names to the fishes. Fishes found in these rocks often had armor instead of scales and many did not have jaws. During the Devonian that followed, many new types of fishes evolved, including sharks and rays, and bony fishes. The Late Devonian also saw the evolution of *Eusthenopteron,* a fish that developed lungs and could walk on land using its strong front fins.

Crinoid

Rare cones

Nautiloids are molluscs and are related to ammonites. During the Ordovician, most had straight, cone-shaped shells, instead of the familiar coiled shells of ammonites. At the end of the Permian period, all the straight cones became extinct. The coiled cones survived, and evolved to produce a variety of ammonites.

Nautiloid

Helovites

Streptelasmid

Hallopora

Protective armor

Some of the Devonian fishes were completely encased in an armor made up of bony plates, while others also relied on scales for protection. The osteostracans did not have armor that covered all of the body; it was limited to the head. The placoderms were a group of armored fishes that evolved many strange shapes. Their heads and forequarters were covered with heavy armor. These species were not very successful and did not survive the Devonian. Some, like *Coccosteus,* were probably good swimmers. Not all Devonian fish had armor; thelodonts and anaspids were covered with small scales.

Ancient corals

Many rocks of the earlier part of the Paleozoic contain the remains of coral reefs. Corals are first known from the Cambrian, but it was not until the Silurian that large coral reefs became common. Two types of coral built the reefs. Colonial corals (for example *Favosites*) are made up of many animals all living in the same stony coral. Solitary corals only have one animal living in them. The reefs were home to other creatures including crinoids, nautiloids, trilobites, and fishes. Ancient corals tended to be larger than today's and lived singly, like sea anemones.

A best-seller
Hugh Miller (1802-1856) was a stonemason from Scotland. He collected many important fossils from the Old Red Sandstone that outcrops in northern Scotland. Many were of Devonian, armored, jawless fish. Miller is famous for a series of popular geology books he wrote in the 1840s and 1850s. These books were best-sellers at the time.

Alive and kicking
Coelacanths are known from fossils in rocks ranging from the Devonian to the Cretaceous, when it was thought they became extinct. In 1938, a strange fish was caught by fishermen off the southeastern coast of Africa. Scientists noticed the similarity between this fish with its leglike fins (called *Latimeria*), and fossils of prehistoric fish, and decided that the coelacanths are still alive today! *Latimeria* lives in the deep waters of the Indian Ocean.

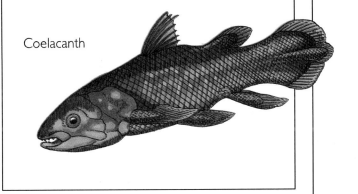

Coelacanth

Favosites

Crinoids (sea lilies), above, are related to starfish and sea urchins. They attached themselves to the seafloor.

Jawless fish

Most of the earliest fish did not have jaws. They belong to class Agnatha, which means "no jaws." They had a simple hole for a mouth and many must have grubbed about for organic debris in the sediment under the water. Today, there are two living groups of agnathans, the lampreys and the hagfish. It is thought that the class Gnathostomata (all of the vertebrates with jaws) evolved from jawless fish. The jaws were formed from some of the bones that supported the gills.

Thelodonts

Osteostracans

Dinithys

Anaspid

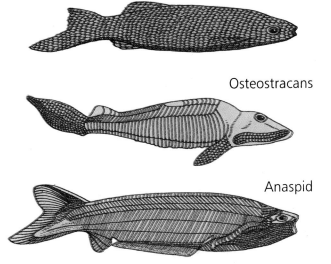

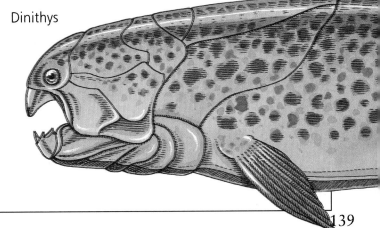

Different objects reflect different colors. This is because of a variety of substances they contain called pigments. Different pigments reflect different combinations of colors. Paints and dyes contain pigments. They can be used to change the color of things by changing the colors they reflect.

BLUE AND YELLOW MAKE GREEN

Many objects contain more than one pigment. You can mix paints to see how the pigments combine to give different colors. Mixing pigments is quite different from mixing lights. The primary colors of pigments are said to be red, blue and yellow — but more accurately they are magenta, cyan and yellow. All colors can be made by mixing these primary colors. Mixing blue with yellow makes green. This is because blue paint (cyan) reflects violet, blue and green light. Yellow pigment appears yellow because it reflects red, orange, yellow and green light. The only color which both pigments reflect is green. Mixing all three primary colors makes black, since between them the pigments absorb all colors of light.

Printed color photographs are made by combining dots of the primary colors on the page. Use a magnifying glass to look at the dots that make up the photograph on the opposite page. Apart from magenta, cyan, and yellow, black is used to give extra contrast.

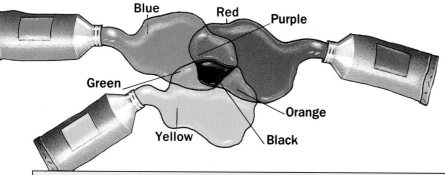

Blue Red Purple Green Orange Yellow Black

▷ These materials have been dyed bright colors to make them more attractive. Dyes can be made from plants or they may be man-made.

USING CHROMATOGRAPHY

You can separate the pigments used in colored pens and inks. This is called chromatography. Cut a strip of blotting paper and draw a line of ink about 2 inches from one end. Hang the strip so that the end nearest the ink just dips into a dish of water. The pigments will soon spread up the paper. Each pigment travels at a different speed and so they separate. When the color is at the top of the paper take it out and let it dry.

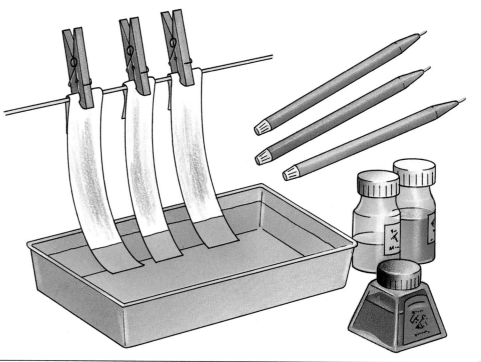

MAKING DYES

You can make vegetable dyes to color material. You can use cherries (red), onion skins (yellow) and spinach (green), as well as many others. Ask an adult to boil the leaves or fruit in a pan with a little water and simmer the mixture for 15 minutes. When it has cooled, put a coffee filter into a funnel and pour the liquid through it into a pan. Leave the material you want to dye in the pan for a few minutes and then let it dry.

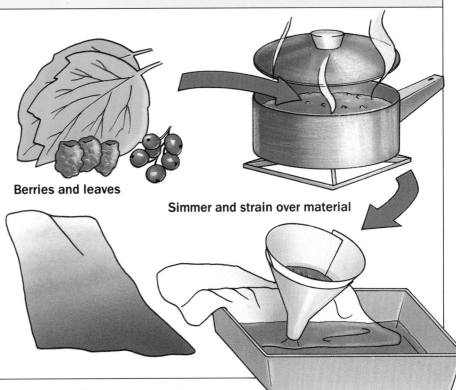

Berries and leaves

Simmer and strain over material

FIGHTING SHIPS

Fighting ships were conceived as fighting platforms for troops to board and capture the enemy vessels. The early Egyptian galleys were probably the first real fighting ships, and although sails were added through the ages, galleys with banks of oarsmen were still in service until the 17th century. The great ships or galleons like the *Mary Rose* (which sank because she was made top heavy) were followed by the ships-of-the-line, like *Victory*. They used their broad sides of cannon fire to cripple opposing ships before boarding and capturing the enemy. The French *Gloire* (1859) was the first warship to carry iron armor plates, followed in 1860 by the English all-iron, screw-driven *Warrior*.

Battleships

In *Warrior* (below), iron replaced wood, steam replaced sail, and guns replaced cannon. *Dreadnought* was one of the first new class of

battleships. It was launched in 1906, had ten 12-inch guns and a crew of 800 men. It was the first steam turbine-powered battleship.

HMS *Dreadnought*

Triremes

The trireme (above) appeared in the Mediterranean around 500 B.C. A typical Greek trireme was about 130ft long and 20ft wide. It had three banks of oars operated by 170 oarsmen, and also carried warriors for combat. It attacked and sank other ships by ramming.

Fire control radar

Bridge

Automatic gun

SAM launcher

Aircraft carriers

The first aircraft carriers were introduced between the two World Wars and during World War II they were the most important ship type.

Modern navies are based around aircraft carriers. The biggest carriers in the world are the *Nimitz* (below) class of the U.S. Navy. Their flight decks are 1080 feet long and they carry about 90 aircraft and helicopters.

New Developments

High-tech developments are likely in naval craft. The U.S. Navy's *Sea Shadow*, shown left, can avoid detection by radar.

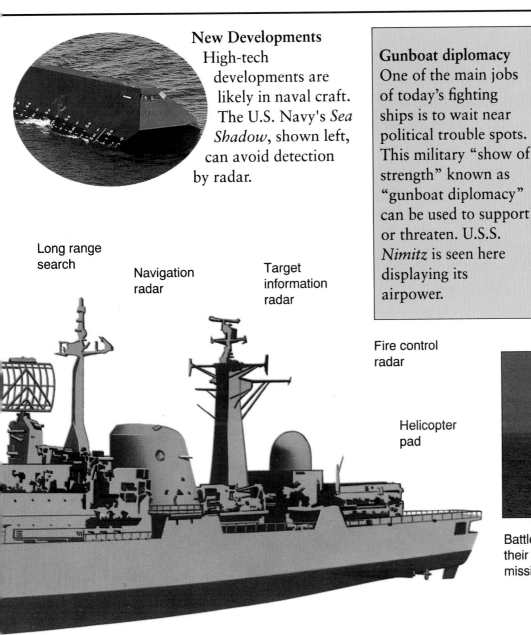

Long range search

Navigation radar

Target information radar

Fire control radar

Helicopter pad

HMS *Glasgow*, a Sheffield (type 42) class destroyer.

Gunboat diplomacy

One of the main jobs of today's fighting ships is to wait near political trouble spots. This military "show of strength" known as "gunboat diplomacy" can be used to support or threaten. U.S.S. *Nimitz* is seen here displaying its airpower.

Battleships in the Gulf conflict used their huge guns and launched cruise missiles.

The modern ship

The use of iron and explosive shells revolutionized battleships. Modern fighting ships, such as the destroyer above, are fast, light, and crammed full of electronics. The gas turbine engines give it a top speed of 29 knots. Armament includes light guns, torpedoes, and surface-to-air (SAM) missiles for attacking aircraft. These are controlled by the computerized fire-control system. A helicopter is carried for antisubmarine operations. In a conflict, the ship's main role is to defend the fleet's aircraft carriers.

High-speed boats

Some countries operate high-speed patrol boats around their coasts. They often include hydrofoils and hovercraft as well as gas turbine boats. Iranian gunboats sank several oil tankers in the Gulf with torpedoes, during the Iran/Iraq war of 1984/1985.

AIR AND THE EARTH

The Earth is surrounded by the atmosphere, a big layer of air which formed about 4,500 million years ago. It is held in place by the pull of the Earth's gravity. The atmosphere works like a shield, keeping out harmful rays from the Sun and reducing the impact of rocks from space as they fly toward the Earth's surface. Life is only possible on Earth because the atmosphere prevents it getting too hot or cold.

Measuring air pressure

Atmospheric pressure is endlessly changing – it pushes on us from all directions because of the gas molecules constantly jostling with each other.

To feel the effect of atmospheric pressure try this simple test. Place a piece of paper flat on a table, by the edge. Then slip a ruler between the paper and the table and lever the paper upward with the ruler. The force you feel working against you is atmospheric pressure.

Colors of the sky

Sunlight is composed of all the colors of the rainbow. Molecules of gas in the atmosphere scatter the blue light more than the other colors. So extra blue light reaches our eyes and we see the sky as blue on clear days.

At sunrise or sunset, the Sun is low in the sky and has to shine through a thicker layer of atmosphere. More light is scattered aside by dust and gas molecules in the air and only the orange and red light gets through.

On the Moon, the sky looks black because there is no atmosphere with dust and gases to scatter the light.

Layers in the atmosphere

The atmosphere can be divided into five main layers, although there are no physical barriers and the gases in the air move freely about. More than 75 percent of the atmosphere is in the troposphere, and all life and weather is in this layer. Above this, the stratosphere contains the ozone layer, which absorbs ultraviolet rays from the Sun. In the upper atmosphere, where the air is very thin, are the mesosphere, thermosphere and exosphere. In the thermosphere the air can reach temperatures as high as 4,000 degrees F.

Space suits

Out in space, there is no air at all, so to travel to and from space or work outside their spacecraft, astronauts wear special space suits. These act as a kind of miniature atmosphere, providing air pressure (blood pressure would cause astronauts' bodies to explode otherwise), temperature control and pure oxygen. The early space suits used for walking on the Moon have been developed into sophisticated Manned Maneuvering Units. First used in 1984, these have an autopilot that keeps the astronaut in position using nitrogen gas-jets.

Exosphere – up to 650 miles

Only 47 percent of the total radiation from the Sun ever reaches the Earth's surface. The rest is absorbed by the ozone layer (in the stratosphere) or is reflected back into the stratosphere by clouds.

Thermosphere – up to 300 miles

Mesosphere – up to 55 miles

Stratosphere – up to 33 miles

Tropopause

Troposphere – up to 14 miles

Altitude

As you go higher and higher above the Earth, there is less and less air and the atmosphere becomes thinner. On high mountains, there is not enough oxygen in the air for climbers to breathe properly so they may take oxygen tanks with them. Mountain animals, and people living at high altitudes, develop large hearts and lungs to enable them to take more oxygen from the air.

Altitude sickness happens when people do not get enough oxygen. They may experience symptoms such as headaches, nausea, coughing, and sleeplessness.

10,000 yards – aircraft cabins are pressurized to the equivalent of 2,000 yards

9,000 yards – maximum height people can survive without extra oxygen

4,000 yards – altitude sickness can occur

INCA RELIGION

Religion cemented the unity of the Inca empire. At its heart was the cult of Inti, the Sun. Other important deities were Mamaquilla (the Moon), Pachamama (Mother Earth), Mamacocha (Mother Water) and Illapa (Thunder). These gods all represented Viracocha, the Creator. The Incas also worshiped holy sites, called *huacas*. The High Priest of the Sun and his assistants belonged to the imperial family. Mamacunas (chosen women) lived in convents. It was their duty to teach the *acllas* (virgins).

The Inca Calendar

The Incas observed the sun, moon and stars. They established a solar calendar of twelve months, in accordance with the sun's position in the sky, which was marked by special stones (below). The Inca calendar cycle was respected throughout the empire.

The Sapa Inca

To assert his power, each ruler claimed to be the son of the Sun. As the Sun ruled the skies, so the Supreme Inca ruled on Earth. When the Sapa Inca died, it was said that the Sun had summoned him. The bodies of dead rulers were mummified and were consulted as oracles (right). Their wishes were interpreted by the living Sapa Inca.

Ceremony and Sacrifice

Religion was the focus for the entire Inca empire. One third of everything was passed on to the cult of Inti and the priests (right), who held an important position in Inca society. Llamas and guinea pigs formed part of this "taxation." If these were free from blemishes they were sacrificed to the air, frost, and water in order to ensure a good harvest. Sacrifices were also made to the Sun as it rose every day over the city of Cuzco.

Egyptian sun worship

From very early times the sun was also worshiped in the Nile Valley. During the Old and Middle Kingdoms of Egypt (c.2666-1640 B.C.), the supreme deity was Ra, the Sun God (below). His symbols were the pyramid and the obelisk, and he was shown sailing the heavens in a boat. The cult of Ra showed itself most clearly in the raising of magnificent temples. For Egyptians, Ra was embodied in the Pharaohs, who were worshiped in the same way as Ra himself.

The cult of the Sun

Inti, the Sun, was worshiped as the "giver of life." Temples for the cult of Inti were built throughout the empire. At Cuzco's main temple the Incas kept gold images of the Sun (main picture). Herds and produce belonging to the Sun were used in rituals and as offerings. The cult's festivals were closely tied to the growing of crops (above). Inti Raimi, the Feast of the Sun, was celebrated on the winter solstice in the month belonging to June.

Mummification

The Incas revered the remains of their ancestors. After the death of each emperor, his internal organs were removed and buried, and his body preserved. Dressed in fine fabrics and surrounded by precious objects, the bodies remained in the palace that each had inhabited in life. Thousands of years before, the Egyptians had also mummified their dead, and in South America, the Paracas people placed mummy bundles in deep caves (right).

WHAT ARE AMPHIBIANS?

Major groups: earthworm-like caecilians (150 species), newts and salamanders (350), eel-like sirens and species with minute limbs (4), frogs and toads (2,700).
Distribution: all wetlands except in polar regions.
Largest: Japanese and Chinese giant salamanders – 1.8m (6ft) long, 65kg (143lb) in weight.
Smallest: Arrow-poison frog – 8.5mm (0.3 in) long.

The name amphibian comes from two Greek words – *amphi* meaning both, and *bios* life. Young amphibians live in water. Like fish, they breathe using gills, use a tail and fins for swimming, and have a lateral line system. Adult amphibians are adapted mainly for life on land. They breathe using lungs or through their skin, have two pairs of limbs for walking or jumping, and have eyes, ears and a nose like those of true land vertebrates. Yet few adult amphibians are entirely independent of water. Most breed in water because their eggs need moisture, and amphibians dry out if their skin cannot be kept moist. Some American tree frogs, for example, spend their entire lives in trees, using rainwater "puddles" that collect at the bases of leaves to keep moist and for laying their eggs.

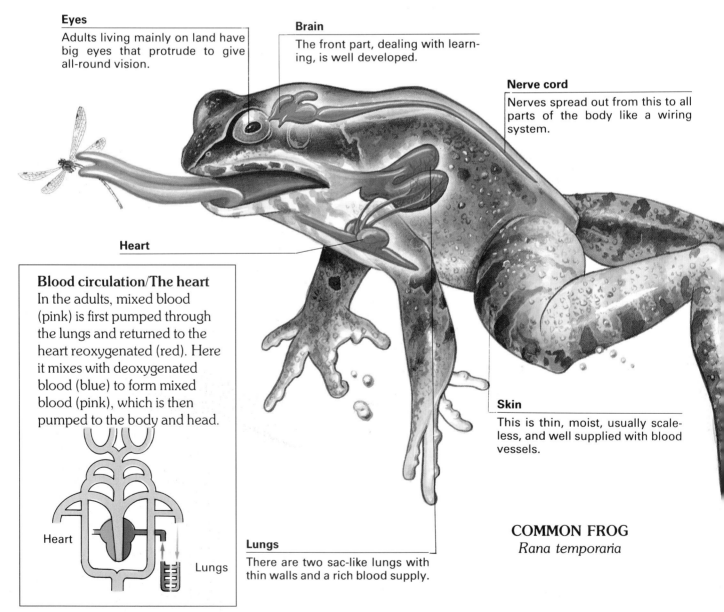

Eyes
Adults living mainly on land have big eyes that protrude to give all-round vision.

Brain
The front part, dealing with learning, is well developed.

Nerve cord
Nerves spread out from this to all parts of the body like a wiring system.

Heart

Blood circulation/The heart
In the adults, mixed blood (pink) is first pumped through the lungs and returned to the heart reoxygenated (red). Here it mixes with deoxygenated blood (blue) to form mixed blood (pink), which is then pumped to the body and head.

Heart

Lungs

Skin
This is thin, moist, usually scaleless, and well supplied with blood vessels.

Lungs
There are two sac-like lungs with thin walls and a rich blood supply.

COMMON FROG
Rana temporaria

Metamorphosis

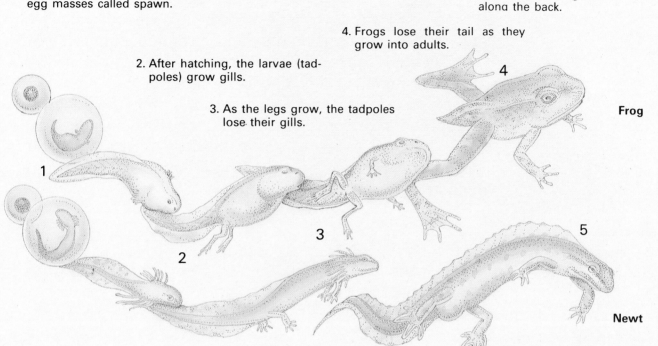

1. Female frogs and newts lay egg masses called spawn.

2. After hatching, the larvae (tadpoles) grow gills.

3. As the legs grow, the tadpoles lose their gills.

4. Frogs lose their tail as they grow into adults.

5. Newts keep their tails and some species grow a frill along the back.

Frog

Newt

A common feature of most amphibians, and certainly of the familiar frogs and toads, is that they undergo a complete change in appearance and internal body structure during their life history. The gradual change from aquatic larva to land-living adult is known as metamorphosis. In newts and salamanders this change is less dramatic.

The adult amphibians breed in water. The female produces eggs (spawn) that are protected by a layer of jelly. After a few days to several weeks the larvae, or tadpoles, hatch. Those of frogs and toads feed on tiny water plants, whereas newt larvae eat insect larvae and small soft-shelled animals. Then, the tadpoles start to take on adult features. They begin to lose their gills, and as their lungs grow they come to the surface to breathe. They start to eat insects such as flies and worms. Legs begin to grow – first the back ones and then the front ones – and the tail gets shorter and shorter (in frogs and toads) until it disappears. The young adults are then ready to come out on land.

Skeleton

Except for lack of ribs, this is like the skeleton of true land vertebrates.

FROG SKELETON

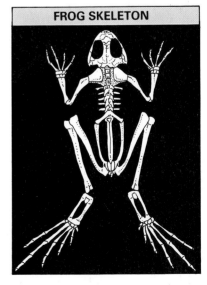

Webbed feet

Skin between the toes of the hind feet helps to push against the water.

CHEMICAL REACTIONS

Have you ever wondered why cakes rise in the oven or what the bubbles in soda are actually made of ? The answer in each case is the same – carbon dioxide. Carbon dioxide is a gas which is formed when two atoms of oxygen join with one atom of carbon. The formula for carbon dioxide is CO_2. There are actually small amounts of carbon dioxide in the air and green plants give out CO_2 during the hours of darkness. The CO_2 in cakes, however, is not drawn from the air. It is produced when acids react with carbonates or bicarbonates which are present in the ingredients.

VOLCANIC ERUPTION

1. Make a volcano which erupts with a foam of vinegar and baking powder. Form a cone shape around an old plastic cup or bowl. Glue the cone firmly to a base.

1

2

2. Cover the cone with 5 or 6 layers of newspaper and glue and leave to dry. Next, cover the base with glue and sprinkle with sawdust or sand. Paint the base and volcano.

3. When dry, a coat of sealing mixture (3 parts water to 1 part glue) will help to protect the paintwork when the volcano erupts. Once again, allow the whole thing to dry well before the next step.

4. Next, prepare the ingredients which will produce the reaction. You will need a small amount of baking powder or bicarbonate of soda and some vinegar mixed with a little red food-coloring.

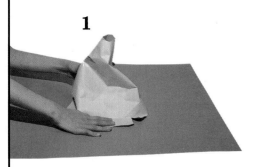

3

5. Put a teaspoon of the baking powder into the volcano then pour in a little vinegar. The reaction should be fast and a red liquid containing carbon dioxide will foam up over the sides of your volcano as it "erupts."

4

5

WHY IT WORKS

The vinegar is an acid and it reacts with the sodium bicarbonate (which is an alkali) in the baking powder. This reaction produces carbon dioxide gas. If you add water to baking powder you would also get a reaction, although it would be a slower one. This is because the baking powder contains acidic salts which become acids when the water is added. These acids react with the sodium bicarbonate to produce CO_2. It is partly this reaction which causes cakes to rise in the oven.

Vinegar   Baking powder   Carbon dioxide

BRIGHT IDEAS

Why not make your own fizzing lemonade? Mix the juice of 4 lemons with 1 quart of water then add sugar until your mixture tastes good. When you want a drink, pour out a glass, add half a teaspoon of bicarbonate of soda, stir, and drink at once!

6. Obviously, the more ingredients you use, the bigger the size of the eruption. A fizzing noise, known as effervescence, can be heard – this is the sound of the carbon dioxide gas being produced.

6

FAMOUS COMPOSERS

The following list of famous composers have written music for piano, flute, trumpet, or violin. Some have written for all of these. The composers below span the Baroque (c.1600-1750), Classical (c.1750-1820), Romantic (c.1820-1900) periods as well as the new developments of the 20th century and present day. The Baroque period featured very elaborate, rich music, with new forms of vocal work. The Classical period emphasized a balance and elegance in the different sections of a piece of music. In the Romantic period composers believed music should be highly imaginative and emotional. The 1900s has seen many developments, such as new ideas in harmony, and popular music such as jazz.

BACH, Johann Sebastian (1685-1750)
A very famous German composer of the Baroque period. He was also a choirmaster and a brilliant organist. He wrote sonatas, suites, and cantatas and other orchestral works for many different instruments. His fugues (pieces in which the notes of a theme follow themselves up and down the keyboard) are particularly famous. Bach wrote much music for the organ, including "chorales" based on old German hymn tunes. He also wrote many works for the flute, including "The Musical Offering," written for Frederick the Great, and the B minor suite.

BARTOK, Béla (1881-1945)
Hungarian composer who developed a national style based on the folk and gypsy music of his country. This is clear in his writing for the violin.

J.S.Bach

BEETHOVEN, Ludwig van (1770-1827)
One of the greatest composers in history. A German composer who was revolutionary in that he broke away from the tradition of writing religious music, and wrote music to be listened to for its own sake. He wrote many dramatic concertos and sonatas for the piano. From the age of 30, Beethoven's hearing began to fail, and some of his greatest works were composed when he was deaf. His violin concerto, a powerful piece, opens with four ominous drumbeats. The virtuoso violin concerto went on to become a very popular form in the course of the 19th century.

BERLIOZ, Hector (1803-69)
A French composer who wrote his violin concerto in memory of a young girl. It begins with just the four open strings.

BERNSTEIN, Leonard (1918-91)
An American composer and conductor whose music is inspired by jazz, Broadway musicals, and traditional Jewish music.

BIEDERBECKE, Bix (1903-1931)
Jazz pianist, cornet-player, and composer, who wrote "Singin' the Blues" and "In A Mist."

BIRTWISTLE, Harrison (b.1934)
A present-day English composer who has written concertos for trumpet with orchestral accompaniment.

Bix Biederbecke

BOULEZ, Pierre (b.1925)
A French composer and conductor whose sonatine contains modern techniques which give the flute a wide range of expression.

BRAHMS, Johann (1833-97)
A great German composer, who has been regarded as the leading composer of Romantic symphonies, concertos, and chamber music. When he wrote his famous violin concerto it was first thought to be unplayable. It was called a concerto "not for but against the violin."

BRITTEN, Benjamin (1913-76)
A versatile English composer who has written work for particular performers, and for amateurs and children, such as "The War Requiem."

BRUCH, Max (1838-1920)
A German composer who wrote two very popular violin concertos.

BYRD, William (1543-1623)
An English composer

Claude Debussy

known for his religious music, and for being one of the first composers of keyboard music. The Renaissance period, between 1400 and 1600, saw the beginning of the great age of keyboard music. Byrd composed for the virginal, a stringed keyboard instrument similar to the harpsichord.

CHAMINADE, Cécile Louise Stephanie (1857-1944)
French composer and pianist whose flute concerto has a delightful Hollywood-style opening and furious technical sections.

CHOPIN, Frédéric (1810-49)
One of the greatest pianist-composers who wrote for solo piano. He discovered a new, poetic character

for the new 19th century piano.

COPLAND, Aaron (1900-1991)
American composer who wrote several film, ballet, and theatre scores.

CORELLI, Arcangelo (1653-1713)
A celebrated violinist and teacher, who was the first to write specifically for the violin. But even the hardest pieces he wrote seem quite easy by modern technical standards.

COUPERIN, François (1668-1733)
Couperin composed music for harpsichord and organ. Today this music is often played on the piano.

DEBUSSY, Claude (1862-1918)
A French pianist-composer. By the 19th century grand pianos had a beautiful sound and touch, and Debussy was very inspired by this. He created musical "impressions" of natural phenomena like rain, sunlight, and snow. His "L'apres-midi d'un faune" begins with a haunting flute solo, and his "Syrinx"

is possibly the best-known solo piece for the flute.

DELIUS, Frederick (1862-1934)
English composer who is famous for his rich harmonies and romantic music.

DVORAK, Antonin (1841-1904)
Czech composer whose symphonies, concertos and chamber music are colorful, and

George Gershwin

dramatic, reflecting the character of Czech music.

ELGAR, Sir Edward William (1857-1934)
A British violinist and composer of the Romantic tradition. He wrote many orchestral works, including "The Enigma Variations."

COMETS

From time to time an object looking like a star with a tail appears in the sky. This is a comet. The solid portion of a comet is a mixture of water, ice, frozen gases, and rock. Comets travel far out in space away from the planets in elongated orbits. When their orbits bring them close to the sun, frozen gases on the rocky body vaporize and form the bright tail which always points away from the sun. Some comets are well known. Halley's comet, for example, returns every 76 years. Amateur astronomers have been very successful in discovering new comets, so keep your eyes and notebooks open.

COMETS
A few comets are visible to the unaided eye. Others have to be viewed through binoculars or telescopes. Although many comets are well known, new comets are spotted from time to time and are always named after the person who first saw and recorded them.

ORBITS OF COMETS

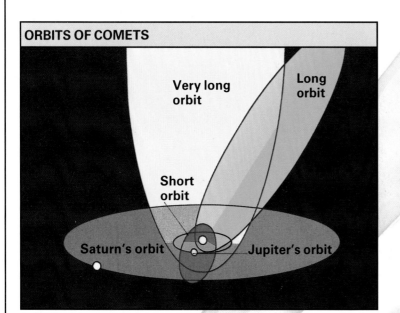

Very long orbit

Long orbit

Short orbit

Saturn's orbit   Jupiter's orbit

INSIDE A COMET
A comet's core is a mixture of water, ice, frozen gases, and rocks.

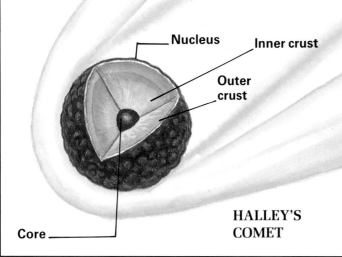

Nucleus   Inner crust

Outer crust

Core

HALLEY'S COMET

ASTEROIDS

There are thousands of pieces of rock and iron orbiting in our solar system. We call them asteroids. One group of vast boulders orbits the sun in a "belt" between Mars and Jupiter. Another group, the Trojans, occupies the same orbit as Jupiter. This includes the largest asteroid, Ceres, which is over 600 miles across. A third group orbits close to Earth. The Martian moons, Phobos and Deimos, may be asteroids that have been captured by the planet's gravitational field.

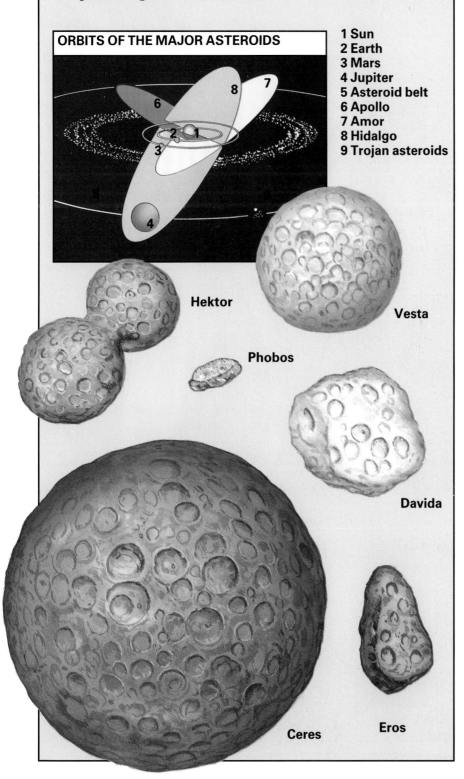

ORBITS OF THE MAJOR ASTEROIDS

1 Sun
2 Earth
3 Mars
4 Jupiter
5 Asteroid belt
6 Apollo
7 Amor
8 Hidalgo
9 Trojan asteroids

Hektor

Vesta

Phobos

Davida

Ceres

Eros

METEORS

Meteors, which are sometimes produced when asteroids collide, appear as streaks of light whenever chunks of debris from space enter Earth's atmosphere and burn up. Meteors can be seen on almost any night. Regular meteor showers also occur when Earth passes through a stream of particles left by a comet. The Orionid shower, for example, (October 16th-26th) is caused by particles from Halley's comet.

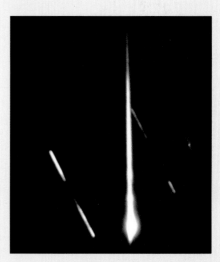

Because of their brief appearance, meteors are also known as "shooting stars."

ROCKS FROM SPACE
A meteor that reaches Earth without burning up is called a meteorite.

THE ALL-SEEING BRAIN

The eyes are the brain's windows on the world. Through them, the brain sees shapes, colors and movements. It identifies familiar objects, investigates strange ones, and keeps a lookout for food, drink, comfort, danger, and computer games.

Eyebrow-raising muscle

Eyelid-closing muscle

BRIGHT OR DIM?

No, not you – the light. The hole in the front of the eye, the pupil, gets smaller in bright light. This prevents too much light from damaging the retina. Eye color is the color of the iris.

Bright light (blue eye) *Dim light (brown eye)*

SPIES ON YOUR INSIDES

BLINKING EYES
Blinking smears tear fluid over the eye surface, to wipe off dust and germs.

The doctor looks into the eye with a light-and-lens instrument, the ophthalmoscope. It shows the retina, blood vessels, and gives clues to the eye's health.

SEEING
The cornea and lens bend light rays to focus a clear image onto the retina.

Cornea

Iris

Pupil

Lens

Object

Cornea and lens

Upside down image

Nerve signals to brain

EYEBALL LAYERS

The sclera is the eye's tough outer layer. The choroid is rich in blood vessels.

Sclera
Choroid

Close-up view of retina

LANDING LIGHT

Light rays land on the retina, the eye's inner layer. It is no bigger (or thicker) than a postage stamp. Here 130 million special cells, rods and cones, detect the light rays and change their energy into nerve signals. These flash along the optic nerve to the brain.

Nerve fibers in optic nerve

Cross-over

Image on retina

CROSS EYES

The optic nerves part-separate and cross. So each side of the brain sees with halves of both eyes!

EYES LEFT, RIGHT

Six long, slim muscles pull on the eyeball to make it look around.

Eye-moving muscle

EXTRA LENSES

If the eye's own lens is too strong or not strong enough, this can blur vision. Glass or plastic lenses, in eyeglasses or as contact lenses, make vision clear again.

Contact lenses

SPARE-PART SURGERY

Ophthalmic (eye) surgeons can put artificial lenses into the eye, if the natural lens becomes cloudy as in cataract. Or they can shave pieces off the cornea with a laser beam, to cure short or long sightedness.

Near sight

Far sight

Flatter cornea

Rounder cornea

157

Exploring the DEPTHS

The early films of Hans and Lottie Hass and Jacques Cousteau allowed many people to explore the wonders of the underwater world on their own TV sets. Now, with modern diving suits and camera equipment, ordinary people can plunge into the oceans and examine their watery secrets for themselves. Louis Boutan, the inventor of the first underwater camera, would have been amazed to see the disposable waterproof cameras now for sale. Some resorts now offer submarine trips rather than boat tours. Soon you may be able to buy a submersible of your own!

PRESSURE SUITS

Wearing some diving suits feels like wearing a submarine! The Wasp *and* Jim *(left) are popular designs, in which a diver can reach 1,650 feet (500 m) with enough air for three days. However, the suits are expensive and clumsy to use.*

Do submarines ever get lost? On September 1, 1973, a small submersible, the *Pisces III*, was rescued from 1,580 feet (480 m) below sea level. Two men had been trapped inside for three days, after losing control of the craft and straying out of radio contact with their surface ship. It took two crewed submersibles and a robot vehicle to find and recover the submarine.

OCEAN FLYERS

Deep Flight One *(above) is a new craft that "flies" underwater. It is very strong, but weighs only as much as a large car. Deep Flight Two may soon take people down to the depths more easily than the clumsy* Trieste.

FISHING THE DEEP

Scientists can catch animals from the deep-sea floor by using special underwater sleds with nets. The sled is towed by a ship over the muddy seabed, on the end of a cable up to 9 miles (15 km) long. It can carry instruments to examine the water, and video or still cameras.

SNAPPING THE OCEANS

Scientists have started dropping their cameras into the sea! The Bathysnap *(left) is a special camera that sinks to the seabed and takes pictures of the mysterious animals that live deep down. When the film is finished, the camera is automatically released from the heavy weights which hold it and floats to the surface.*

Say "Cheese!"

Louis Boutan took the first underwater photograph in 1893 (left), but his camera was heavy and clumsy. Today's cameras are small and light and have brought many of the ocean's mysteries to life. Special lamps emphasize colors and scenery. Remote-controlled still and video cameras can explore the seabed, sending back images to scientists on research ships. These pictures can be transmitted live to laboratories and museums worldwide.

YELLOW SUBMARINE

The British scientist Robert Leeds has recently designed a small "yellow submarine" (right), shaped like a flying saucer, for commercial use.

It will be tested in 1996 and, if it is declared safe, you may soon be able to hire one and go fish-watching down to a depth of 165 feet (50 m).

USING HOLOGRAMS

Holograms are used in three main ways: as an art form, to record information, and as a security measure to prevent something being copied. Some shops now specialize in selling holographic works. Holograms have even been added to the exhibitions of painting and sculpture in major art galleries.

One of the most important uses of holograms in the future will be to store information. The 3-D image in a hologram contains much more detail than a normal photograph. It can be turned to show parts of the image that are normally hidden and to reveal how different objects or parts of objects relate to each other in space. Information can also be recorded in a hologram in the on-off binary code computers use.

Until recently, holograms were only made in laboratories in small numbers and they could only be viewed in laser light. Today, holograms can be made in large numbers and they can be seen in daylight. Because of this, holograms will become common in packaging, store windows and street signs.

Although holograms can be made more easily now by specialist companies, they are still almost impossible to copy. This is why they are printed onto security items, for instance credit and identity cards. In this way, holograms help to prevent fraud.

Holograms like this bird are often printed on credit cards to make it difficult to copy them.

Science has helped to create the new visual art forms of our age – photography, movies, television and now holography (as seen in the gallery above). Holograms are increasingly being used to record 3-D images of complex objects. Designers and architects can now produce holograms which show how their work will look from computer programs, and dentists can keep holographic records of patients' teeth or dental plates (below).

Information stored as holograms

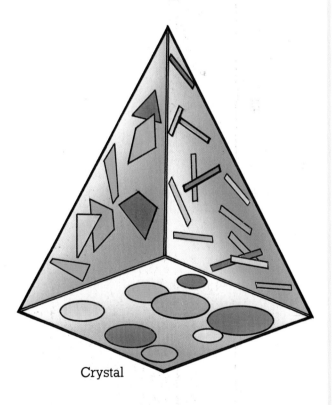

Crystal

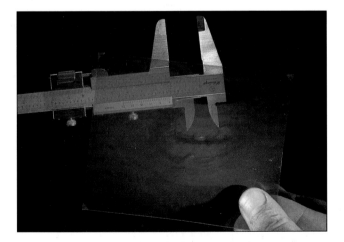

Crystals are materials with a regular geometrical shape formed from sheets (or planes) of particles. Some crystals can store a different hologram on each plane. In 1969, the

U.S. Bell Laboratories found that 1,000 holograms could be stored in a crystal of lithium niobate. As the crystal is tilted, the hologram on each plane appears.

161

THE AGE OF THE KNIGHT

Between about 900 and 1400 the mounted knight was the most valued European battle weapon. Knights were more than just warriors. They formed a privileged group at the top of society. The division of land was geared to the cost of putting an armored knight into the field and knightly behavior, known as *chivalry*, was held up as an example for everyone to follow.

Nevertheless, the importance of mounted knights in battle is easily exaggerated. They looked magnificent and could make devastating charges. But medieval warfare was primarily about capturing enemy castles, not cavalry attacks.

Commanders usually avoided battle if they could. Besides, in an extended fight a knight with his head inside a steel helmet often had no idea what was going on!

A SOLDIER OF FORTUNE

Until 1300, some lords paid for their knights' equipment, but as the cost of armor and a war horse rose, the practice stopped.

Soon being a knight cost an arm and a leg in more ways than one. The enormous expense of putting an armored, mounted warrior in the field restricted knighthood to all but the wealthiest families.

Knight in 1200

CASTLES COUNT!

Large-scale battles between mounted knights were rare and usually of little significance.

The capture of mighty Château-Gaillard from French King John (*above*) in 1204, for example, had more impact on the history of France than any cavalry conflict.

Château-Gaillard (above) *dominated the countryside for miles around.*

The Sword in the Stone

British director John Boorman used the name Excalibur – *Arthur's magical sword* (right) – *as the title of his remake of the legend* (left).

Arthur found the weapon sticking into a stone and returned it to the Lady of the Lake when he died.

The Power of the Sword

The sword, ideal for stabbing and slashing, was the basic weapon of every knight.

THE LEGEND OF KING ARTHUR is a blend of ancient British and French myth, spiced with Christianity, and a dash of fact.

The real Arthur may have been a Romano-Briton who fought the Anglo-Saxon invaders in the 6th century A.D. Arthur, the romantic hero of Camelot was created by the 12th-century monk Geoffrey of Monmouth.

Geoffrey set the tales in his own time, with his own religious message. This is why they feature knights in armor, Christian chivalry, and glamorous ladies in long pointed hats!

Knight in 1500

CHAOS AT BOUVINES (*above*)

King John lost his French possessions with the fall of Château-Gaillard. When he tried to get them back, he was heavily defeated in 1214 at Bouvines, Flanders (modern Belgium).

The battle was a rare example of a major conflict between mounted knights. After the first assault, the fight deteriorated into total chaos!

WHAT ARE REPTILES?

There are probably more than 10 million different kinds, or species, of animals in the world. About 6,500 are reptiles – "cold-blooded" creatures with a bony internal skeleton and scaly skin, that breed by laying eggs. Despite their small proportion of total animal species, reptiles are one of the best-known animal groups. They include slithering snakes, speedy lizards, slow tortoises, flippered turtles, and fearsome crocodiles. Those giants of the distant past, the dinosaurs, were also reptiles.

Reptile eggs

Reptiles are vertebrates – animals with backbones. Like another group of vertebrates, birds, they lay tough-shelled eggs. The shell houses and protects the baby animal as it develops inside, using the food store in the egg known as yolk. The eggs of turtles, snakes, and most kinds of lizards have tough, leathery, slightly flexible shells. Those of tortoises, crocodiles, and lizards such as geckoes have hard, brittle shells, more like a bird's egg. However, some lizards and snakes do not lay eggs. The young develop inside their mother and are born fully formed.

Hatching

Baby reptiles have a hard, horny scale on the mouth, called the egg tooth. They use it to crack their way out of the egg.

The lizard group

There are about 3,750 species of lizards, from tiny wall and sand lizards to big, sturdy monitors and iguanas. Lizards are the most widespread reptile group.

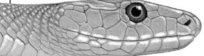

The crocodile group

There are about 22 species of crocodiles, alligators, caimans, and gavials, called crocodilians. They have powerful tails and mostly live in swamps, lakes, and rivers.

A reptile puzzle

The worm lizards are a small group of reptiles, with about 140 species. Neither worms nor lizards, they are in a reptile group of their own, called the amphisbaenids. Most have no legs and live in tropical and subtropical places, burrowing in the soil of forests to prey on worms, insects, and other creatures. The biggest amphisbaenids are 30 ins (75 cms) long.

The skeleton

The skeleton of a reptile is similar to other vertebrates, being composed of a skull, a line of bones called vertebrae making up the spinal column, and four legs. The vertebrae carry on past the hips to form the tail.

Skull

Leg bones

Main vertebrae (backbones) of spinal column

Front foot bones

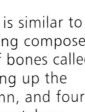

Dragons galore

Myths, legends, and stories from all over the world feature dragons, sometimes called "great worms."
The typical dragon is a reptile-like creature. It has scaly skin, breathes fire, flies on vast wings, guards stolen treasure, attacks humans, and is evil and cunning. One of the most famous is Smaug, the huge and terrible dragon from J R R Tolkien's exciting folk story *The Hobbit*, written in 1937.

Inside a reptile

A reptile such as this crocodile has all the main internal parts common to other vertebrate animals, like frogs, birds, or mammals such as yourself. These include a brain, heart, stomach, intestines, kidneys, and the bones of the skeleton.

The snake group

There are about 2,400 species of snakes, from tiny thread snakes to huge pythons. They have long, slim, flexible bodies, and most lack all traces of legs.

The turtle group

There are about 240 species of turtles, tortoises, and terrapins, called chelonians. Many have domed shells of bone and horn.

Snakeless zone

The island of Ireland has no snakes. Christian legend says that they were banished by Saint Patrick (389-461 A.D.), patron saint of Ireland, because they were evil. A more likely biological explanation is that snakes have never managed to spread to Ireland from mainland Britain because of the wide barrier of the Irish Sea.

FUTURE CITIES
DESIGNING BETTER CITIES

Most of the world's population live in cities; and the cities we live in were almost all built before the invention of the car, the telephone, or electricity.

As a result, most cities are congested and polluted, and use energy inefficiently. Designing better cities is difficult because technology moves so fast: what makes sense on the drawing board may be out of date by the time the city is built. To escape from 19th century squalor, 20th century planners went for clean, "garden cities" in which workplaces and homes were placed far apart. That forced people into cars, replacing factory pollution with exhaust fumes. Housing developments on the edges of cities provided good houses, but a boring environment that bred crime and disillusionment. *Lu Jia Zui*, a new plan for a district of Shanghai by the Richard Rogers Partnership, attempts to design a future city without these problems. Grouped around a park, *Lu Jia Zui* will

One solution to expanding urban populations could be to build out into the sea (below). Land has been reclaimed from the sea in the past, but the concept of a floating city – like a futuristic Venice – looks more and more probable. Reclaimed land could also provide the wide open spaces of parkland that may no longer exist in the older cities.

be served by steetcars and a light rail system, with frequent stops so that nobody will have to walk more than a quarter of a mile. The plan for *Lu Jia Zui* is flexible, to allow for change. A computer program allows changes in population, parking, energy-use, and the

movement of people to be analyzed and incorporated into the design. Housing and commercial developments are mixed in all six sections of the city. To maximize the daylight admitted to the buildings, a model was tested for summer and winter conditions.

Lu Jia Zui (right) will lie close to the famous Shanghai waterfront, the Bund. A light rail system will circulate around the central area, with parking for cars, and connections to the Shanghai subway.

S A V I N G   S P A C E
G O I N G   U N D E R G R O U N D

As the population of the world increases, space has become more and more valuable. Building downward instead of upward is one solution to an over-populated and over-polluted environment. This vision of the future (below) shows what an underground city might look like. Shielded from the outside weather conditions by a huge, glass dome, the underground city can create its own climatic conditions. Air from the outside could be cleaned and filtered before being pumped around the multi-story city, while natural light penetrates the building through a central atrium. Natural insulation from the surrounding earth would help to save the energy usually needed to heat or cool a conventional building above the surface.

Energy (right) would be provided both as heat, and as electricity, with all the buildings designed to be energy-efficient. The buildings have been arranged to maximize natural light, which cuts energy costs by 15 percent. All areas of the city are within easy reach of open spaces, with private cars banned from the inner areas.

HOW SOUNDS ARE HEARD

When sound waves enter our ears, they strike the eardrum which vibrates back and forth. This in turn causes tiny bones called ossicles to vibrate. These vibrations are turned by our "inner ear" into electrical signals that pass along nerves to the brain. When the signals reach the brain, we hear sounds. People cannot hear some sounds because they are too high or too low – not everyone can hear the high-pitched squeak of a bat. Dogs can hear higher pitched sounds than people, and a scientist called Sir Francis Galton (1822–1911) invented a whistle for calling dogs which was too high for people to hear. This kind of sound is called ultrasonic sound, or ultrasound.

WHY IT WORKS

The sound waves from your friend's voice make the plastic wrap vibrate. These vibrations are transmitted into your cardboard "ossicles" and can be seen by watching the mirror for movements. This is a simple model of how a real ear works.

Vibrations in the air (sound waves) enter the outer ear and make the eardrum itself vibrate. The three bones, the malleus, the incus, and the stapes, together known as the ossicles, transmit the vibrations through the middle ear

to the oval window, or vestibular fenestra. The force of the vibrations on the oval window is over 20 times greater than that of the original vibrations on the eardrum. The oscillations (or vibrations) of the stapes makes the fluid in the part of the inner ear called the cochlea vibrate. The cochlea also contains fibers that pick up the vibrations and send messages along nerves to the brain. Other parts of the ear control our balance – these are called semicircular canals.

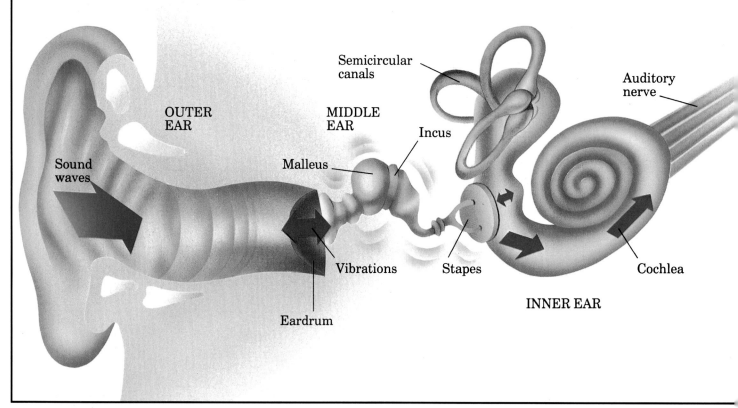

Semicircular canals

Auditory nerve

OUTER EAR

MIDDLE EAR

Incus

Malleus

Sound waves

Vibrations

Stapes

Cochlea

Eardrum

INNER EAR

HEAR THIS?

5. Shine a light onto the mirror and ask a friend to talk into the ear. Watch the mirror for vibrations.

5

1

1. To make an eardrum, stretch a piece of plastic wrap or a piece of an old balloon across the end of a tube. Fix in place with a rubber band.

3

2. Make a set of "ossicles" with two disks and a fork shape of thin cardboard held together with double sided tape.

2

3. Attach a small mirror or a disk of shiny foil to one end, and attach the other to the plastic wrap "eardrum" on the tube. Your middle ear is complete.

4. Make an outer ear from a cone of cardboard with a hole at its end. With careful use of pink tissue paper you can achieve quite a realistic look!

4

BRIGHT IDEAS

☀ Watch the oval window of your ear again. How does it respond to shouting, whispering, whistling etc? The vibrations of your oval window could be a result of blowing on the eardrum, rather than the vibrations of sound waves. Use a radio to create sound without blowing.

☀ A hundred years ago, people who suffered from hearing loss used ear trumpets. Find out about these devices! Can you make your own?

☀ Listen to sounds blindfolded. Put your hand over one ear and try to tell which direction a sound is coming from. Listen to the same sound with both ears. Can you hear a difference? It is easier to hear the direction of sound with both ears.

BEFORE THE DINOSAURS

The earth had already passed through most of its history before the dinosaurs appeared. Earth is about 4,600 million years old, and the first dinosaurs came on the scene 230 million years ago. The first living things were tiny creatures, like viruses or bacteria, which lived in the warm oceans 3,500 million years ago. Their fossils can only be seen through a microscope. Larger plants and animals arose 1,000 million years ago, and familiar forms, like shellfish, corals, and fish, existed by 500 million years ago. Fish were the first animals with backbones, and they gave rise to land-living amphibians 375 million years ago, and reptiles a little later. The reptiles ruled the earth from 275 million years ago until mammals became dominant over 65 million years ago.

Early views of dinosaurs

The first dinosaurs were named in England in 1824 (*Megalosaurus* from Oxfordshire) and 1825 (*Iguanodon* from Sussex). The only fossils at that time were odd bones and teeth, and scientists originally thought that these new animals were either large lizards, or rhinoceros-like giants. It was only later, when complete skeletons were found, that the mistakes were realized. Long before the dinosaurs were named in England, fossilized bones and teeth had been found in China. Written records of "dragon bones" and "dragon teeth" exist from the third century.

An early illustration of Iguanodon shows a ferocious, dragonlike monster.

Cretaceous Period
The last phase of the age of dinosaurs, a time of great success. Flowering plants came on the scene and, with them, social insects such as ants and bees.

TODAY

65 mya

mya= million years ago

Cainozoic Era
The most recent phase of earth history, the last 65 million years of the Age of Mammals. During this time, all modern plants and animals appeared, including humans.

It is hard to understand the huge amounts of time involved in the history of life on earth. When you remember that the first cars ran on the roads only 100 years ago, think how much can happen in spans of millions of years. This chart shows some of the main divisions of geological time over the past 400 million years, and some of the common backboned animals.

Devonian Period
Fish were abundant, and amphibians appeared.

Carboniferous Period
Amphibians, like bloated crocodiles, were the common backboned animals. They lived in warm coal swamps.

360 mya

Permian Period
A drier time in many parts of the world, and ruled by various kinds of reptiles.

286 mya

245 mya

208 mya

Triassic Period
Dinosaurs arose halfway through this time, about 230 million years ago.

Jurassic Period
The age of the giant dinosaurs, the great long-necked plant-eaters. Also time of origin of the birds.

144 mya

Dating rocks
Layers of rock can be placed in order by looking at the fossils in them. But, the exact ages, in millions of years, are worked out by studying the radioactive decay of rock particles. When the elements that made up the earth were formed, all possible particles were present. Now, the older the rock is, the more the radioactive elements have decayed. It is possible, therefore, to give an age to rocks by looking at the rates of radioactive decay.

Geological periods
The units of geological time were named during the 19th century. The names reflect something of the life at the time, or commonly refer to a part of the world. The main units are the eras: Paleozoic (ancient life), Mesozoic (middle life), and Cei nozoic (recent life). The Mesozoic Era, the Age of Reptiles, includes three periods: the Triassic, Jurassic, and Cretaceous. Triassic (three parts) refers to the three main divisions of rocks of that age in Germany. Jurassic was named after the Jura Mountains in Germany, and Cretaceous is based on "Creta" (chalk), a common rock of that particular age in history.

Rock strata

WHAT IF A BAT COULDN'T HEAR?

Clicks
Echoes

Bat sonar

The bat's sound pulses are so high-pitched that you or I couldn't hear them. However, a bat's hearing is so sensitive, it can hear these clicks and their echoes. The bat can find its way and catch its flying food even in complete darkness. The system is like radar, but with sound waves instead of radio waves. It's known as sonar or echolocation.

It would fly through the dark night – and crash into things! Mammals possess an amazing array of senses to detect the outside world. Hearing is only one of these. They are able to see in very poor light, smell the very faintest odors, taste an enormous variety of different foods, and detect touches and vibrations that are as light as a feather.

Dolphin sonar

Predatory members of the whale group, such as dolphins and killer whales, have a sonar system like the bat's (above). The sound pulses are concentrated, or focused, into a beam by a large lump in the forehead, the melon.

melon

What if whales could sing?

All whales make underwater sounds, varying from shrill clicks and squeaks and squawks, to haunting low moans and groans. Beluga and humpback whales are so noisy that their calls can be heard underwater more than 125 miles (200 km) away. The "songs" of a whale can last between 6 and 35 minutes, and are used by the whales to communicate with each other.

Nighttime eye-shine

If you've ever shone a flashlight into a cat's eyes, you will have seen that they appeared to glow in the dark. A cat's eye has a mirrorlike layer inside, the tapetum. Light rays come into the eye and some are detected by the light-sensitive layer, the retina. Others pass through the retina, bounce off the tapetum, and get sensed by the retina on the way out. This gives the eye two chances to detect light rays. Other nocturnal (nighttime) animals, such as opossums, have this too.

The pupil opens wider in dark conditions, to let in more light.

The retina detects light and turns it into nerve signals, which go to the brain.

The tapetum is a layer behind the retina. It reflects the light back onto the retina.

What if a lion had eyes on the side of its head?

It would leap at its prey, and probably miss! Most hunters, such as seals, cats, and foxes, have two forward-facing eyes at the front of the head. This gives them overlapping fields of vision (right), and allows them to judge distances well, for pursuit and pounce. Most hunted mammals, such as deer, zebras, and rabbits, have eyes on the sides of their head. Although this means that they can't judge distances well, it does give them a good overall view for spotting any predators that may be creeping up on them (right).

Something in the air

Dogs sniff everything, from the food they eat, to other dogs, especially when it is time to mate. The scent in the air enters the nose and attaches to an organ called the *olfactory bulb*. This is very large and very sensitive in a dog's nose. It then sends signals to the brain.

Olfactory bulb

HIEROGLYPHICS

The Ancient Egyptians spoke a language related to the languages of the Middle East and North Africa. Those who could, wrote using a system of picture writing, called hieroglyphics. The Egyptians began using hieroglyphics in about 3000 B.C., shortly after the first known examples of writing appeared in Sumer (now southeastern Iraq). Each picture, or hieroglyph, could stand for an object and a sound. Some represented one letter; others up to five letters. These were always consonants. Vowels were not written down.

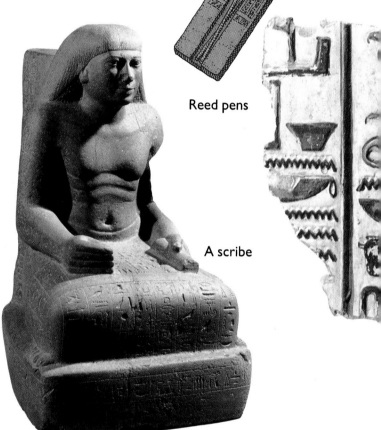

Ink blocks

Reed pens

A scribe

Breaking the code
Hieroglyphics were last used in about A.D. 394. For more than 1,400 years no one could read or understand them. In 1799, however, a soldier in Napoléon Bonaparte's army in Egypt found a large stone slab — the Rosetta Stone. On the stone was a text carved by Egyptian priests in 196 B.C. to mark the crowning of King Ptolemy V. The same text was written out in Ancient Egyptian hieroglyphs, demotic script (a simpler form of hieroglyphs), and Greek. By comparing the three, a French scholar called Jean-François Champollion, was finally able to crack the code in 1822.

Champollion

The Rosetta Stone

Writing hieroglyphs
The word "hieroglyph" is Greek for sacred carvings. Egyptian hieroglyphs were usually written or carved by highly trained men called scribes. Egyptian society was based on keeping records, and scribes were therefore very important. Many rose to positions of great authority because they could read and write. Use the symbols below to write your own hieroglyphic message.

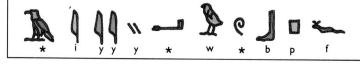

*   i   y   y   y   *   w   *   b   p   f

Papyrus paper

The Egyptians wrote on a paper-like material, called papyrus, made of reeds. The pith was taken out of the reeds and cut into strips. These were laid flat in layers, covered with cloth, and pounded with heavy stones or a mallet to weld them together. The papyrus was then polished to give a smooth, flat surface. Sheets of papyrus were often put together to form a roll.

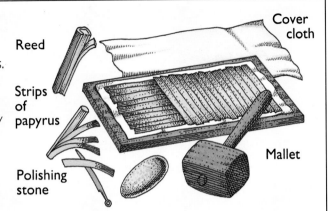

Reed

Strips of papyrus

Polishing stone

Cover cloth

Mallet

Hieroglyphs (above) were not used in everyday life. They were reserved for important inscriptions, such as those on tombs and temples and for affairs of state.

For daily use, two simpler, less formal shorthand scripts were created. Hieratic script (left) was used in the Old Kingdom. By about 700 B.C., demotic (from the Greek word *demotikos,* meaning "popular") script was in use.

B

B

There were many different ways of writing hieroglyphs. They could be written from left to right, right to left or top to bottom. If an animal faced right (A), you read from right to left. If it faced left (B), you read from left to right.

A

A

The name or symbol of a ruler appeared in hieroglyphs within an oval frame called a cartouche (shown left).

K L I O P A D R A

Champollion solved the puzzle of the Rosetta Stone using names like Ptolemy and Cleopatra (left and above). See if you can spot which letters appear in both names.

P T O L M Y S

*No translation

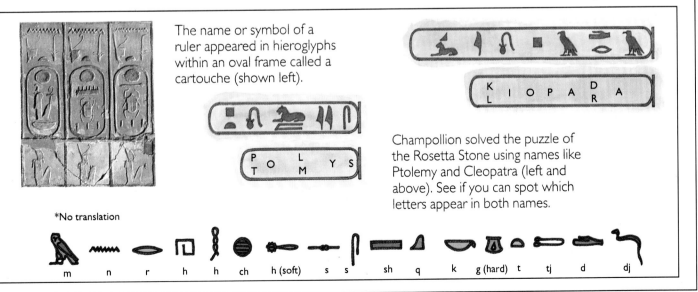

| m | n | r | h | h | ch | h (soft) | s | s | sh | q | k | g (hard) | t | tj | d | dj |

DOGS

The dog family, or Canidae, includes dogs, wolves, jackals, and foxes. Dogs tend to take advantage of any situation, feeding on carrion, insects, and even fruit and leaves, if they cannot hunt. They can all run at speed for long distances, but are less agile than cats. Dogs are intelligent, sociable animals and most live as tightly-knit family groups or packs, at least for part of the year. They communicate by sounds, body postures, and their highly developed sense of smell.

Domestic Dogs

The earliest remains of a domestic dog are believed to be over 11,000 years old. Abandoned wolf pups may have been taken into the home as pets, guard dogs, or hunters. Dogs treat the families they live with as members of their pack, taking their place in the hierarchy. As with other domestic animals, many different breeds have been produced, each with different characteristics.

Big Bad Wolf

Wolves have had a bad image for centuries because they kill domestic animals and game if they have to. There are many stories, but few proven cases, of attacks on people. Fairy stories about the Big Bad Wolf and legends of werewolves (right) reflect the fear of wolves. It has lead to centuries of persecution. Today the gray wolf, which once roamed most of the northern hemisphere, is an endangered animal. Efforts to re-introduce it involve improving its image.

Hot and Cold Foxes

The Arctic fox, as its name suggests, lives in the cold Arctic tundra. It can survive temperatures as low as -58°F. It has a coat of thick fur all over its body, even on the pads of its paws, and on its small, rounded ears. They are so well insulated that they loose very little heat.

Pavlov

Ivan Pavlov was a Russian doctor who spent a lot of time finding out how the human body works. He used dogs for his experiments. He discovered he could train them to salivate with a bell, not just in

response to food. When the body learns to perform a function in response to an artificial cue it is called a conditioned reflex.

Peter and the Wolf

The Russian composer Prokofiev wrote this musical fairy tale for children in 1936. The story is told by a narrator and all the characters – Peter, his grandfather, the wolf, the bird, the cat, and the duck – are played by different musical instruments from the orchestra. The wolf is portrayed by three horns.

Wolf

Coyote

Jackal

Canine Relatives

The closest relatives of the domestic dog are wolves, coyotes, and jackals. Members of a wolf pack hunt together cooperatively to bring down large prey. The North American coyote is one of the few wild animals that is increasing in numbers today. An adaptable animal, it eats anything it can find. A breeding pair of African jackals stay mated for life.

Working Dogs

Many domestic dogs work for their living, helping on the farm or with field sports, racing and guarding or guiding their owners. Huskies, bred for their strength and resilience, work together in teams, pulling sleds across the snow.

The tiny Fennec fox, the smallest of all the wild dogs, lives in hot African deserts. It keeps itself cool by sleeping in a burrow during the hottest part of the day. It uses its huge ears as radiators to get rid of excess body heat. They are also useful for listening to the sounds of the tiny animals on which it feeds.

Spooky PLACES

Stonehenge is only one of many mysterious places. Ancient sites often seem to attract supernatural events, such as sightings of ghosts and aliens. One theory is that standing stones and earthworks (banks of earth built by early peoples) were placed at the crossing points of the magnetic energy lines that cross the Earth, to form a bridge to the sky. *Ley lines* are a network of straight lines which seem to link sites such as standing stones and barrows (mounds of earth covering graves) with holy places. Ancient trackways follow these lines; some scientists believe that they match the lines of force around the Earth's surface.

THE VANISHING CREW
On a calm afternoon in December 1872, the Mary Celeste *was seen drifting in the Atlantic Ocean. Her log ended on November 25. The entire crew had vanished. Had they been attacked by a giant octopus, sucked into a whirlpool, abducted by aliens...or simply drowned?*

MYSTERIOUS MONUMENTS
On the slopes of Easter Island, in the Pacific Ocean, stand dozens of giant stone statues. They were probably made in A.D. *1000–1500, in the quarries of the extinct volcano Rano Raruku. They are believed to represent spirits of ancestors, who magically protected the islanders.*

Bermuda

Florida

Puerto Rico

What was Stonehenge used for? Scientists believe that this great monument was a tribal gathering place and religious center, although no one can be sure. It is thought that the layout of the stones was used to predict important astronomical events. Tribal ceremonies were probably held there at certain times of the year.

DEADLY TRIANGLE
Off the coast of Florida is an area known as the Bermuda Triangle, where over 200 ships and planes have vanished mysteriously. Some disappearances can be explained as the result of unusual weather, but the rest are a puzzle. Many people think that there could be strange energies at work there.

PICTURES IN THE SAND

In 1927, a pilot, flying a light aircraft over the Nazca plains of Peru, looked down and saw thousands of vast lines and pictures drawn in the desert. The pictures included a spider, a monkey, and a hummingbird with a wingspan of 200 feet (60 m, above). Archaeologists think they were created 1,000–2,500 years ago by the Nazca people, who moved the dark stones to expose the light sand underneath.

Visitors from the skies

In 1969, Erich von Däniken wrote a book called *Chariots of the Gods?*, in which he suggested that aliens had visited Earth 10,000 years ago.

He claimed that they came from an advanced civilization and created many ancient wonders, like the Easter Island statues and Stonehenge. He said that some South American carvings (above) and a cave painting in Australia's Kimberley Mountains were images of alien visitors. Von Däniken said that early peoples worshiped the aliens and that many ancient myths were reports of their arrival in fiery chariots or spaceships.

POWERFUL STONES

The standing stones at Carnac, France are just one ancient site apparently chosen to match the Earth's energy lines. Thousands of huge stones are arranged in parallel rows, but no one knows why.

THE LOST CONTINENT

The ancient Greek philosopher Plato described a vast continent in the Atlantic known as Atlantis, which suddenly vanished. Huge undersea walls, from about 9500 B.C., have been found in the Bahamas. Could these have been the walls of Atlantis? Or did the legend arise from the flooding of the island of Crete in 1950 B.C.?

Bacteria are so small that they can be seen only with the aid of a microscope. They have cells with a very simple structure. The cells of plants and animals are more complex and measure between 0.001 and 0.002 inches across.

The amount of oxygen in the atmosphere gradually increased with the greater number of cyanobacteria. At first it probably killed off many of the bacteria, but gradually they adapted to use the oxygen for their own purposes. The development of different types of bacteria led to the evolution of other organisms that obtained their energy simply by feeding off more primitive ones. The next important stage occurred when more complex cells acquired the ability to photosynthesize through the development of chloroplasts (see below). These were the first true plant cells.

Simple to complex cells

The cells of plants and animals are much more complicated than those of bacteria. Plants, for example, have tiny egg-shaped structures called chloroplasts inside their cells. By separating them from the rest of the cell, scientists have shown that they do the work of photosynthesis – using sunlight to make food. What is most striking about chloroplasts is how much they resemble cyanobacteria – the single-celled creatures that originally pumped oxygen into the air. It is now believed that chloroplasts are the descendants of cyanobacteria that made a home inside larger cells many millions of years ago.

Plant and animal cells include other egg-shaped structures known as mitochondria. These are responsible for the reactions in which food is broken down and oxygen is used to produce energy. Like chloroplasts, mitochondria are probably descended from bacteria that had learned to cope with oxygen, and which then began living inside larger cells that had "swallowed" them.

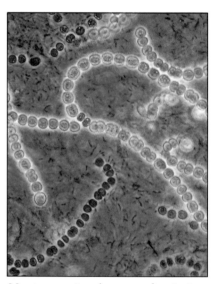

Nostoc, a simple cyanobacterium

PLANT CELL

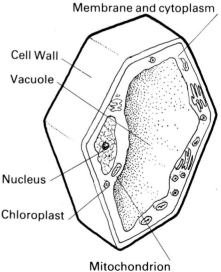

- Membrane and cytoplasm
- Cell Wall
- Vacuole
- Nucleus
- Chloroplast
- Mitochondrion

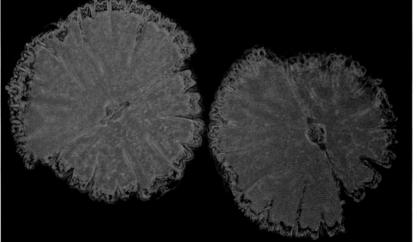

Single-celled desmids have a cellulose cell wall.

Plant evolution

The first plants were single-celled organisms formed when cyanobacteria took refuge inside larger cells. Those larger cells already contained mitochondria, descended from other bacteria. From their point of view, there was a lot to gain by giving the bacteria a home. The mitochondria helped them to cope with oxygen, and the chloroplasts made food for them.

These ancestral plants probably lived at the surfaces of seas and lakes, as many of their descendants – the unicellular algae – do today. In time, the single-celled plants began to evolve into many-celled forms, by dividing into two without separating. Some formed balls of cells, others hollow cylinders, and some formed strings of cells. Many organisms with these arrangements (shown below) live today as pondweeds and seaweeds.

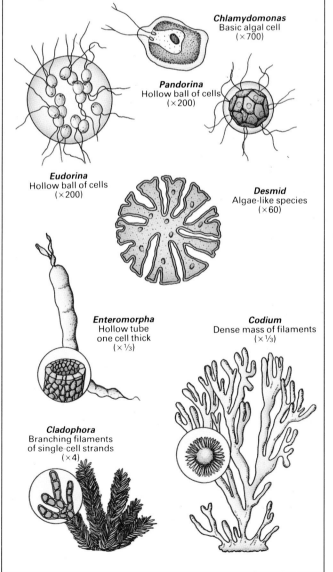

Chlamydomonas
Basic algal cell
(×700)

Pandorina
Hollow ball of cells
(×200)

Eudorina
Hollow ball of cells
(×200)

Desmid
Algae-like species
(×60)

Enteromorpha
Hollow tube
one cell thick
(×⅓)

Codium
Dense mass of filaments
(×⅓)

Cladophora
Branching filaments
of single-cell strands
(×4)

On to land

For millions of years, algae were the only forms of plant life. Like today's algae, they were largely confined to water because they would dry out on land and because they had no supporting structure to hold up their leaf-like fronds. To begin with, therefore, there were no plants on land. Then a small alga began to grow around the edges of ponds, just out of the water. In time, it evolved a semi-waterproof covering, and developed root-like structures to draw up water from the soil. These pioneering algae gave rise to the mosses, simple plants which still need damp places in which to grow. Later on, more advanced groups of plants such as ferns appeared. These had a waterproof covering on their leaves and were the first plants to develop roots and woody stems, allowing them to grow taller.

Mosses need a layer of moisture to reproduce.

The cycad is an ancient primitive plant.

WHAT ARE FLOODS?

Floods are the waters which cover an area of land that is normally dry. They have affected almost every corner of the earth at some time or another, but those which cause the greatest amount of damage are the result of extreme weather conditions.

Tropical storms, which are called typhoons, hurricanes, or cyclones in different parts of the world, whip up the winds over the oceans and create huge waves. These waves, known as storm surges, race toward the shore and crash onto the coastline. The country of Bangladesh has suffered serious flooding on many occasions, as cyclones in the Bay of Bengal send huge sea waves crashing over the low-lying coastal areas. Other enormous waves which produce severe flooding are the so-called tidal waves, or *tsunamis*, which result from earthquakes or volcanic eruptions.

The millions of tons of rock, soil, and mud unleashed during a landslide can block a river valley or dam, causing water levels to rise dramatically. Flooding can also follow a seiche, the violent movement of lake waters following an earthquake. The most frequent cause, however, is when heavy rains and melting snow and ice make inland rivers and dams burst. This problem is made worse in areas where large numbers of trees have been cleared. Stripped of their vegetation, the hillsides cannot hold the excess water, which runs off and causes flooding in lowland areas.

◄ During powerful storms, strong winds whip up high waves that pound down on the coastline. Sea defenses are often smashed to pieces, causing serious flooding in areas along the coast and extensive damage to property.

▶ **Sudden, violent bursts of water surging down narrow mountain valleys or dry river beds are called flash floods. These raging torrents of water, such as the one shown right at El Oued in Algeria, can flood an area for just a few hours, or even minutes, before subsiding.**

Heavy rain falls during the summer monsoon season.

Volcanoes and earthquakes on the ocean bed cause *tsunamis.*

Swollen rivers burst their banks.

Storm surges cause flooding of lowland areas.

SAMURAI WOMEN

Samurai women followed the same code of honor as the men. They were expected to show the same obedience to their fathers and husbands as a *samurai* would to his master. Women were often forced into arranged marriages in order to increase the power of their families.

It was considered very important that a *samurai* had a son to inherit his possessions. Sometimes the *samurai* would take another wife if the first one did not give birth to a boy.

One *samurai* woman, Tomoe Gozen, fought alongside her husband, Yoshinaka, in all his battles. Her story is told in the long poem *Heike Monogotari*.

Some *samurai* women learned to fight and they defended their homes against enemies. One *kabuki* play tells of two, sisters, Miyagino and Shinobu, whose father was murdered by a *samurai* called Shiga. They swore to avenge their father's death. In secret they trained themselves to fight, then they went to the local leaders and asked permission to challenge Shiga to a duel. In the fight that followed, Shiga was killed and the family honor was satisfied. The story of Miyagino and Shinobu is still performed on the Japanese stage to this day. It shows the courage of *samurai* women.

SAMURAI CHILDREN

In the Edo period, schools were set up for the sons of *samurai*. Calligraphy and Chinese writings were the main subjects taught, as well as the *samurai* codes. Girls learned *ikebana*, the art of flower arranging, and the tea ceremony from their mothers. At the age of 13, boys had the front part of their heads shaved. This was a sign that they had become men.

Girls wore their hair parted in the middle and falling over their shoulders. By the time they grew up, it touched the ground. Boys liked to catch dragonflies and make them fight each other. Girls caught fireflies and kept them in jars to use as lanterns.

13 year-old boy

Young boy

Young girl

BIRDS

Birds, the champions of the air, are the most plentiful of the earth's warm-blooded animals. Scientists have estimated that there may be over 100,000 million birds in the world altogether. Their success is largely due to their ability to fly, which gives them versatility in finding food and places to live. Birds come in all different sizes and colors.

Brilliantly colored macaws live in noisy flocks in the world's rain forests. The species shown here are endangered in the wild.

Blue and yellow macaw

Scarlet macaw

The first birds
All living things change over thousands of years to improve their chances of survival. This process of change is called evolution. Birds evolved from reptiles about 150 million years ago. Their feathers developed from the scales which covered their ancestors. Wings gradually evolved from front legs. One **Archaeopteryx** of the first birds was *Archaeopteryx* ("ancient wing"). It was about the size of a gull and had the sharp teeth of a lizard. It was a poor flier and used to climb trees and then glide away.

Legend and symbol
Birds have been so successful that they can be found virtually everywhere. Over the years, different cultures have come into contact with birds and attached various meanings to them. Bird flight has always inspired awe in earthbound humans. Birds have often been viewed as bearers of good fortune. However, crows, vultures, and other carrion-scavenging birds are commonly associated with evil or horror.

The phoenix
This bird was worshiped in ancient Egypt, but exists only in legend. The phoenix was said to set itself on fire and then rise from its own ashes.

The dove
The dove as a symbol of peace originated with the biblical story of Noah, who sent a dove from his Ark to find dry land.

Skull

Wing bone — Vertebrae

Ribs

Wishbone
(Collarbone)

Tailbone

Breastbone

Pelvis — Leg bone

Hyacinth
macaw

Scarlet
macaw

Inside a bird

Birds are vertebrates, with an internal skeleton and backbone. Flying birds have very light skeletons, to reduce the amount of weight they have to carry in flight. Many of their bones are hollow. The inside of the bone looks like a honeycomb. Birds also have lightweight beaks, instead of heavy, bony jaws.

Bird records

There is an amazing variety of different bird species. Although all birds share similar body structure, they differ enormously in color, size, and shape. Some birds are so plentiful that they become pests. Others, like the California condor, are extremely rare.

Largest and smallest

The ostrich is the largest bird in the world. It can grow up to 9 feet (2.7m) tall. The smallest bird is the bee hummingbird of Cuba, which is no larger than a bumblebee.

Ostrich

Most common

The domestic fowl, also known as the chicken, is the world's most common bird. In the wild, the red-billed quelea of Africa is the most numerous bird.

Domestic
fowl

Mute
swan

Heaviest

The heaviest flying bird ever recorded was a mute swan that weighed 50 lb (23 kg). The Kori bustard can also grow to this weight.

The white stork

In Europe, the stork is a symbol of good luck. In legend, the stork delivers newborn babies to homes.

The pelican

The pelican got its reputation for being a dutiful parent in the Middle Ages (5-15th centuries). It was fabled to pierce its chest and feed its young with its blood.

THE REUSABLE SPACECRAFT

Conventional rockets are used just once, then thrown away. The space shuttle is different; it takes off vertically, like a rocket, enters space as a spacecraft, and then returns and lands on a runway like an aircraft. The idea was to make spaceflight simpler and cheaper, but the results have been disappointing. To put a satellite into orbit with NASA's space shuttle costs up to $250 million, no less than a conventional rocket. The popular dream of ordinary people paying for a space ride is still many years away.

Development

The design of the shuttle drew on experience from a series of rocket planes developed in the United States. The first of these, the Bell X-1, launched in mid-air from beneath a B29 bomber, was the first aircraft to exceed the speed of sound in 1947. Later models (below) showed the rounded shape and V-shaped delta wings of the shuttle, designed to resist the intense heat of reentry and then to glide swiftly to a landing.

X-15

The Bell X-15 rocket plane (above), tested in the 1960s, reached speeds of more than 4,000 mph and attained heights of 67 miles, the very edge of space.

X 24A

M2F3

X 24B

The shuttle

The shuttle is built of aluminum alloy, covered with ceramic tiles to protect it from the heat of reentry. The cargo bay is 60 feet long by 15 feet wide, which is about the size of a railway freight wagon. The doors are made of carbon-fiber reinforced plastic. The stubby wings allow the shuttle to glide, though very fast, and land at more than 200 mph The flight deck is the upper level at the front, with the galley and sleeping berths below in the mid deck area. Each shuttle costs about $1.1 billion.

Satellite payload

Fuel tanks

Payload handling controls

Airlock

Oxidizer tank

First flight

The space shuttle Columbia lifted off for its maiden flight in 1981. In general, the shuttle program has been successful. It launches satellites regularly, carries out experiments in space, and also does secret military work. It has made dramatic rescues.

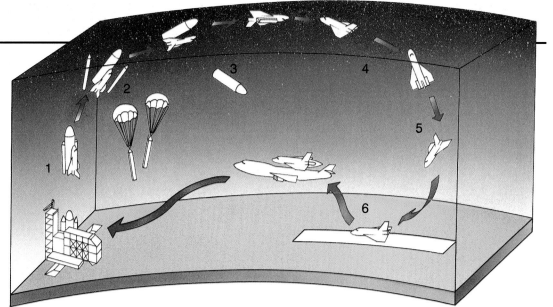

Space radiator

Forward control thrusters

Nose wheels

Flight plan

The flight sequence of the shuttle appears above. For lift-off (1), the shuttle uses its three main engines, plus two boosters. Extra fuel is carried in a huge internal tank. After two minutes, the boosters burn out and parachute into the sea (2). Six minutes later, the main engines stop, and the fuel tank is released (3). The final step into space is made by smaller orbital engines (4). After landing (5), a Boeing 747 returns the shuttle to the launch pad (6).

International rescue

In 1992 (below) three shuttle astronauts spent more than eight hours on a space walk, wrestling a four-ton communications satellite, Intelsat-VI, into the cargo bay. There they fitted a new rocket motor and sent the satellite off on its true orbit, 22,300 miles above the Earth.

Disaster

In America's worst space disaster, hot gases leaked through a joint in the booster casing during the launch of Challenger in 1986. A tongue of flame burned into the main tank and ignited the fuel, blowing the shuttle to pieces and killing its seven crew members, among them Christa McAuliffe, a teacher. The disaster set back the program by nearly three years, as engineers struggled to prevent it from ever happening again.

USING PENCILS AND PASTELS

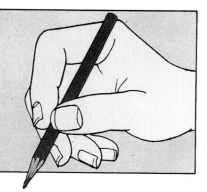
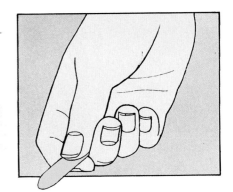

Colored pencils
Colored pencils are one of the most basic coloring tools. Many bright and wonderful colors are available. Artists like David Hockney frequently choose to use them. Although they are often used as colors in their own right, they mix and can be laid down on top of one another to achieve different effects.

Chalk pastels
Chalk pastels are pure pigment bound together with gum. They blend well if you rub them with your finger – this is messy, but effective. Pastel can be put on smoothly with the side of the chalk, or quite thickly if you press firmly with the end. As with most drawing materials, price and quality vary.

Colored pencil and wash
Water-soluble pencils are fun to experiment with. Lines drawn with them will blur to make an area of flat color if you lay a wash of clean water over them with a paint brush.

COLOR THEORY

The six colors you can see in the color wheel on the left are divided into two groups. Red, yellow and blue are called the *primary* colors. Orange, green and purple are the *secondary* colors, and are a mix of the two primaries on either side. In fact nearly all colors can be mixed from the primaries; some ways of mixing colors are shown below. The more colors are mixed together, the duller they become. The colors that are opposite each other on the color wheel are known as *complementaries*. When placed side by side, they bring out the best in each other. For example, red looks redder next to green, and vice versa.

△ *"Make a color wheel for yourself with the primary and secondary colors. Then try again, blending the secondaries from your primary colors."*

Colors can be mixed in various ways. In *cross-hatching*, shades of colored pencil are laid on top of each other.

Colors appear darker or lighter, depending on how hard you press down with your pencil or crayon.

Strokes of yellow wax crayon laid over blue produce a light green. Blue laid over yellow makes a darker green.

Wax crayons can be blended with a finger. If colors are rubbed too much, they will get dirty.

Felt-tip colors can be blended by over-lapping groups of tiny dots. This technique is used in color printing.

WHAT IS ENERGY?

Energy is the ability to do things. Without it we couldn't get up in the morning, or turn on the lights, or drive the car. Plants wouldn't grow, the rain wouldn't fall, the Sun wouldn't shine. Everything we do needs a supply of energy, which is used to make things work: The word energy is Greek, and means "the work within." Energy comes in many forms, which can be stored and used in different ways.

The universe was born 15 billion years ago in an incredibly hot ball of energy (left). It began to expand at an astonishing rate, creating matter, and cooling rapidly as it grew. After 10,000 years, atoms appeared and in two billion years began to group together to form stars and galaxies. Whirling gases around the stars condensed into the planets, like Earth and Mars, about five billion years ago.

Matter and energy

Energy and matter seem very different, but they're not: in fact, matter can be turned into energy. This is how the Sun produces its enormous energy, and how nuclear power stations and nuclear bombs work. The physicist Albert Einstein showed that the amount of energy produced is given by the equation $E = mc^2$, where E is energy, m is mass, and c is a very large number – the speed of light.

The energy we need comes from food. Some foods, like sugar or fat, contain more energy than others. In the body, food is digested to release its energy, which then flows through the bloodstream to the muscles. An active person needs more food than somebody who sits down all day.

Aristotle and Galileo

The Greek philosopher Aristotle (384-322 B.C.) was among the first to try to explain energy. He believed that a heavier stone would fall faster than a lighter one – but he never tested it. If he had, he would have found that both fell at the same rate. They did not fall simply because they were heavy, but because they had energy from being lifted. It was the Italian physicist Galileo Galilei (1564-1642) who first began to understand this and to challenge many of Aristotle's incorrect theories.

All machines need a source of energy. Viking longboats were driven by muscle power, which is limited. But the gasoline or diesel engines in a modern mechanical digger are far more powerful. Until the invention in the 19th century of engines that could turn heat from coal or oil into work, the methods by which people altered their environment were very different.

Energy expressions

There are many sayings which use ideas about heat and energy. To "get into hot water" means to get into some kind of difficult situation. To "go full steam ahead" means to do something with all your energy. To "blow hot and cold" is to change your attitude toward something many times. Do you know these sayings: to "be too hot to handle." to "be firing on all cylinders?"

Tidal waves

The energy of earthquakes under the sea can travel across the oceans as huge waves called tsunamis. The tsunamis, or tidal waves, are barely visible out at sea, but when they reach land they sweep ashore, causing destruction. Systems around the Pacific Ocean warn people to move if a tsunami approaches.

Sound is a form of energy, created by vibrations, such as the sound of a tuning fork. It is transmitted through the air in waves, which travel at about 700 mph (1,126 kph). The vibrations of the air are picked up by our ear drums, which vibrate in time, sending signals to our brains.

CLIMATE CHANGE

Weather changes from day to day, season to season, and even over longer periods of time. The climate of a region may change altogether. For example, the Sahara used to be a grassland thousands of years ago. Now it's a desert. Because of the pollution we continually pump into the atmosphere, we could be drastically changing the atmosphere ourselves. Recent winters in the Alps have seen many places without their usual cover of snow. This could be a sign of climatic change.

Some heat escapes.

Cities and factories produce waste gases.

THE GREENHOUSE EFFECT
The amount of carbon dioxide in the atmosphere has increased slightly in the last 100 years. It is believed this increase is caused by the burning of fossil fuels and destruction of rainforests. If the buildup continues, more heat will be trapped in the atmosphere and an increase in the average temperature over the earth may occur (global warming).

ICE AGES

There have been several Ice Ages when the climate of the earth was colder than average. Ice that spread from the poles and glaciers covered much of Europe and North America. The last Ice Age ended 10,000 years ago. Some scientists think that the world is returning to an Ice Age climate. But more people fear global warming.

Heat is reflected back toward the earth.

Heat radiation from the sun

CFCs

CFCs are chemicals used in aerosol cans, refrigerators and in making styrofoam. If released into the air, they break down when exposed to ultraviolet light, giving off chlorine. The danger is that this chlorine may attack the ozone that forms a protective layer from ultraviolet radiation in the atmosphere. Already, environmentalists have detected ozone damage.

Rainforest destruction

WEATHER WATCH

You can keep tabs on the weather in your area. You can make a rain gauge and measure how much falls each day. You can record wind direction, either with a weather vane or a wind sock. You may be able to estimate wind speeds, too. How damp is the atmosphere? You can get complicated instruments to measure this, or you could just use an old pinecone, and notice whether it is open (dry) or closed (damp). Measure the temperature, too. Put a thermometer outside, but in the shade. You could make a chart of temperature and rainfall for each month. You would need to keep up your record for a long time, though, before you could even begin to guess whether the climate was changing!

Homemade rain gauge made from a plastic bottle that has the top cut off and sitting upside down in the base.

Make a card for each month and measure temperature, rainfall and record other observations such as animals seen or trees.

Take average rainfall and temperature and make graphs for each. Use symbols for such things as falling leaves.

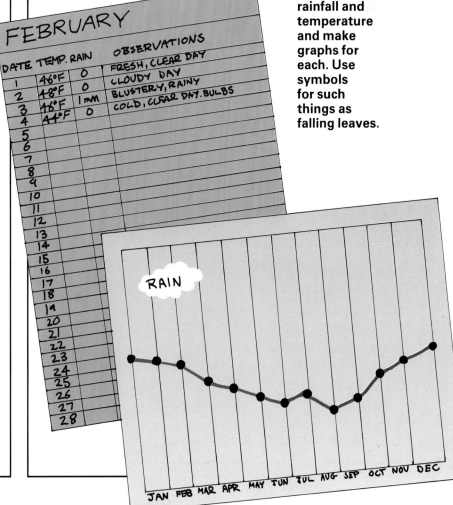

FEBRUARY

DATE	TEMP.	RAIN	OBSERVATIONS
1	46°F	0	FRESH, CLEAR DAY
2	48°F	0	CLOUDY DAY
3	46°F	1mm	BLUSTERY, RAINY
4	44°F	0	COLD, CLEAR DAY. BULBS
5			
6			
7			
8			
9			
10			
11			
12			
13			
14			
15			
16			
17			
18			
19			
20			
21			
22			
23			
24			
25			
26			
27			
28			

RAIN

JAN FEB MAR APR MAY JUN JUL AUG SEP OCT NOV DEC

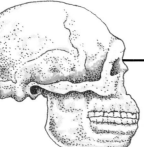

THE FIRST HUMANS

It is very difficult to identify a single line of development from *Australopithecus* to the first true humans called *Homo*. Fossil finds in Kenya show that *Australopithecus*, *Homo habilis* and *Homo erectus* were all alive 1.5 million years ago. *Homo habilis,* who evolved around 2 million years ago, was the first to make tools. *Homo erectus*, who evolved around 1.5 million years ago, cooked food on fires and hunted large animals. Such hunting would have required detailed planning and effective communication within the group.

Out of Africa
Homo erectus was the first human to move out of Africa. About 1 million years ago, they moved into North Africa, and across the Middle East to Asia, and later to Europe.

| | 1.7 million year-old sites |
| | 1 million year-old sites |

Fossil sites of *Homo erectus*

Homo erectus foraged for leaves, roots, and fruits as well as hunting for meat. The relationship between *habilis* and *erectus* is not clear, though it is thought that the first gave rise to the second.

Illness and health
Early humans lived dangerous and exposed lives. They did not have clothing or proper shelters to protect them from extreme heat or cold, and they suffered from many diseases. Some diseases, such as arthritis and tuberculosis damage the bones, and so have been detected in fossils. Food was often scarce, and this must have caused illness too. In many societies today, people commonly live for more than eighty years, but early humans were lucky to reach the age of forty.

Homo habilis

Homo erectus

Habilis and erectus

Homo habilis ("handy man") evolved 2 to 1.5 million years ago, and *Homo erectus* ("upright man") evolved 1.5 to 0.5 million years ago. *Homo habilis* had a rounded head, flat nose and projecting jaws. *Homo erectus* had a bigger brain and body than *habilis*, and an extremely thick skull.

Hunter or scavenger

There is no doubt that *Homo habilis* ate meat, but scientists are still not certain whether they hunted large animals actively or whether they scavenged animals. They may have let a larger predator do the killing and then moved in to claim the meat. A site in Africa shows that *erectus* humans took the carcasses of the animals they hunted to their home base and cut the meat off with stone tools. This is shown by the cut markings that have been found on fossilized animal bones.

Sabre-toothed tiger with its prey

A family of *Homo erectus* (left) make a fire to cook meat and keep away predators. One of the men is making some stone tools, perhaps to help cut the meat. Evidence of fires was first found in excavations of Peking Man, a Chinese *Homo erectus* who lived 1 million years ago.

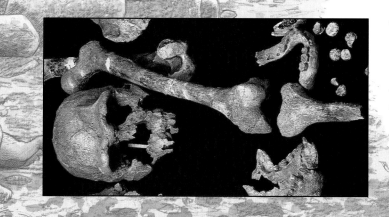

Three skeletons

During the 1970s and 1980s Richard Leakey discovered skulls of *Homo habilis*, *Homo erectus* and *Australopithecus* (left), all dating from the same era. The finds proved that all three species were alive around 1.5 million years ago, putting an end to the idea that humans, unlike any other mammal, had evolved without any variation in species.

THE LEGACY OF ROME

Even today, over 1,500 years after the decline of the empire, Rome still has an enormous influence over our lives. Many of our buildings were copied from the Roman style of architecture. Our legal and political systems can be traced back to Roman times. In addition, there is a huge quantity of historical evidence, from literature and coins, to surviving roads and aqueducts, to keep the memory of Rome well and truly alive.

The Radcliffe Camera is a library in Oxford, England. Its architect, James Gibbs (1683-1754), modeled it on a Roman basilica. The dome, the pillars, and the ornate, classical style are reminiscent of many of the magnificent buildings of the Roman Empire. Several major cities have been built on sites chosen by the Romans. For example, Londinium (modern day London) was founded by the Romans in A.D.43 as a seaport. Can you find out any other examples of towns or cities which were built by the Romans, and which remain today?

The Roman revival
In the early 15th century, writers, artists, sculptors, and architects began to draw inspiration from ancient Greece and Rome. Ruins were studied and statues were dug up. Ancient myths and legends were used as the basis for paintings, such as the French artist Claude's depiction of Aeneas at Delos (shown right). Latin literature also provided inspiration for Renaissance writers. The English poet Pope was greatly influenced by the Latin writer Juvenal throughout his work.

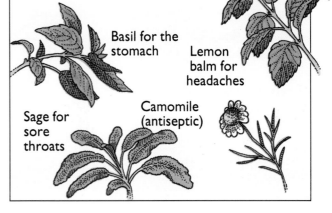

The European Community flag

The period of Roman Empire demonstrated the possibility of one government controlling large areas. Roman citizenship gave people a sense of identity. Today the European Community can be seen to reflect Roman ideals of unity, albeit with modern goals of a single monetary and taxation system, and a central government.

Herbal medicine

For centuries, the healing properties of plants and herbs have been used by different cultures, including the Romans. Try growing your own herbs from seed in a patch of garden or in a small pot. Place them in a sunny, sheltered spot and remember to water them well. Some of the medicinal properties of herbs are listed below.

Basil for the stomach

Lemon balm for headaches

Sage for sore throats

Camomile (antiseptic)

Pompeii

Much of the evidence that we have today about ancient Rome comes from archaeological excavations such as Pompeii (below). The town has been well preserved under the volcanic ash and lava which engulfed it in A.D. 79. Its forum, basilica, theaters, temples, lavish villas, and tiny sleeping quarters offer a complete picture of Roman life. The ruins also provide us with a valuable insight into many aspects of Roman civilization and culture.

The archaeological remains of Pompeii, which was destroyed by the volcano, Vesuvius, in A.D.. 79.

The French Empire

The Imperial system used by the Romans was later copied by rulers of other European countries. The Frankish king, Charlemagne, revived the idea of the Roman Empire in the West. It was termed the Holy Roman Empire by subsequent Frankish and German leaders. The Holy Roman Empire was destroyed by Napoléon Bonaparte who modeled his own empire on that of Rome and even called himself emperor.

WHAT IF AN ELEPHANT HAD NO TRUNK?

The long trunk is one of the main features of the animal, and it couldn't survive without it. The trunk is the nose and upper lip, that have joined together and grown very long. The elephant uses its trunk for many vital actions, especially eating and drinking. Without a trunk, this plant-eater would not be able to pick up grass and leaves to eat. It also uses the trunk to smell, breathe, feel, and to suck up water. If the elephant crosses a deep river, it can even use its trunk as a snorkel!

Trunk call
The hairy tip of the trunk is very sensitive to touch. The two holes are nostrils that lead to the long nose tube. Through this the elephant breathes and trumpets its calls. Muscles bend the trunk in any direction.

Sniffing and smelling
Elephants lift their trunks high to sniff the air for predators, fire, and other dangers, and to catch the scent of their herd and other creatures. They also smell food before eating it.

The daily grind

Long, thin, sharp, fang-shaped teeth are good for catching, killing, and ripping up meaty prey – but they are no good for chewing or grinding up leaves, grass, fruits, and other plant parts. Herbivores (plant-eaters) need wide, broad, fairly flat teeth to mash and pulp their food thoroughly. This is because plants are made from tough fibers that need to be broken down, so that a herbivore's intestines can extract the nutrients.

Feeding

The elephant has a short neck, so its head cannot reach down to the ground or up to the trees. But the trunk can. It curls around juicy grasses and leaves, rips them off, and stuffs them into its mouth.

Communicating

Elephants touch and stroke their fellow herd members, to greet them and keep up their friendships. They also trumpet and make noises with the help of their trunk. These forms of communication are very important to the herd.

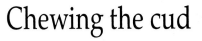

Chewing the cud

Some mammals are able to swallow their food quickly, and then bring it up again to chew over slowly. They are called *ruminants*. They include cows, antelope, and llamas.

When the food is first swallowed it goes into the rumen, the first part of the four-chambered stomach (below). The animal can then bring up this half-digested food, called *cud*, to chew over more leisurely. The cud is then swallowed into the reticulum, and then into the intestines.

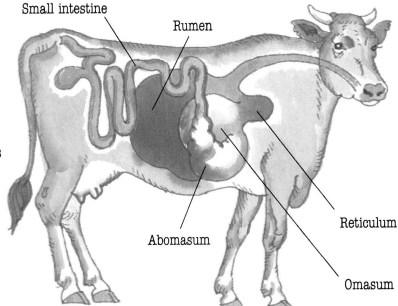

Small intestine

Rumen

Abomasum

Reticulum

Omasum

Drinking and bathing

The trunk's long nasal tubes allow the elephant to suck up enormous amounts of water. This can then be flung over its back when it wishes to cool off at a watering hole. Alternatively, the elephant may be thirsty, and then it will empty its trunk into its mouth to take a drink.

Fantastic VOYAGES

With the development of the rocket, people's dreams of space travel finally came true. Rockets burn fuel to produce gases that escape through a nozzle, causing the rocket to thrust forward. Their engines are the only kind that can work in space, and they must carry all their fuel and oxygen to burn it. The secret of reaching space is the multi-stage rocket, in which various parts burn out and fall off, one after another. Since the first rockets went into space, spacecraft have explored the solar system to its very limits, and people have walked on the Moon.

A VISION OF THE FUTURE
The French author Jules Verne was well known for his futuristic visions. In 1865 he wrote a book about a journey to the Moon. His space travelers were fired from a gun – which in real life would have killed them – and had to fly around the Moon, and then come back, because they had no way of landing.

THE ROCKET PIONEERS
The principles of rocketry were developed by Konstantin Tsiolkovsky, a Russian teacher, at the beginning of the twentieth century. Robert Goddard, an American physicist whose early rocket is shown bottom left, and Werner von Braun (above) from Germany went on to build and launch successful rockets. Von Braun's V-2 rocket (top left) was used by the Nazis as a devastating weapon during the last year of World War II (1939–1945).

NASA

The National Aeronautics and Space Administration (NASA) put the first person on the Moon in July 1969. But unstaffed NASA missions to the planets have taught us more. For example, the landings on Mars by Viking spacecraft found no signs of life there, despite many people's claims that it could exist.

Can we make time stand still?
If we can ever design a spacecraft that is able to travel at the speed of light, time on board will stand still, according to Albert Einstein's theories. An astronaut could travel for 1,000 years and come back no older than the day he or she set off. But it is unlikely that technology will ever develop enough to build such a fast craft.

ALONE IN SPACE

The first person in space, Major Yuri Gagarin, was launched by the former Soviet Union in Vostok 1 on April 12, 1961. He completed a single orbit of the Earth, and landed safely.

PROBING DEEP SPACE

The first space probes to leave the solar system were Pioneer 10 and 11, then two Voyager spacecraft. The Voyager craft took closeup pictures of Jupiter and Saturn in 1979, then Voyager 2 went on to visit Uranus and Neptune. The latest mission, Galileo, was launched in 1989 but will reach the outer planets slowly, by a complicated route.

LITTER-BUGS

The landscapes of the solar system are dotted with equipment left behind by various expeditions.

EARTH'S CALLING CARD

Pioneer 10, which was launched in 1972, carries a plaque of information, or "calling card," in case it should ever meet other intelligent life. It has a diagram showing what human beings look like, and a sky map to identify where our solar system is.

TRUMPET AND BRASS

Your trumpet is a member of a large family of trumpets, all named after the notes they correspond to on the piano. Your instrument is probably a B^b trumpet; there is also a C trumpet, a D trumpet, and so on. The higher the trumpet, the shorter the instrument will be.

Try the following test with a piano. Play the first open note of a scale, your middle C, on your trumpet. Now play a B^b on the piano, or ask someone to play it for you. The notes should sound the same on both instruments. Your C equals the piano's B^b, so your trumpet is called a B^b trumpet. An E^b trumpet playing the same open note would sound the same as E^b on a piano.

PICCOLO TRUMPET

E^b TRUMPET

C TRUMPET

ROTARY VALVE TRUMPET

The trumpets that are mostly used in the United States and Britain are known as piston trumpets. This name refers to the type of valve that is used in the instrument to produce a wider range of notes. In countries such as Germany and Austria, rotary valve trumpets are played instead. Rotary valves look similar to the valves used on French horns. Although they look different from piston trumpets, rotary valve trumpets are played in almost the same way.

204

BRASS FAMILY

The **euphonium** (right) has a warm, deep, lyrical sound. The **trombone** (below) is the only modern brass instrument that uses a slide to produce a full range of notes.

The **sousaphone** was invented by John Philip Sousa for marching bands. The **tuba** (below) is another large member of the brass family. It was invented 150 years ago, for Russian military bands.

The **French horn** is a descendant of a hunting horn. It would measure over 16 feet (5 m) long if stretched out. The musician places one hand in the bell to improve the sound.

The **tenor horn** is used mainly in the brass band, where its warm, soft sound adds color. You can expect to see three or four tenor horns in many brass bands.

LOUIS ARMSTRONG

Louis Armstrong was one of the strongest influences in the history of jazz. He learned to play while at reform school (he had been arrested for firing blanks from a pistol in the street). He was soon in demand as a cornetist, and eventually formed his own bands. His influence on many musicians is widely acknowledged.

205

WHAT IS LIGHT?

Light is a mixture of electrical and magnetic energy that travels faster than anything else in the universe. It takes less than one tenth of a second for light to travel from New York to London. Light is made up of tiny particles of energy called photons. The light moves along in very small waves that travel forward in straight lines, called rays. Light can travel through air and transparent substances, but can also travel through empty space. This is how sunlight reaches the earth. Light is similar to other forms of electromagnetic energy which have different wavelengths.

Radio waves
These have the longest wavelength. They are used for satellite communication and to carry TV and radio signals.

Visible light
Appears white or colorless, but is made up of colors, each with a different wavelength.

Radio	Micro	Infrared	Visible

Electromagnetic spectrum
This shows different kinds of electromagnetic energy arranged in order of their wavelengths. Wavelength is the distance between two consecutive waves.

Infrared rays
Invisible rays, but we can feel the heat from them. They can be used to detect cancer and arthritis, or to take photographs in the dark.

Microwaves
Very short radio waves used in microwave ovens. They are also used in radar.

Different ways of seeing
Most animals see visible light like we do. However, others have evolved sight which detects different wavelengths along the spectrum. Some insects see in ultraviolet light, which is invisible to most mammals and birds (except pigeons). Insect-pollinated flowers have lines which guide insects to their nectar. These lines only appear in ultraviolet light. The insects follow the guide lines to the nectar, scattering pollen on the way. This process helps the flowers to reproduce.

Bees cannot see the color red. They are strongly attracted by yellow and blue flowers which usually have strong ultraviolet markings. These markings attract bees to the flowers, and even pinpoint the location of the nectaries.

Ultraviolet rays

These cause us to tan and help the skin to produce vitamin D. Large amounts are dangerous and may cause skin cancer, although most ultraviolet light from the sun is absorbed by the ozone layer.

Gamma rays

These have the shortest wavelength. They are given off by naturally radioactive materials, such as uranium, and are part of the fallout after a nuclear explosion. They can travel through lead and cement, and damage living tissue.

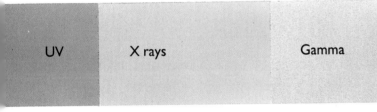

UV	X rays	Gamma

X Rays

Called "X" by their discoverer because he was unsure of their nature. They pass through flesh, but are absorbed by bones and teeth, causing them to show up on x ray film. Small doses are safe, but large amounts are harmful to living tissue.

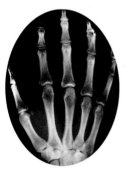

Taking the straight path

Try this experiment to prove that light travels in straight lines. Cut out two pieces of cardboard, about 8 in square. Make a hole in the center of each piece of cardboard, and stick a knitting needle through both holes, ensuring that they are aligned. Fix the cardboards onto a flat surface with modeling clay. Turn off the light and shine a flashlight through the holes. What happens? Try putting certain materials like cellophane, paper, or a book, between the two cards when the flashlight is on. Describe what happens to the ray of light.

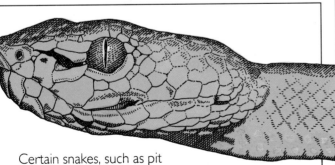

Certain snakes, such as pit vipers and pythons, detect prey by sensing the infrared light or "heat" they give out. They have special heat sensors which form an image from the infrared emissions. This helps them to hunt at night.

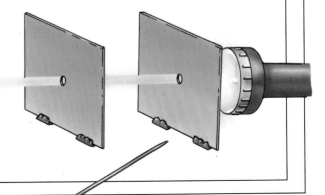

WATER POLLUTION

Humans use enormous quantities of water. Not only do we drink it, we use it to wash and bathe. We irrigate farm crops and gardens. We use it to flush away waste in the sewage system. Flowing water provided the first source of energy to power machines. Today's factories still use water to make things, or sometimes just to cool machinery. Hydroelectric power is an important source of energy in some countries. Our need for water makes it hard to find enough. We dam valleys to trap water in reservoirs – but this may disturb a river's flow. We sink boreholes – but these may dry out the land and stop springs flowing. Many human activities leave water dirty, and sometimes full of unwanted and dangerous chemicals. How to stop this pollution is one of the biggest problems we now face.

POLLUTING WATER

Detergents and poisonous chemicals are an obvious danger to water. But even chemicals that make things thrive, such as fertilizers, can create problems. If they run off the land into water they can make tiny water plants grow too well. These may use up all the oxygen in the water.

Sewage plant discharges into river.

Boreholes reduce the underground water level.

Factories discharge waste into rivers.

Oil tankers and refineries leak oil into the sea.

SEWAGE TREATMENT

Water and solids flow into the sewage treatment plant (1). This is filtered to remove solids and germs (2). Solid sludge may be stored to rot (3), or dried and used as fertilizer or burned (4). The remaining liquid is cleaned and returned to a nearby river (5).

1

2

3

4

5

Rain can be acid.

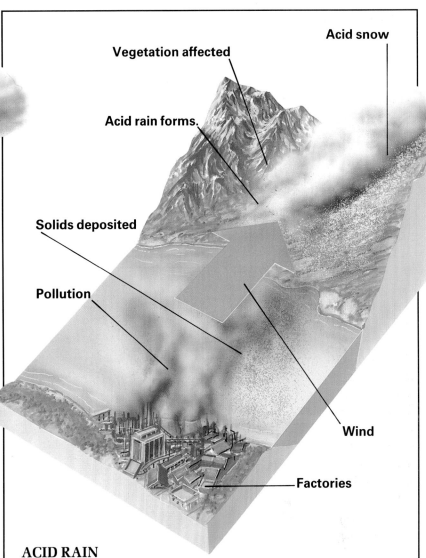

Vegetation affected

Acid snow

Acid rain forms.

Solids deposited

Pollution

Wind

Factories

Dams disrupt a river's flow.

Fertilizers, pesticides and animal wastes spread on land may be washed into water.

ACID RAIN

Power plants produce sulfur dioxide and nitrogen oxides when they burn coal. If these are not filtered out, they are pumped into the air from huge chimneys. Carried by wind, polluted clouds can make rain very acidic hundreds of miles away. This rain can kill trees, damage other plants, and make water too acidic for fish. Acid snow can also damage countryside.

DANGER IN THE FOOD CHAIN

Some substances that are used to control pests break down soon after they are used. But some do not, and these may be passed up the food chain to animals which are not the original target of the poison. The poison can build up to harmful levels in animals at the top of the chain.

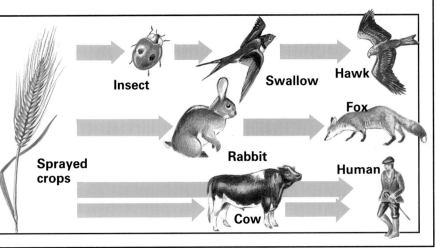

Insect

Swallow

Hawk

Fox

Rabbit

Human

Sprayed crops

Cow

WHO WERE THE VIKINGS?

The Viking Age lasted from the end of the eighth century A.D. until the end of the eleventh century A.D. The Vikings, or Norsemen, came from Scandinavia, from the present-day countries of Denmark, Sweden, and Norway. The Vikings are most famous as fierce warriors who looted and conquered many parts of Europe in a series of terrifying raids. However, they were also successful and adventurous traders and explorers, talented poets, and skilled shipbuilders and craftsmen.

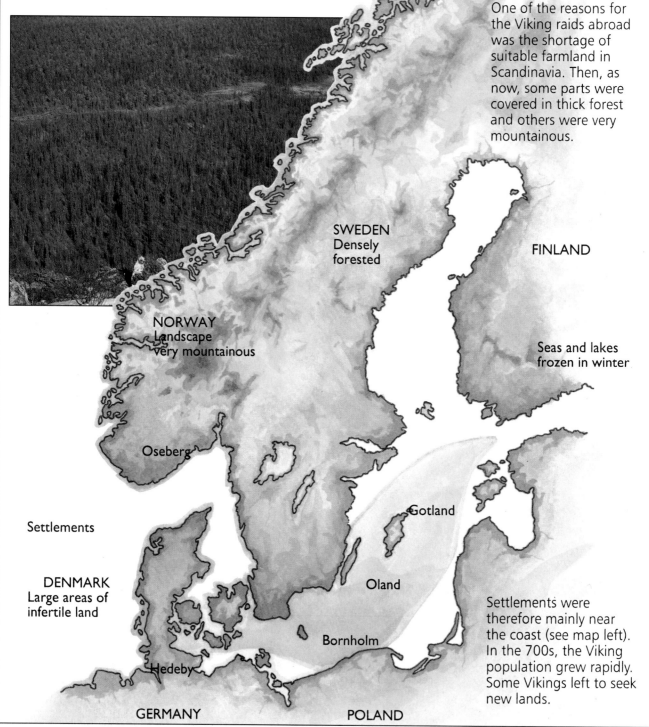

One of the reasons for the Viking raids abroad was the shortage of suitable farmland in Scandinavia. Then, as now, some parts were covered in thick forest and others were very mountainous.

SWEDEN
Densely forested

FINLAND

NORWAY
Landscape very mountainous

Seas and lakes frozen in winter

Oseberg

Settlements

Gotland

DENMARK
Large areas of infertile land

Oland

Bornholm

Settlements were therefore mainly near the coast (see map left). In the 700s, the Viking population grew rapidly. Some Vikings left to seek new lands.

Hedeby

GERMANY   POLAND

Classes of society

Viking society was divided into different classes, based on wealth and land ownership. A king, or chief, ruled over each community. Below him came the rich noblemen, or jarls. The English word "earl" comes from the word "jarl." The kings and jarls were the most powerful landowners. Below them came the freemen, or karls. They included farmers, merchants, and craftsmen. At the bottom of the ladder were the slaves, who were known as thralls.

JARLS
Noblemen

KARLS
Freemen

THRALLS
Slaves

The Viking name

The Scandinavians did not call themselves Vikings. This was a name used by early writers. The word "Viking" may come from the old Icelandic word "vik.," meaning bay or creek. The phrase "a-Viking" also means to go exploring.

The first raid

"*...never before has such terror appeared in Britain as we have now suffered from this pagan race...*"

This account by the Northumbrian priest Alcuin marks the beginning of the Viking reign of terror after their attack on the Holy Island of Lindisfarne in June, A.D. 793. The Vikings looted the monastery there, killed some of the monks, and carried others off to be slaves. The attack on Lindisfarne was terrifying because it was a holy place, known and respected throughout Europe. Also, like other monasteries around the coast of Britain, Lindisfarne had believed itself to be immune to attacks from the sea.

The original monastery at Lindisfarne was completely destroyed by the Vikings. It was later rebuilt (below).

Vikings at work

The majority of Vikings spent quite short periods away from home on raids. They worked as farmers, growing oats, barley, rye, and vegetables, and tending cattle, pigs, sheep, and goats. Fruits, such as apples, and hazelnuts and walnuts were also grown and stored for use during the winter. Reindeer, rabbit, hare, and wild bears were hunted by the Vikings, and cod, salmon, and trout were plentiful in the Scandinavian fjords and rivers. Other Vikings were merchants, traveling far and wide to trade their goods. Some were specialized craftsmen – silversmiths, blacksmiths, and woodcarvers. Most famous of all were the skills of the Viking shipbuilders and sailors.

The Gila Monster of the North American deserts is a lizard with a venomous bite. Its venom is powerful enough to subdue its bird and mammal prey.

The Australian Stump-tailed Skink is able to store food in its tail, as fat, and can go for months without food.

Gila Monster

Stump-tailed Skink

Desert Lizards

The Lizard group is by far the largest group of reptiles living today. Lizards can be found in many different environments. Many species of lizards live in the deserts. Lizards are well adapted to living in dry habitats. Their bodies are geared to retain water; they have very dry and scaly skin which loses water at a very slow rate.

Lizards also burn fat very slowly, therefore they are able to go for long periods of time without food. This is useful in dry desert areas where food is quite scarce.

A Frilled Lizard runs on its back legs to keep its body away from the hot sand. ▷

SUBMARINES

Most of the world's submarines are warships. They are designed to carry and fire torpedoes and missiles, or to lay mines, to destroy enemy vessels. Only the smallest submarines, called submersibles, are used for non-military, or civilian, work. Submersibles are built for repairing oil rigs, laying pipes on the seabed, and to study the underwater world.

There are two main types of submarine. The most common is the diesel-electric. This is powered by a diesel engine when on the surface of the water and by an electric motor when submerged. The second type is the nuclear submarine. This is powered at all times by a nuclear reactor. Diesel-electric submarines are the easiest and cheapest to build.

Military submarines are given code letters that describe their engines or the weapons they carry. For example, diesel-electric attack subs are coded SS, and nuclear powered ones SSN. Attack subs are designed to find and destroy enemy warships. Submarines that carry missiles which can be guided to a ship or target on land are coded SSG or, if nuclear powered, SSGN.

The nuclear powered hunter-killer submarine is fast and well-armed.

A submersible – for underwater research.

A nuclear missile-carrying submarine.

Submarines range in size from submersibles less than 6m (20ft) long to the 170m (558ft) Soviet Typhoon class submarine. This is nuclear powered and carries "ballistic" missiles (SSBN class).

A diesel-electric submarine.

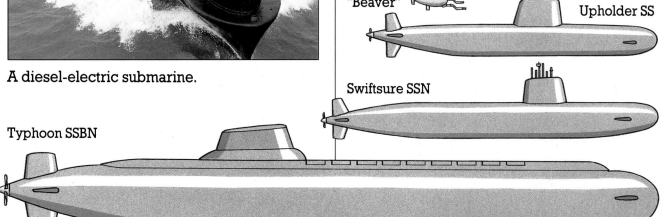

"Beaver"

Upholder SS

Swiftsure SSN

Typhoon SSBN

WORKING WITH PHOTOS

"From this day on, painting is dead." Many people believed this when photography was first invented. Artists today haven't actually given up painting, but a great many have used photographs in picture making.

Picture puzzles

Cutting up and reassembling a photograph is a little like making your own jigsaw puzzle. This process will produce a new image which can be intriguing, bizarre or funny.

You will need a collection of images from postcards or magazines. These pictures can be cut up, using scissors or a craft knife. Cutting paper with a craft knife held against a metal ruler will produce a clean edge. There are many ways in which the pieces that you cut can be reassembled. A few are shown here, and others are suggested for you to try.

Squares, strips and fans

Photographs can be cut into squares, as described below, or they can be cut into straight strips or curves. Curved strips can be spread out evenly, or shaped into a fan. Fanning will elongate your image. On the right, fanning has emphasized the curve of the goose's neck. This technique is very effective with photographs of figures in action.

Two into one *will* go

Another project with strips is shown at the bottom of the opposite page. This project works best with two images that complement each other, as the shape of the bird's head and the hill do there. Cut both pictures into strips, and intersperse the two images. When the pictures are combined, the shapes will interact with one another.

◁ *"The image on the left is composed of squares. To cut squares more accurately, mark out the lines on the back of your image first.*

The illustration shows only one of the many ways in which the squares can be reassembled. Try rotating each square by 90°, and see what happens. Try again, rotating all the squares by 180° and sticking them upside down."

△ *"Here the photograph from the opposite page has been treated very differently. Try replacing strips like these in reverse order, or removing every other one and putting the rest together again."*

▽ *"The round hill echoes the shape of the bird's head below. Look for similar shapes for your own collage."*

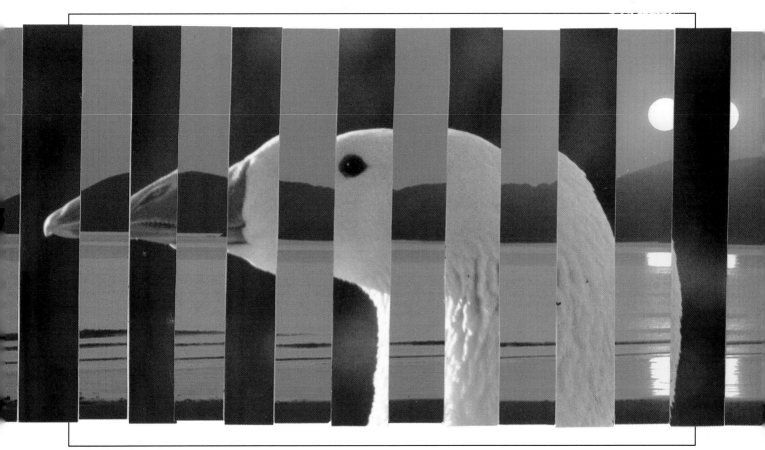

SOUND WAVES

Sound waves are similar to light waves in some ways. Like a beam of light can be reflected from a mirror, so a sound can be reflected from a surface like a wall. If you shout loudly in your school hall, the sound waves travel to the wall and are bounced back, reaching your ears a split second later – this is an echo. Bats make use of echoes when finding their way, or hunting. They give out a very high pitched sound that bounces back from objects or insects, telling them how far away things are. We can also use this method to find objects that we cannot see. Sonar uses sound to locate objects at the bottom of the sea, such as shipwrecks and shoals of fish.

FIRING WAVES

1. This cannon will send a narrow "beam" of sound waves. Begin by making a pair of wheels for your cannon using circles of cardboard, paper plates, thread spools, and a wooden stick.

3

3. The front of the cannon is a disk of stiff cardboard with a 1 in hole in the center. You could decorate this with a disk of colored paper.

1

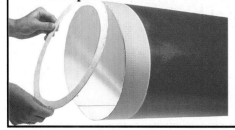

2. Make a large tube of stiff cardboard for the cannon itself, 18-20 inches in diameter, and four feet long. Make the back of the cannon by covering a circle of cardboard with plastic wrap. Attach **2** with tape.

5. Fix the tube to the wheels with tape, and weight the back end of the cannon so that it does not tip forward. Aim the cannon at a wall and tap the plastic wrap quite firmly – from a distance you should get an echo. Make a curtain from 0.5 in strips of foil. Fire your cannon at the curtain. You should see the sound waves making the foil vibrate.

5

4

4. Tape the ends of the cannon firmly with double sided tape – this will enable you to fix the ends onto the tube and not into it.

WHY IT WORKS

When you strike the piece of plastic wrap (diaphragm) on the cannon, the vibrations lead to sound waves being formed. The waves travel outward from the diaphragm, making the air particles around move back and forth in the same direction. When the waves leaving the front of the cannon meet a solid object, some of them are reflected while some continue traveling through the object, making it move slightly like the air particles. A bat uses sound to find objects in the dark. It produces sounds and then listens for the echoes to be reflected. This is called echolocation.

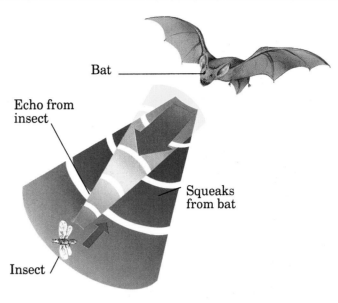

Bat

Echo from insect

Squeaks from bat

Insect

BRIGHT IDEAS

☀ Which surfaces are best for echoing? Can you make an echo in a bathroom, a kitchen, a cafeteria, a hall, a subway? Try other places, too. Do you think hard surfaces are better than soft surfaces for giving echoes? Which sounds echo the best?

☀ Try shouting, knocking two stones together, banging two blocks of wood together, whistling, and talking. Do short, sharp sounds echo better than long soft ones?

☀ The cannon channels the sound waves in one direction. Make a megaphone to channel your voice. Make a narrow cone, and then a wide cone. Shout to a friend through each cone. Shout again, aiming the megaphone 30 feet to their side. What happens? Which cone makes your voice sound louder, and which can you hear best from the side? Can you figure out why?

SAVING ENERGY

In the 1970s, the oil-producing nations twice increased the price of oil. Though it has since declined, the shock made many nations think carefully about saving energy. More efficiency, less waste, and greater efforts to recycle materials are the results. Homes, offices, and factories now use less energy, while the fuel consumption of cars has improved. More could be done, but the high cost of saving energy is often seen as a disadvantage.

Industry has always recycled valuable materials; a quarter of every new car is made of metal from old cars. Paper can also be used again, once it has been bleached to remove ink. Recycled paper is never as clean and crisp as new paper, so it can't be used for high-value products. Often, it may simply be cheaper to plant more trees and use them as raw material.

Insulation
A simple experiment shows the value of insulation in saving energy. Use two identical mugs and wrap an old scarf around one. Fill both with hot water at the same temperature. Take the temperature of each at regular intervals and plot them on graph paper. Also try a thermos flask. Why is that so much better?

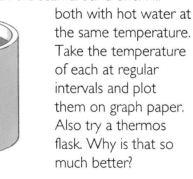

BMW has produced a totally recyclable car, in which every item can be dismantled and re-used.

Pedal power
Bicycles are the most energy-efficient form of transportation in towns. They don't burn fuel and are quicker in heavy traffic. The police in Seattle use bicycles instead of cars. The biggest drawback is the danger from other vehicles.

Scientific research has shown that the lead in car exhaust fumes is dangerous to the body, even in small quantities. Lead-free gasoline was introduced to reduce pollution but it doesn't save energy because it burns less smoothly than leaded gas.

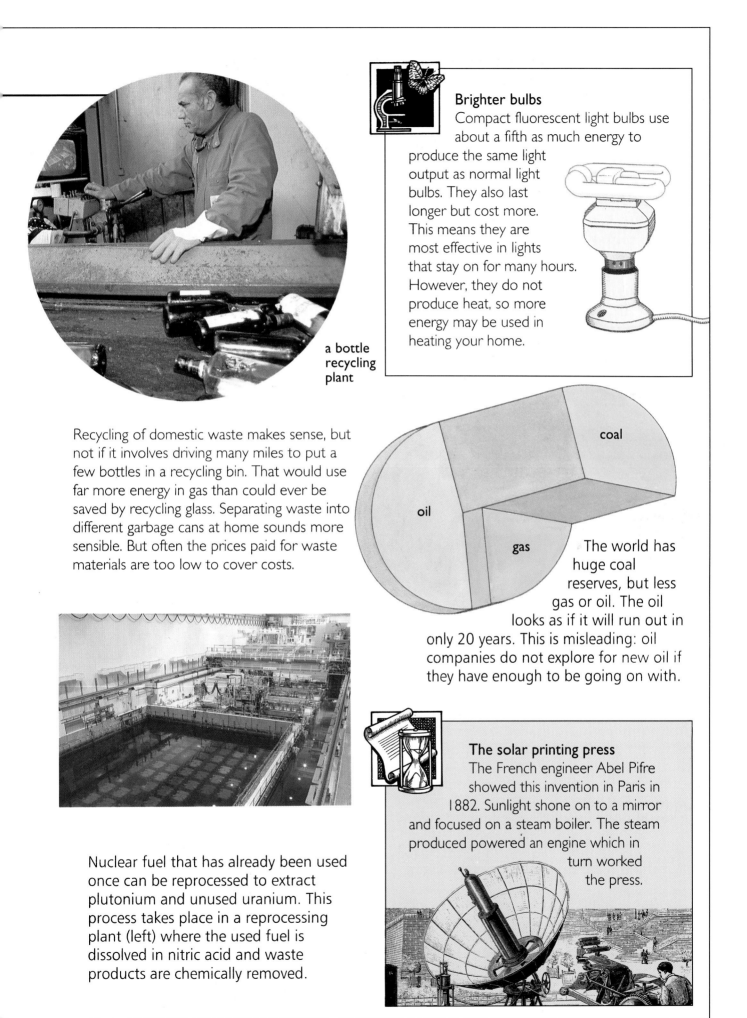

a bottle recycling plant

Brighter bulbs
Compact fluorescent light bulbs use about a fifth as much energy to produce the same light output as normal light bulbs. They also last longer but cost more. This means they are most effective in lights that stay on for many hours. However, they do not produce heat, so more energy may be used in heating your home.

Recycling of domestic waste makes sense, but not if it involves driving many miles to put a few bottles in a recycling bin. That would use far more energy in gas than could ever be saved by recycling glass. Separating waste into different garbage cans at home sounds more sensible. But often the prices paid for waste materials are too low to cover costs.

coal

oil

gas

The world has huge coal reserves, but less gas or oil. The oil looks as if it will run out in only 20 years. This is misleading: oil companies do not explore for new oil if they have enough to be going on with.

Nuclear fuel that has already been used once can be reprocessed to extract plutonium and unused uranium. This process takes place in a reprocessing plant (left) where the used fuel is dissolved in nitric acid and waste products are chemically removed.

The solar printing press
The French engineer Abel Pifre showed this invention in Paris in 1882. Sunlight shone on to a mirror and focused on a steam boiler. The steam produced powered an engine which in turn worked the press.

THE PIRATE SCHOONER

Pirates operated in every kind of ship, from galleys to junks. Usually they had no choice – they sailed in whatever vessel they captured. The type of schooner shown here was built from the mid-18th century onward. It was an ideal craft: fast, maneuverable, and with a shallow draft that allowed her to hide in rivers and bays. The sail plan, with square sails only at the tops of the masts, allowed the boat to sail close to the wind. "Schooner" comes from the American verb scoon, meaning to skim along

Captain's Cabin
Placed at the stern, this was out of the worst of the weather and could be easily defended in case of mutiny. It was also the store-room for charts and money.

powder *wadding* *shot*

UNDER FIRE

Cannons (*above*) were loaded through the muzzle with powder, wadding, and shot. A gun's recoil, capable of breaking a man's leg, was absorbed by ropes. A single cannon ball weighed 20 lb (9 kg). To get greater range and hit a vessel on the waterline, gunners skimmed shots off the sea (*below left*). Double balls and shrapnel (*below right and middle*) were used against the rigging to do the most damage.

Sail Locker —
A storm could carry away the entire rigging, so all ships carried spare sails. They had to be kept dry to prevent rotting.

Stores and Armory
These were kept at the bottom of the boat due to their weight. To prevent damage they were tied down in rough weather.

A schooner with all sails set

CHART POWER An accurate chart of a stretch of newly discovered coast could prove more valuable than gold! In 1682, Bartholemew Sharpe and two friends were tried for piracy before the High Court of the Admiralty. Despite having killed 200 people, sinking 25 ships, and doing damage valued at 4 million pieces of eight, all three were found not guilty. The reason – Sharpe had captured a book of charts of the South American coastline. On his return to England he had presented them to King Charles II. The king himself made sure Sharpe came to no harm.

Galley
The galley was the ship's kitchen. Due to the risk of fire, the stove was built of brick and iron, with a bucket of sand always at the ready to put out the fire in rough weather.

Rigging
A ship carried many hundreds of feet of hemp rope, as well as pulleys (blocks), sails, and spars (the beams from which sails were hung). The mainstays (shrouds) of the masts were crossed with ratlines.

Show a Leg!
The hammock was invented by native Caribs and adopted by sailors as a bed on board ship. The phrase "show a leg," meaning "get on with it," was originally a command for sailors to get up out of their hammocks (below).

Windlass
The mainsails and their spars were tremendously heavy, especially when wet. The windlass enabled a few men to raise them quickly. It was also used for lifting the anchor.

Ballast
kept the ship upright.

Anchor
An absolutely essential piece of equipment used when there was no safe harbor or jetty nearby.

The Toilet!
When pirates wanted to relieve themselves, they went to a rope cage suspended over the sea in the bows.

WHAT ARE INSECTS?

Insects are the most successful of all animal groups, making up 85 percent of the whole animal kingdom. There are as many as 10,000 insects living on every square yard of the Earth's surface. There are many different kinds of insects, but all share a common body design, adapted to cope with every possible environment, and to eat every possible kind of food. All adult insects have a segmented body which is divided into three parts: head, thorax, and abdomen.

An insect's skin is made of a tough substance called chitin. This forms a hard shell, or exoskeleton, which protects the insect's organs. The leg and wing muscles are securely anchored to the exoskeleton. It is waterproof, and prevents the insect from drying out. But it does not allow air through. Holes in the skin, called spiracles, lead to breathing tubes. The exoskeleton does not grow. As an insect gets bigger, it must shed its old skin, and grow a new one. The outer skin, or cuticle, is patterned and colored for camouflage or warning.

Antennae

Compound eye

Mouthparts

Thorax

Six jointed legs

Emperor dragonfly

Common cockroach

Bush cricket

Firebug

All insects have three pairs of jointed legs, and most have four wings. Insects from some easily recognizable insect groups are shown above.

Preserved in stone
Insects first appeared on Earth about 370 million years ago. Early species had no wings; they fed on the sap and spores of the newly-evolved land plants. Insects were the first creatures to conquer the air, 150 million years before birds first flew. This is a fossil of an early dragonfly that lived 300 million years ago, in the steamy Carboniferous forests with the ancestors of the dinosaurs.

Wings

Abdomen

Spiracles carry air inside the body.

Biblical insects

The Bible contains many stories about Samson, a hero possessed of great strength. One story tells how he killed a young lion which threatened him. Later he noticed bees flying from the lion's body and found honey inside it. He made his discovery into a riddle: "Out of the eater came forth meat, and out of the strong came forth sweetness." No one could guess the answer. In fact, the insects were probably not bees at all, but carrion flies that live on rotting flesh. The explanation of the honey is still a mystery!

Samson discovers the bees.

The head contains a simple brain which receives messages from the sense organs and controls the muscles. The thorax is made of three segments fused together. It carries the legs and wings. The abdomen contains the organs for digestion and reproduction.

Seven-spotted ladybird (beetle)

Bluebottle (fly)

Privet hawkmoth

Wood ant

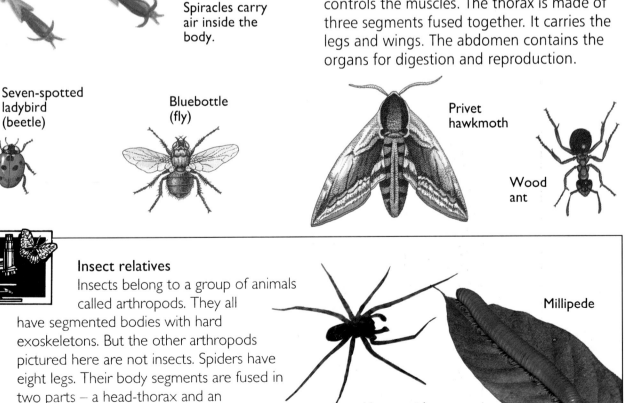

Insect relatives

Insects belong to a group of animals called arthropods. They all have segmented bodies with hard exoskeletons. But the other arthropods pictured here are not insects. Spiders have eight legs. Their body segments are fused in two parts – a head-thorax and an abdomen. Millipedes and centipedes have many body segments, with legs on each.

House spider

Millipede

THE FIRST MOTORISTS

After the experiments of the 1880s, the first car-making factories were set up in Germany and France during the 1890s. Engineers improved Daimler's engines, making them more powerful and reliable. Frenchman Emile Levassor was probably first to think of the car as a machine in its own right, and not just a cart without a horse. In 1891 he moved the engine from the back to the front, away from the mud and stones thrown up by the wheels. He also replaced the belt drive between engine and road wheels, with a clutch and a gearbox. The car as we know it today was quickly taking shape.

Napier 1913

Fun for the family
A trip in the car was an enjoyable outing, provided the rain stayed away. Early cars had no heaters and little protection from mud, dust, or the weather.

Roads to run on
Cars were faster than horse-drawn carts, so they needed better roads. Instead of packed-down layers of earth and stone (top right), engineers devised smooth surfaces of tarmac or asphalt.

Drainage trench

Smooth asphalt surface

Graded gravel layers

Base of crushed stone

A sign of status
Big houses, fine furniture and beautiful horses had been signs of wealth for centuries. Around 1900 a new symbol of status appeared: the car. As yet, the car was not a useful means of transportation. Roads were muddy, rutted cart tracks, and refueling places were scarce.

Flying the red flag

Under a law passed in Britain in 1865, steam traction engines were allowed to lumber along roads, provided they did not exceed 4 mph (6.5 kph) and a man with a red flag walked about 170 feet in front. The red flag was abandoned in 1878, but a footman still had to walk 60 feet in front. This law applied to any similar vehicle, including the first cars. In 1896 the footman was abandoned too, and the speed limit raised to almost 12 mph (20 kph).

Gas pump 1905

Buying a car

At first, only the rich could afford a car. But many people gathered in car showrooms to gaze at these newfangled pieces of machinery, which seemed to have little practical use.

Stopping for fuel

In the early days many car owners carried cans of spare fuel with them. There were no detailed maps and finding a gasoline station on a long journey was mostly a matter of luck.

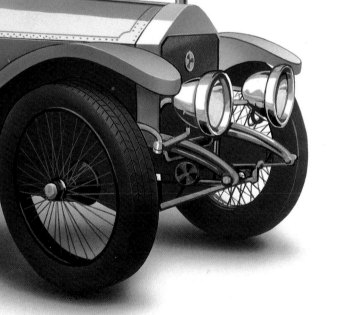

The maker's name

Car manufacturers were soon competing to produce the best, fastest, or cheapest vehicles. Companies such as Buick and Austin designed easily recognized nameplates.

Advertising

The growing car business involved designers, engineers, manufacturers, mechanics, and of course advertisers. As roads became busier, they became valuable places for posters, advertising the latest cars to drivers.

SCALES, SHARPS, AND FLATS

Some scales have natural notes, which are the white keys on a piano. A scale is C major, when it starts on C. Scales that begin on other notes use sharps and flats, which are the black keys on the piano.

The sign for a sharp is shown on the left. A sharp raises the pitch of a note by a half step. A flat sign is shown below left. It lowers the pitch of a note by a half step. Sometimes sharps or flats appear in the "key signature" near the treble clef. They tell us the scale or key that the music is based on.

If no sharp or flat appears in the key signature, the key is C major. In the second line below, the key is G major, with F$^\#$ in the key signature.

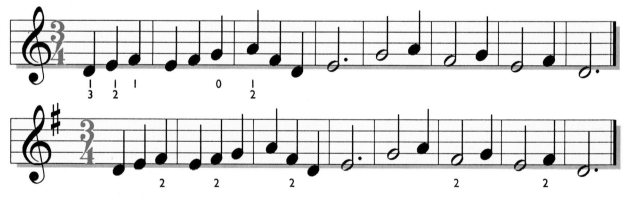

For every major key there is also a minor one. The first exercise below is in F major; the second is in D minor. Both have B^b in the key signature.

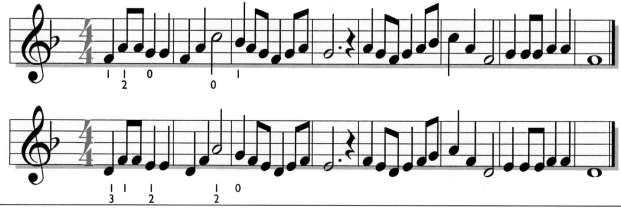

KEY SIGNATURES

Sharps or flats in the key signature do not appear in the music itself. The scales of D major and B minor have F$^\#$ and C$^\#$ in the key signature.

The scales of B^b major and G minor both have B^b and E^b in their key signature. Remember to play these notes flat in the music itself.

Practice the exercises below, looking out for the key-signature. See if you can tell if they are written in a major or a minor key.

MAJOR AND MINOR

In the Middle Ages early forms of scales, or "modes," were used by choirs of monks in Christian churches. The monks would sing just one melody line, with no accompaniment. By the 13th century the music was sung in two or more parts; what we call "harmony" was born. Many modes gradually disappeared, leaving us with mainly the major and minor scales that we recognize today.

UFOs and ALIENS

40 million UFO sightings have been recorded since 1947, when the first "flying saucers" were reported. The most common sightings are of glowing balls of light, moving quickly. There have been reports of crash landings by mysterious objects and of alien abductions. In 1948, the U.S. Air Force set up an investigation into UFOs. By 1969, when the project ended, about 12,000 incidents had been recorded. A quarter were caused by natural phenomena or known objects, but the rest remained unidentified. It has yet to be proved that there are intelligent life forms elsewhere in space – or that they are visiting Earth.

KIDNAPPED!
People who claim to have been abducted by aliens often describe strange noises, flashing lights, and blackouts. Some say they were examined, losing hair and fingernails, and developing strange marks on their skin.

TIME TRAVELERS
No other planet in our solar system can support life, so UFOs must come from planets orbiting another star like our Sun. It would take thousands of years to reach us from the nearest star. Some people think that aliens can "beam" their ships across space and time.

MYSTERY AT ROSWELL
In 1995, British ufologists unveiled an old film showing U.S. scientists examining the corpse of an alien (below). It has been linked to a reported UFO crash near Roswell, NM, in 1947. The U.S. government claimed the wreckage was a weather balloon, but others said they were hiding a "spy" balloon...or a UFO. The film is now being tested – perhaps the truth will be known at last.

TOP SECRET

Where do UFOs come from?
Most ufologists believe that aliens visit Earth from distant galaxies which human science and technology are not yet advanced enough to find. However, some people have a theory that UFOs come from a hollow area in the center of the Earth and fly into space through a hole at the North Pole!

CLOSE ENCOUNTERS

UFO sightings are called Close Encounters. A Close Encounter of the First Kind is seeing a UFO. The Second Kind includes evidence such as landing marks. The Third Kind is when a witness sees or meets alien beings. In 1947, a pilot saw some strange disks in the sky. He told reporters that they looked like "saucers" and the name "flying saucers" caught on.

FACING THE ALIENS

UFOs appear in many shapes and sizes! On April 24, 1964, a police officer claimed that he saw an egg-shaped craft land and two small, human-like creatures climb out. The aliens saw him, rushed back to the ship, and took off. Scorch marks were later found where the ship had been standing.

Tracking alien beings

Everyone has seen imaginary UFOs in films such as *Close Encounters of the Third Kind* (below), but ufologists investigate UFO sightings by real-life witnesses. They use hi-tech equipment to measure radio waves and magnetic effects which might be caused by UFOs, and track mysterious craft on radar screens. Amateur ufologists watch the skies using telescopes and cameras. If they spot a UFO, they record its position, movement, color, and shape, and send this data to UFO organizations. Permanent observers now keep watch for UFOs around the world.

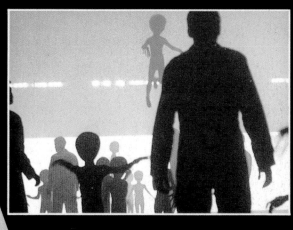

ENCOUNTER OVER IRAN

On September 9, 1976, a UFO was seen over Iran. Two planes went to investigate, but their controls jammed. The UFO, which was about 160 feet long, seemed to fire at them before speeding away.

WHAT IS A HURRICANE?

A hurricane is a large, spinning wind system that develops over warm seas near the equator. These areas are known as the tropics. Technically, hurricanes are called tropical revolving storms, but they also have local names. They are called hurricanes when they occur over the Atlantic Ocean, typhoons in the Far East, and cyclones in the Indian Ocean. By definition, all are characterized by rotating winds that exceed speeds of 75 mph on the Beaufort wind scale.

The tropics are the hottest parts of the world, and experience the most extreme weather conditions. Air heated by the sun rises swiftly, which creates areas of very low pressure. As the warm air rises, it becomes loaded with moisture that condenses into massive thunderclouds. Cool air rushes in to fill the void that is left, but because of the constant turning of the earth on its axis, the air is bent inward and then spirals upward with great force. The swirling winds rotate faster and faster, forming a huge circle that can be up to 1,200 miles across.

▲ The typhoon that hit Manila in the Philippines in 1988 caused severe flooding. People were forced to cling to items like tires to survive.

► The shattered remains of Darwin in Australia after Cyclone Tracy hit the area on Christmas Day in 1974. Tracy's winds reached 150 mph and battered the city for over four hours. 48,000 inhabitants were evacuated and 8,000 homes destroyed.

Extreme conditions

A spectacular part of tropical storms is the long, low thunderclouds that can be seen rolling across this landscape. The tinges of gray-black at the edges of the clouds are the result of undercurrents of cold air that force the moisture in the warmer air above to condense very quickly. It is these clouds that bring the torrential downpours of rain that accompany most thunderstorms. Thunder and lightning can also occur.

EARLY MAMMALS

Mammals evolved from a group of reptiles that existed long before the dinosaurs. Throughout the Triassic, certain carnivorous reptiles, the cynodonts, grew to resemble mammals. These mammallike reptiles were fairly small, about the size of a dog. The first true mammals were small, shrewlike beasts, such as *Megazostrodon* (below). It was probably covered with hair and was "warm-blooded." Today, mammals can be divided into three groups: the monotremes, marsupials, and placental mammals.

Megazostrodon

Barylambda lived in the Early Tertiary.

What is a mammal?

Mammals are "warm-blooded" animals covered in hair. They are able to produce heat inside their bodies. Most give birth to live young, although the monotremes lay eggs. All feed their young milk. Some mammals look after their young in special pouches. Such animals are called marsupials, and include the kangaroos and wallabies. Mammals have adapted to live on land, in the sea (for example, seals, porpoises, and whales), and in the air (for example, bats).

A marsupial protects and feeds its underdeveloped embryo in a pouch.

Causing a sensation

William Buckland (1784-1856) worked as Professor of Geology at Oxford University and as the Dean of Westminster, England. He was an eccentric character who kept many strange pets, including a bear and a jackal. He is most famous for describing the carnivorous dinosaur *Megalosaurus*. He also described the first Jurassic mammal, *Amphitherium*. His announcement that mammals had lived at the time of great reptiles caused a great sensation at the time!

William Buckland

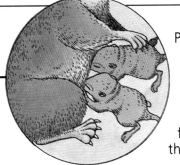

Placental mammals (such as humans and rodents) feed their unborn young through a placenta. They produce milk to feed their young after they are born.

Mammalian evolution

From the Triassic period until the end of the Cretaceous, 155 million years later, mammals were very small, never growing larger than a cat. At the start of the Tertiary period they evolved very quickly and filled many of the niches left by the dinosaurs. Today, mammals are found on every continent and have even traveled to the Moon!

Meniscotherium

Lions

Monotremes are mammals that lay eggs. Their oldest fossils are known from Early Cretaceous rocks. Today, monotremes like the spiny anteater and duck-billed platypus live in Australia.

Mammals vs dinosaurs

Mammals and dinosaurs shared the Earth for 155 million years. For many years, it was thought the mammals were responsible for the extinction of the dinosaurs. Scientists described the dinosaurs of the Cretaceous as slow and stupid, claiming they were not able to compete with the active and intelligent mammals. We now know that mammals did not kill off the dinosaurs, even though they would have eaten dinosaur eggs given the chance!

Echidnas resemble large hedgehogs.

Planetetherium

Earliest mammals

The earliest known true mammals, from the end of the Triassic, 190 million years ago, were found in South Wales, China, North America, and Southern Africa. During the age of dinosaurs, they hunted at night and many of their rodent descendants are still nocturnal.

AZTEC RELIGION

The Aztecs regarded themselves as "the people of the sun."
Huitzilopochtli (hummingbird-on-the-left) was the god of war
and the sun, and was the most important god to the Aztecs. They
did, however, worship many other gods, including Tezcatlipoca
(smoking mirror), and Quetzalcoatl (plumed serpent). The Aztecs
believed it was essential to offer the gods a stream of
human sacrifices, in order to regenerate the cosmos and help the sun
on its daily journey across the sky.

The gods

Aztec deities were depicted in gold,
jade, stone, clay, wood, and other
materials. Tezcatlipoca's emblem was an obsidian
mirror. His mask was made from a human skull
decorated with a mosaic of turquoise, lignite,
and shell. Quetzalcoatl was the plumed serpent
god. His turquoise mosaic mask (top) has a pair
of serpents entwined around the eyes, nose, and
mouth. Mictlantecuhtli was Lord of the Region of
Death. This sandstone carving (right) shows him
with a skull mask.

Mictlantecuhtli

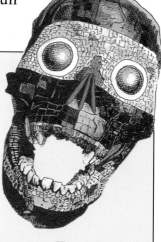

Tezcatlipoca

Human sacrifice

Human sacrifice was practiced by
the Aztecs on a huge scale. Victims,
regarded as the gods' messengers, were
thrown on the sacrificial stone and their
hearts cut out (right). Sacrificial knives (left) were
highly decorated, inlaid with turquoise, jade, and shell.

Temples

The Aztec city was dominated by the
great double temple of Huitzilopochtli
and Tlaloc (right). To mark its
inauguration in 1487, 20,000 captive
warriors were sacrificed. This huge
monument, dedicated to warfare
and agriculture, was built in
seven stages. Aztec builders
increased the size of the
massive pyramid by
building each new
construction onto earlier ones.

Time and the cosmos

The Aztec Calendar Stone (right) commemorates the five world-creations. To count time, the Aztecs used a solar calendar of 365 days and a sacred calendar of 260 days. The combination of these led to cycles of 52 years. Each year had many festivals, such as the Flying Dance, which saw five men climb a pole. While one played music, four "flew" to the ground, suspended on ropes (left).

Pyramids

Egyptian pyramids were monumental tombs. Built of stone with a rubble core, they covered or contained a burial chamber, and were thought to guarantee the well-being of kings in the afterlife. Early pyramids had stepped sides (bottom), but later ones were given straight sides to represent the sun's rays. Although they knew nothing of Egyptian pyramids, the Maya of ancient Mexico and the Aztecs after them built very similar structures. These stepped pyramids had temples at the summit, unlike Egyptian pyramids and were rarely used as tombs (right).

WHALES AND PORPOISES

There are 2 major types:
Toothed whales (66 species), including river dolphins, beaked whales, dolphins and porpoises.
Whalebone (baleen) whales (10 species), including gray whale, rorquals and right whales.
Biggest species: Blue whale – more than 100 ft (30 m) long and weighing 140 tons.

The whale family comprises mammals completely adapted to life in water. The majority of the 80 or so species live in the open seas, and of these, many inhabit warm tropical waters, while others spend much of their lives in the cool polar seas. All are mammals that during evolution returned to the sea, where animal life began. They still have a fish-like appearance. Among them are the biggest animals ever to have lived on Earth, with the Blue whale at 140 tons. Whales have no hind limbs or external ears. Their forelimbs take the form of paddles, and they have a tail with flukes. Beneath the skin is a layer of blubber, or fat, which helps to conserve body heat in the water.

Breathing

Whales can stay under water for an hour or more. Yet they breathe air with their lungs and must surface to replace the oxygen their bodies need. They store oxygen in their muscles and on a dive use this and the oxygen in their lungs to stay alive. As they surface, they open the blowhole on top of their head and blow out the used air. Then they take one or more deep breaths. Underwater, the blowhole is closed by a valve and the windpipe is sealed off from the throat to prevent water entering the lungs when the animal feeds.

A fin whale blows water out of its blowhole.

Birth

Most whales do not reach maturity for many years. Pregnancy lasts from 8 months, for small dolphins, to 16 months or more for the big whales such as the blue, fin and sperm whales. Mostly only one offspring is produced. The baby is born under water tail-first. Immediately it surfaces, or its mother nudges its head out of the water, to take its first breath. The baby suckles milk from nipples hidden in folds on the mother's underside. Care of the young lasts weeks or months and is often carried out by all the females in a group.

A mother dolphin and her offspring

Feeding

Whales are divided into two main groups by the different types of jaws and feeding methods.

Toothed whales have narrow lower jaws and, as adults, cone-shaped pointed teeth in the lower or both jaws. The teeth number from 2 to 120 depending on the species. In narwhals, one of the two upper jaw teeth is greatly enlarged to form a spirally twisted tusk 6.5 feet (2 m) in length. Toothed whales feed mainly on fish and squid.

Baleen, or whalebone, whales lack teeth and the upper jaws V-shaped and has up to 300 plates of horny material similar to matted hair and fingernails. These plates of baleen hang down from the jaw and act as strainers to sift out plankton, the tiny aquatic animals and plants. When baleen whales are not feeding, the plates are enclosed within the broad lower jaw.

A southern right whale feeding on plankton

A killer whale hunts in the Arctic Ocean.

Migration

There tend to be many separate populations of whales. Some inhabit just the Northern Hemisphere, others the Southern, and within each there are Pacific, Atlantic and Indian Ocean groups. Within each area, groups of whales may migrate many thousands of miles each year, following definite circuits. These sometimes take them close to the mainland or among the pack ice of polar regions. Most toothed whales migrate to keep up with the movements of the fish on which they feed. Among baleen whales, the males move north in summer and return to the tropics in winter for the breeding season.

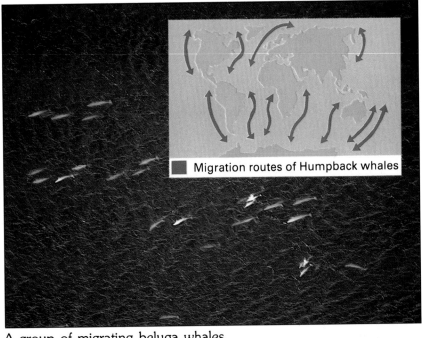

Migration routes of Humpback whales

A group of migrating beluga whales

NEW BICYCLES
CHANGING CONCEPTS

The shape of the bicycle, unaltered for nearly a century, has been transformed in the past ten years.

New materials, new designs, and wind tunnel testing have made bikes lighter, stronger and faster. Designing bikes is like designing aircraft: both have to minimize wind drag, maximize efficiency, respond quickly to the controls, yet be as light as possible. The key to the bike is the frame. Nowadays, the tubes in a racing-bike are made of aircraft-grade aluminum alloy, the gears of titanium, and flat disks are used instead of spoked wheels to reduce wind resistance. Brakes and gear mechanisms may be combined so that less time is needed to switch from applying the brakes to changing the gears.

The Lotus bike replaces the normal frame with a solid "wing" made of reinforced carbon-fiber. Designed for racing on a circular track, it has no gears or brakes. The rear wheel is a flat disk to minimize drag, but the front one is spoked. The flat handlebars allow the rider to lie almost horizontal.

Rider's seat

Rear wheel

British inventor, Clive Sinclair's Zike is a recent attempt to produce a light, powered bike. Batteries in the frame produce electricity to drive the Zike, which can also be pedaled. Designed for town use, the Zike has small wheels and a suspension system.

Rider's seat

Drive chain

Suspension forks

Handlebars are a key factor, because they control the position of the rider. The lower the rider, the less wind resistance; but careful wind tunnel testing is needed to create optimum airflow. Riders in races like the Tour de France use drop handlebars with a curved horseshoe-shaped bar on top, which they can tuck their elbows behind for sprinting. These became popular after American cyclist, Greg Le Mond, won the 1989 tour using them. Clipless pedals, which operate like ski bindings, are safer than the traditional toe clip.

The most expensive mountain bikes, like the Cannondale Super V, use air-sprung shock-absorbers to soak up the bumps. The movement of the front suspension can be adjusted.

Solid "wing"

Three-pronged front wheel

MAVIC
3G

SAILING ON A BICYCLE
HOW THE LOTUS BIKE WORKS

Most bikes lose speed in a crosswind. That is because drag increases sharply when the air is flowing past them at an angle. The Lotus bike, by contrast, is designed to go faster in those conditions by using its flat frame as a sail, taking advantage of the wind.

To achieve this result, the bike was put into a wind tunnel with its rider, Chris Boardman, in the saddle, and wind resistance was measured at different angles. By adjusting the shape and curvature of the frame, and ensuring that it and the solid rear wheel acted as a unit, it was predicted that on a circular track, a fraction of a second would be gained every lap. Boardman went on to win an Olympic Gold at Barcelona. The precise position of the rider, allowing air to flow between him and the bike, was also perfected.

The world's oddest bike is Behemoth, designed by Steve Roberts. It has 105 gears, carries four computers, a satellite navigation system, a refrigerator and solar cells to power them all. Behemoth – it stands for Big Electronic Human-Energized Machine Only Too Heavy – is a mobile office on which Roberts has pedaled 19,311 miles across the United States.

MAKING CARTOON STRIPS AND ANIMATION

Cartoon strips

Cartoon strips are a sequence of individual cartoons that tell a story. From cave paintings to the Bayeux tapestry, from Mickey Mouse to Superman, the principle is to show developing action through a series of images. Have a look through some of your own cartoon books to see the vast range of styles that can be used.

We often enjoy strip cartoons without noticing the techniques artists use to show closeup or long distance views, to indicate drama, tension, or a change of pace. Filmmakers and animators use similar techniques to produce the same kinds of effects.

Cartooning in color

Cartoon strips are usually in color. Many color materials are available. Colored pencils are easy to use. You can create pale and dark tones by pressing lightly or heavily, and new colors by laying one color over another (left). Watercolor and gouache (middle picture) are both good for cartooning. Watercolor is washed on thinly and is transparent. Gouache is denser and opaque. For both you will need to use thick paper, as thin paper will wrinkle up.

Felt-tips (right) are also versatile. Chunky, wedge-shaped ones cover the paper quickly and evenly; thin ones are good for outlines.

Animation

Animation is a way of bringing pictures to life by making them appear to move. When we watch a modern cartoon film, we seem to see a smooth sequence of movement. It's hard to believe we are actually looking at thousands of single pictures, each one slightly different from the last. They change in front of our eyes so quickly we can't see when one image replaces another.

Later in the book we will look at the techniques animators use. You can practice some of these tricks yourself. If you enjoy being precise and working carefully, you can get some very impressive results.

Painting on acetate

For the purposes of animation, cartoons are painted on sheets of clear plastic called acetate. Both sides of the acetate are used, as shown below. The image is drawn on one side with a special oil-based pen called an o.h.p. (overhead projector pen). The image is colored in on the other side using gouache or acrylic paint. This may be done quite messily, because when the acetate is turned over again, the brush marks will be invisible. Small pads of acetate are available and can be bought in art stores. Try cartooning on acetate yourself; the result will look very effective positioned on a window with light shining through it.

MEDICINE

If you had a headache, would you let someone drill a hole in your skull to release the "evil spirits?" Medicine started like that! Most people nowadays expect doctors to cure them of life's aches and pains, and to heal serious diseases. Good medical care is sometimes not appreciated. It is just taken for granted.

Medicine began in the mists of prehistory. Some people found that they could cure an illness with a potion of plant juices, or a smear of animal fluids. They were the first doctors.

Some skulls over 10,000 years old have holes bored in them. The bone had grown back after being drilled, so these people must have survived after their "operation," trepanning.

A few early treatments worked, but many did not. Some were very harmful. Even so, if a medicine worked, people had respect and wonder for the doctor. As a result, doctors became powerful, and some were made into gods.

Trepanned skull

The father of medicine
One of the first proficient doctors was Hippocrates of Ancient Greece. He tried to rid medicine of magic and superstitions, and make it more scientific. He taught that a doctor's main aim was to help the patient, by finding the cause of an illness, and treating it. The results should be checked, so medicines could be improved. Hippocrates' main ideas are still followed today.

Hippocrates

Deadening pain
Surgery has been around for thousands of years. The only way of deadening the pain of the knife and saw was to get the patient very drunk on alcohol or to use opium. In 1842, Dr. Crawford Long operated on a patient using ether as an anaesthetic, to deaden pain and other sensations. Today we could not imagine even a very small operation, without an anaesthetic.

Joseph Lister

Killing germs on the body
Until the 1860s, patients who had operations often suffered and died, because their wounds became infected with germs. British surgeon Joseph Lister began to use antiseptics (germ-killing substances) to clean his operating instruments and the patient's cuts. Within a few years, surgery became much safer.

Alexander Fleming

Killing germs in the body
In 1928, British scientist Alexander Fleming discovered a substance which could kill bacteria (types of germs). It was made by a pinhead-sized mold called *Penicillium*, so he named it penicillin. This was the first antibiotic (bacteria-killing) drug. Many other antibiotics have been discovered, and they have saved millions of lives.

Seeing inside the body

X rays were discovered by German professor Wilhelm Roentgen in 1895. People were amazed that they could pass through the body, except for bones. Soon X rays were showing up broken bones and suspicious lumps and bumps.

Doctors have many modern methods of seeing into the body. CAT scans and NMR scans show the inside parts in amazing detail. Thin tubes called endoscopes can be pushed into the body, to examine and photograph the insides.

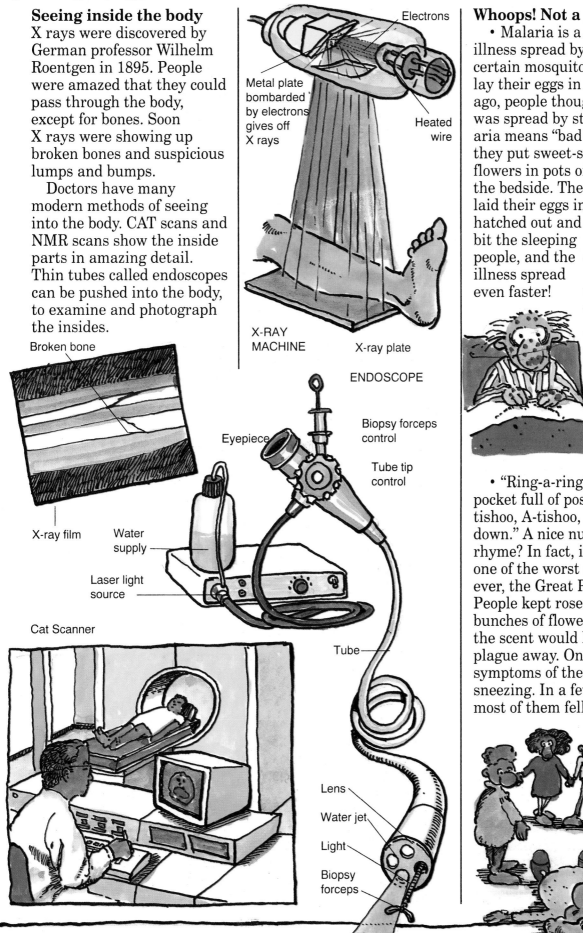

Electrons

Metal plate bombarded by electrons gives off X rays

Heated wire

X-RAY MACHINE

X-ray plate

Broken bone

X-ray film

ENDOSCOPE

Eyepiece

Biopsy forceps control

Tube tip control

Water supply

Laser light source

Cat Scanner

Tube

Lens

Water jet

Light

Biopsy forceps

Whoops! Not a good idea

• Malaria is a serious illness spread by the bites of certain mosquitoes, which lay their eggs in water. Years ago, people thought malaria was spread by stale air (malaria means "bad air"). So they put sweet-smelling flowers in pots of water by the bedside. The mosquitoes laid their eggs in the water, hatched out and bit the sleeping people, and the illness spread even faster!

• "Ring-a-ring-a-roses, A pocket full of posies, A-tishoo, A-tishoo, All fall down." A nice nursery rhyme? In fact, it is about one of the worst diseases ever, the Great Plague. People kept roses and bunches of flowers, hoping the scent would keep the plague away. One of the first symptoms of the plague was sneezing. In a few days, most of them fell down dead.

NATURE'S BALANCE

The living world performs a delicate balancing act. Living things can only exist where conditions are right and they depend on each other for survival. Only a few living things can survive without oxygen from the earth's atmosphere. They all need water. They need the right climate and the right temperature, not too wet and not too dry, not too hot and not too cold. Above all, each living thing forms part of a system, depending on others for survival.

Biome

ECOSYSTEMS IN SCALE
Parrots in a rainforest and fish on a coral reef are part of different ecosystems. Taken together, creatures, plants and their habitat make up an ecosystem. The largest ecosystems into which the earth's land is divided are called biomes. For example, the tropical forest biome, which includes all tropical forests on every continent, takes up about one-fifth of all land. A community consists of the animals and plants in a small area. Within a community are populations, for example, all the rabbits in one wood.

Community

Two populations

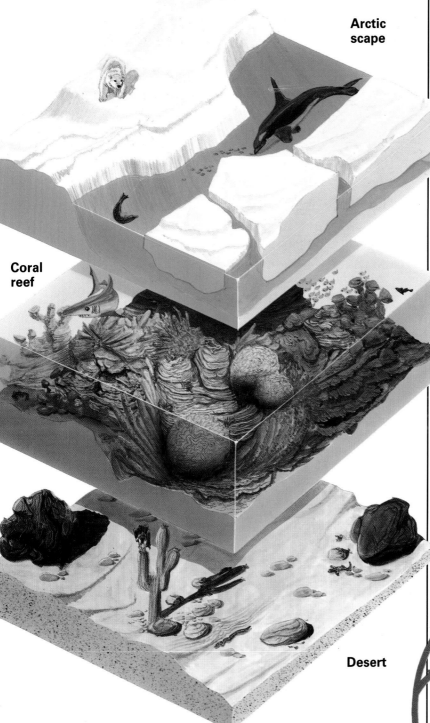

Arctic scape

Coral reef

Desert

FOOD WEBS
In a simple food chain an underwater plant makes its own food. A shrimp comes along and eats the plant. A fish eats the shrimp, which is eaten in turn by a seal. Later, a whale eats the seal. People catch and eat the whale. In fact, food chains are very rarely as simple as this. Most animals eat several different foods. Several other animals may eat them. Food chains are all interwoven, forming a food web, like the one shown below. These can sometimes be very complicated indeed. But they show how living things in an ecosystem depend on each other for survival.

FOOD WEBS

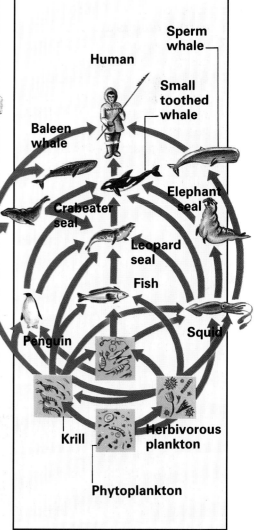

Sperm whale

Human

Small toothed whale

Baleen whale

Crabeater seal

Elephant seal

Leopard seal

Fish

Penguin

Squid

Krill

Herbivorous plankton

Phytoplankton

MAKING A LIVING
Some ecosystems are more complex than others. A desert has few kinds of animal and plant life. This is partly because conditions are so harsh. But there are also few ways of making a living here. In a tropical forest, on the other hand, there is a bounty of trees, flowers, and other plants. Birds, monkeys, frogs, snakes and vast numbers of insects will all coexist.

The way that an animal makes its living is known as its "niche." Coral reefs, perhaps the oldest ecosystems, are teeming with niches. Taking up just a small space on the planet, they support one-third of all fish species. In the Arctic, where there are few niches, things look simpler. But even the simplest ecosystem has a lot going on in it.

MODERN HUMANS

Modern humans all belong to the species *Homo sapiens*. It is thought this species evolved in Africa about 200,000 years ago. Between 100,000 and 35,000 years ago, Europe was home to the Neanderthals, whose brain was the same size as *Homo sapiens* and who some scientists believe were a sub-species of *Homo sapiens*. The Neanderthals were gradually replaced by the Cro-Magnon peoples, *Homo sapiens* who migrated to Europe from the Middle East.

Neanderthals

Neanderthals were strongly built people, who hunted woolly mammoths and rhinos. They made advanced tools and weapons with flint and bone. The Neanderthals disappeared when the ice sheets withdrew from Europe.

Body types

Modern humans show a great range of body sizes and shapes which are suited to the terrain and climate in which they live. Neanderthals, who lived during the Ice Age were short but strongly built, and with much body fat, so they could withstand the cold. Today, modern Inuit (Eskimos) are also short and stocky because they live in the cold. Cro-Magnon peoples were taller, but not as tall as some Modern African peoples, such as the Masai.

Neanderthal

Modern Inuit

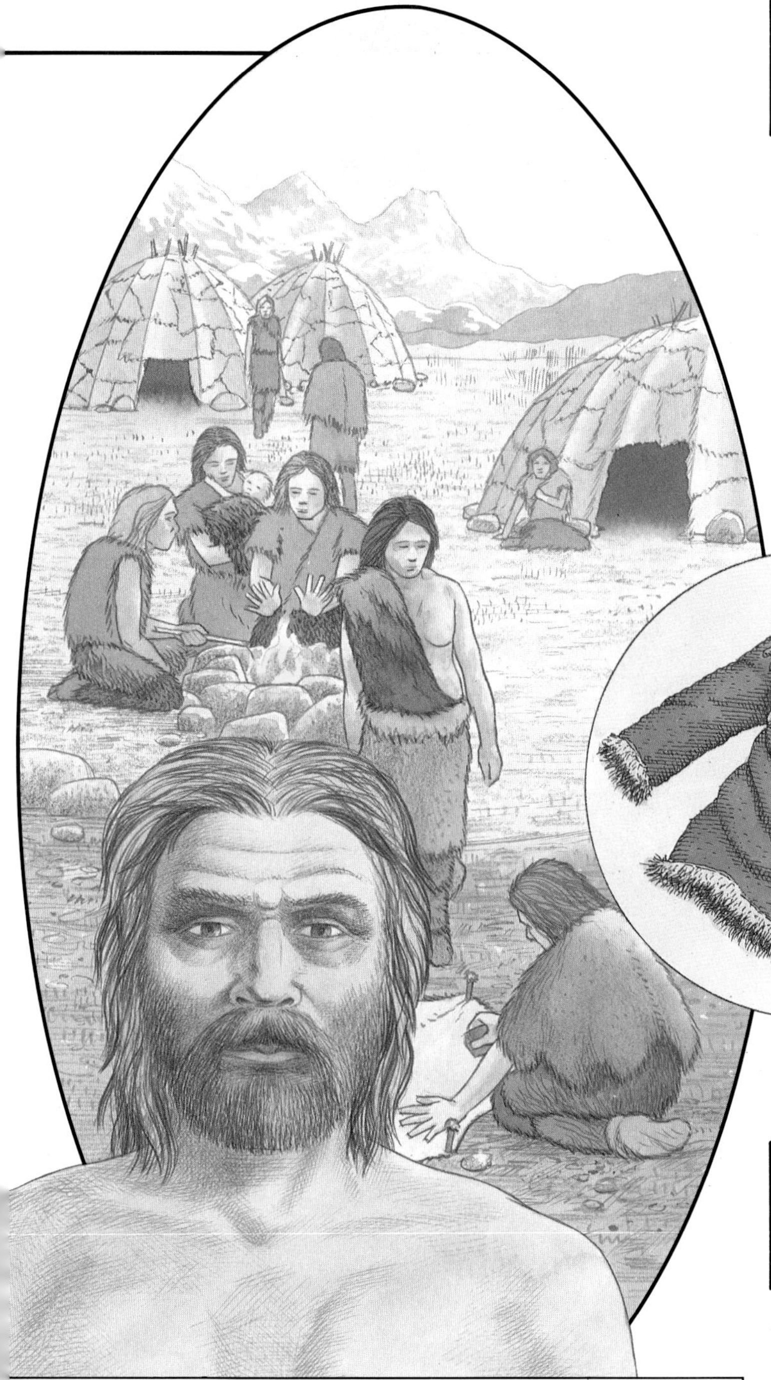

Rafts

Neanderthals and Cro-Magnons made rafts by strapping together logs with thongs made from animal hides. With these simple boats they were able to fish from the middle of lakes or rivers.

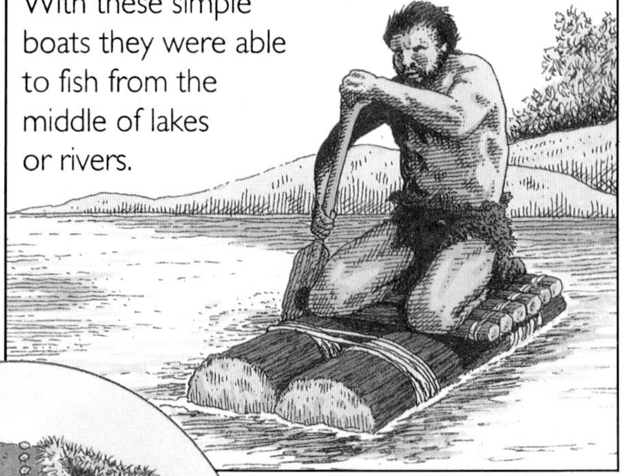

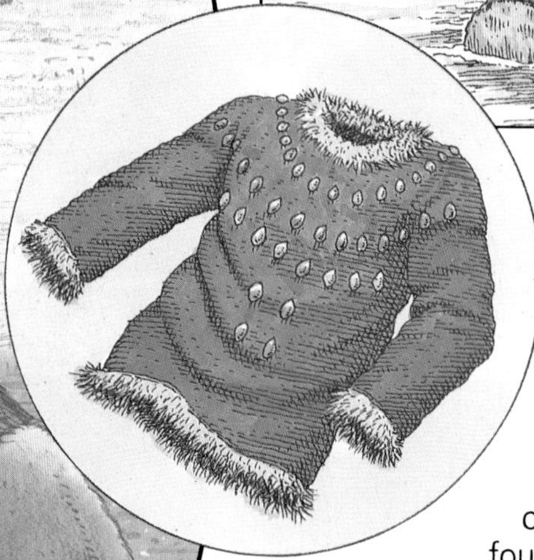

Cro-Magnons

The Cro-Magnon peoples lived between 35,000 and 8,000 years ago. The name comes from the Cro-Magnon cave in France where the first skeletons of Cro-Magnons were found. They produced delicate carvings and paintings and made clothes from animal hides, evidence of which have been discovered on dig sites.

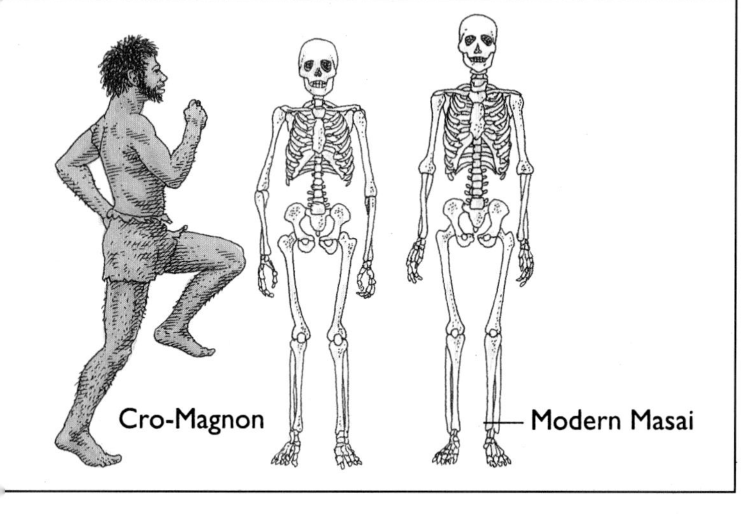

Cave art

The Cro-Magnons left beautiful paintings in caves in France and Spain. Many of the images are of animals and sometimes people. The paintings, which date from 20,000 to 10,000 years ago, show that their makers had high artistic skills and exceptional powers of observation.

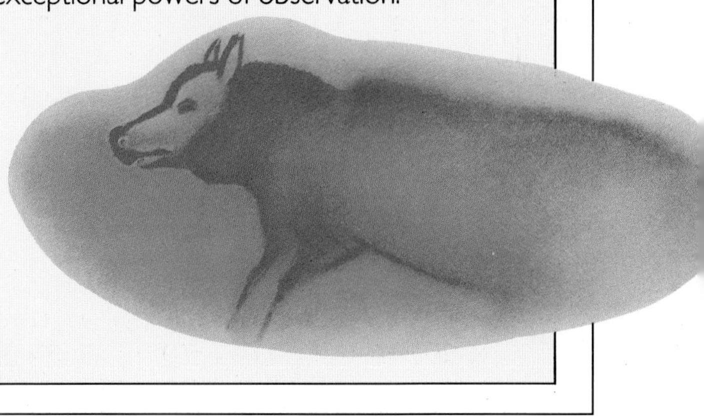

Early Explorers
AND DISCOVERERS

A SENSITIVE APPROACH

Sir William Flinders Petrie (1852-1942) is regarded as the father of modern archaeology. He dug sites carefully, recorded everything in detail and published his results. His first job in Egypt was to measure the Great Pyramid.

EARLY ADVENTURER

Jean de Thevenot (1633-67, below) was one of the first explorers of ancient Egyptian sites.

Throughout history, people have tried to understand the pyramids. Early Christians thought they were places where priests watched the stars. In the nineteenth century, some people believed that the measurements of the Great Pyramid were inspired by God, and that from them they could predict the future! But by then, scholars could read ancient Egyptian writing and they had started to dig up historic sites. The pyramids were finally known to be the last resting places of Egypt's ancient Kings.

THE BURIED SPHINX

In Egyptian legend, the Sphinx (the statue which guards the pyramids) appeared to a prince in a dream. It promised to make him king if he cleared away the sand covering its body. He did so, and became Tuthmosis IV.

NAPOLÉON'S NIGHTMARE

Napoléon Bonaparte, the Emperor of France, led an invasion of Egypt in 1798. Legend has it that he ventured into the Great Pyramid alone, only to emerge pale, shaken, and gasping for air. What secrets did he encounter in the darkness? We will never know...

TREASURE HUNTERS
In the early nineteenth century, great damage was done by collectors and their agents. They entered the tombs in all sorts of ways, including blasting their way in. Giovanni Belzoni was a former circus strongman, who was hired by a collector to gather ancient Egyptian artifacts. He had no idea of preservation – one of his writings describes how he clumsily crushed Late-Period mummies as he forced his way into a tomb.

Preserving the treasures
Many museums and universities have carried out excavations in Egypt. The objects found are treated by experts, then stored for future research. X rays, medical scanners (below), robot photography and many other modern techniques are used to help scientists understand the secrets of the tombs.

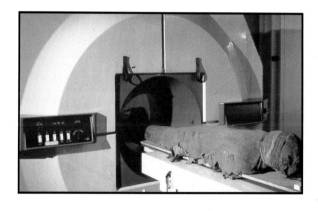

ÆGYPTVS ANTIQVA

THEB LA IDIS

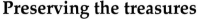
BELZONI 1816

PYRAMID GRAFFITI
Belzoni even carved his name on the stones of the pyramids!

When did tourists start to arrive?
In 1869, Thomas Cook, a British travel agent, bought a steamboat in Egypt and offered a new service – a package vacation.
He charged one amount to cover everything – travel to Egypt, a Nile cruise and a guide. Until then, visitors to Egypt had to arrange all these details for themselves, which could be both very difficult and extremely expensive.

UNCHARTED TERRITORY
After the Arab invasion of Egypt, few people were able to visit the country. Little was known about the pyramids, the Nile Valley and its surroundings, or the culture and history of ancient Egypt.

WHAT IF A TIGER HAD NO TEETH?

Carnassial teeth

It would soon go hungry and starve. The tiger uses its claws to catch and scratch prey. But it needs its teeth to deliver the deadly bites, and to slice the meat off the bones for eating. The tiger has two main kinds of teeth for these jobs. The long, sharp canines or "fangs" are at the front of the mouth. They stab, wound, and skin the victim, making it bleed, suffocate, and die.

The large, ridge-edged carnassial teeth at the back of the mouth come together like the blades of scissors when the tiger closes its jaws. These very strong teeth carve off and slice up the meat, and can even crunch gristle (cartilage) and soft bones.

Canine teeth

Purr-fect claws

A cat's claws are vital for its survival in the wild. With these incredibly sharp weapons, the hunter can slash, stab, and pin prey that will become its food. However, these deadly claws need to be kept razor sharp for the next kill. To ensure this, most cats can withdraw, or retract, their claws into sheaths in the toes.

This allows the cat to run, walk, and jump without scraping its sharp talons along the ground. It keeps them sharp, unbroken, and clean. It keeps them from getting blunt or getting tangled in twigs, grass, bark, and other things. When the cat needs its claws to climb a tree or to slash and pin its prey, it makes them stick out of the toes.

Claws indoors
The cat's claw is equivalent to your fingernail or toenail. But the claw can swing or pivot on its toe bone. A muscle in the lower leg pulls on a long, stringlike tendon that is attached to the bone and claw. This pulls the sharp claw out of its protective sheath.

Bone

Tendon

Claw

Plant-eating carnivore

When the giant panda of China was first discovered, it posed a problem to scientists. It has the sharp, fanglike teeth of a carnivore (meat-eater), and is indeed a close relative of the meat-eating raccoon. However, its diet consists almost solely of bamboo shoots. Even though it can eat meat, the panda chooses the young shoots of this type of grass. Unfortunately, bamboo is very low in nutritional value. As a result, it must spend nearly all of its time sitting around, lazily eating in order to consume enough to survive.

Highly-sprung hunter

The fastest hunter on land owes its speed to its flexible backbone. Without this powerful spring running along its spine, the cheetah would not be able to catch and kill the nimble prey that it hunts, such as gazelle and springbok.

As this big cat sprints, the spine flexes, stretching the body out, and allowing the legs to cover even more distance with each stride. This makes the cheetah the world's fastest runner, at over 60 mph (100 km/h).

As the cheetah's legs come together, the spine bends up in the middle.

As the cheetah extends its legs, the spine flattens and arches backward.

As a result the legs can stretch further apart, letting the cheetah run faster.

VIRTUAL REALITY
COMPUTER ILLUSIONS

Computers have been used to create three-dimensional images for many years. "Virtual reality" allows us to take a walk inside those models, to make us feel that we are really there. Virtual reality technology uses computers to work directly on our senses – particularly vision, hearing, and touch – to create the illusion of reality, being in a computer-created spaceship or at Cluny Abbey. The user wears a special headset fitted with goggles. Computer-created images are sent to the headset. As the user moves, sensors feed data back to the computer, so that the view of the image changes, just as it would if you were moving through a real building or landscape.

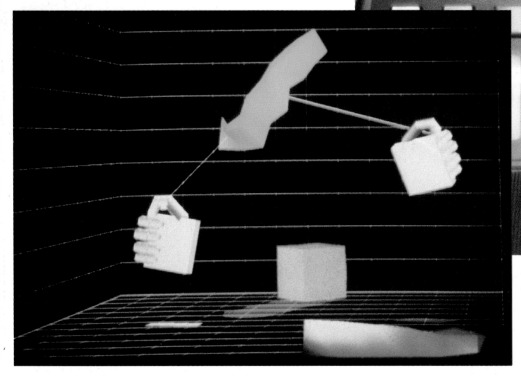

In some virtual reality systems, it is possible to pick up imaginary objects, using a glove fitted with sensors that give the impression of gripping and lifting.

Virtual reality environments like the one above have many uses. Engineers have used virtual reality to plan telephone networks.

Architects have been using three-dimensional computer-aided design programs for several years. But a virtual reality design program like the one used to create Cluny Abbey would enable them to walk inside their buildings before they are constructed.

Virtual reality can be used for entertainment or for serious scientific research. Scientists at the University of North Carolina use it to build up molecules of drugs. Virtual reality not only allows them to see how atoms bind together but to feel when they don't.

The 1000SD is the first virtual reality computer game. Put on the headset and you find yourself in a computer-generated world. The design of the headset allows you complete freedom of movement. All your actions are controlled by a joystick.

The nave of Cluny Abbey, France (below), has been rebuilt inside a computer as an exercise in virtual reality. From the archaeological discoveries, and drawings made before it was knocked down, experts created the model with the help of IBM France.

CLUNY MONASTERY
RECONSTRUCTING THE

Virtual reality is a powerful tool for archaeologists. It is now possible to re-create from plans and sketches what it felt like to walk through buildings long since lost. The monastery at Cluny, in southeast France, was a great center of culture and learning during the 11th and 12th centuries. What is known of Cluny comes from excavations during the 1900s. Virtual reality still has some way to go before it is truly convincing. The graphics alone present some big problems. The headset has to respond to your movement and to send images to your eyes at least as fast as a movie.

THE KEYBOARD FAMILY

The keyboard was one of the most important musical inventions. The system of scales and keys we know today is largely based on it. The keyboard has been used in a wide variety of instruments besides the piano and the older harpsichord, just some of which are shown here.

French musician Jean-Michel Jarre (above right) pioneered the use of synthesizers and electronic sounds.

ELECTRIC KEYBOARDS

Electric organs and pianos are played very like an ordinary piano, but the sounds, like those of the synthesizer, are electronic. These instruments are very popular with jazz musicians and pop groups.

ELECTRIC ORGAN

Electric organs began to appear in movies and theaters in the 1920s. They were technically very advanced for their time, and could produce many extraordinary sounds. Visually these organs made a dramatic impact on audiences, as they rose up from the pit in front of the screen or stage during intervals in performances, with their many lights flashing.

SYNTHESIZER

Synthesizers (above) generate electronic signals which are fed though amplifiers and speakers. These signals can produce many different sounds.

CELESTA
The keyboard of a celesta plays a set of tuned metal bars inside the instrument. Tchaikovsky's "Dance of the Sugar Plum Fairy" is written for it.

ACCORDION
The accordion (right) is a kind of portable organ, with a keyboard down one side. Learning to play the keyboard at this angle takes a great deal of practice.

CHURCH ORGAN
A large church or concert organ (right) often has three or four keyboards (known as "manuals"), plus a pedal keyboard, which is played with the feet. There are also a variety of "stops" — knobs or handles that the organist pulls out or pushes in to select whole groups or sets of pipes. All these devices are needed because many organs have a large number of pipes, with a range of different sound qualities, as well as notes of different pitch. Electric organs which were used in movies or theaters are now sometimes used in churches. The organ shown on the opposite page is reused in this way.

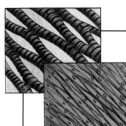

MUSCLES AND MOVEMENT

All the body's movements are powered by muscles. Muscle tissue is specialized to contract, or get shorter. The body has three main kinds of muscles. One is the skeletal muscles, attached to the bones of the skeleton, which you use to move about. There are more than 600 skeletal muscles, from the huge gluteus in the buttock to tiny finger and toe muscles. The other kinds of muscles are cardiac muscle in the heart (top left above) and smooth muscles in the stomach, intestines and other internal organs (left above).

Inside a muscle

A skeletal muscle has a bulging central part known as the body. This tapers at each end into a rope-like tendon, which anchors the muscle to a bone. As the muscle contracts, the tendons pull on their bones and move the body. The muscle body is divided into bundles of hair-fine fibers called myofibers. These long cells contain proteins that slide past one another to make the cell shorter in length.

Muscle sheath

Tendon

Myofiber
(muscle
cell)

Bundle of
myofibers

Front
shoulder
muscle moves
shoulder and
upper arm.

Neck muscle
moves head.

Biceps
contracts
and
bends
elbow.

Muscles in
forearm
bend
fingers.

Front thigh
muscle
straightens
knee.

Shin muscle
bends ankle
by pulling
up foot.

Changing fashions

Bulging muscles have been in and out of fashion through the centuries. A few hundred years ago, plump bodies were seen as desirable. Today some men and women like to look slim. Other people work hard at body-building, training and lifting weights in the gym. They strive to increase the thickness of their muscle fibers through special exercises and diet.

258

Stories of the strong
Legends from many different cultures tell of well-muscled, strong men and women. Some are heroes, others are villains. Hercules of Ancient Greece had to undertake 12 "herculean" (very difficult) tasks or labors. In the Bible, the boy David fought and killed the giant Goliath with his slingshot. Samson was a hero who fought the Philistines, but he lost his strength when Delilah tricked him into having his hair shorn. Blinded and chained, he pushed the columns of the Gaza Temple and brought it crashing down on himself and his captors, as pictured right.

Triceps contracts, straightening elbow. Biceps relaxes and stretches.

Master of art and science
During the Renaissance period, from about the 14th century, there was a rebirth of fascination in the beauty of the human form, and a scientific interest in the structure and workings of the body. Foremost in this field was the genius of art and science, Leonardo da Vinci (1452-1519). He performed amazing dissections of the body, especially the muscle system, and drew them with unparalled skill and mastery, as shown here.

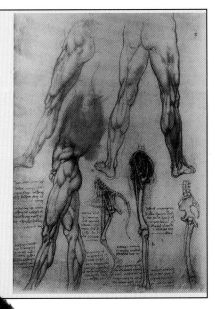

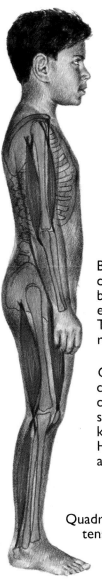

Biceps contracts, bending elbow. Triceps relaxes.

Quadri-ceps contracts, straightening knee. Hamstring muscles relax and stretch.

Quadriceps and hamstrings tensed to maintain crouched position.

Muscle pairs
A muscle contracts to pull on its bone. But it cannot do the reverse – actively get longer and push the bone the other way. So many of the body's muscles are arranged in opposing pairs, attached across the same joint. One partner of the pair pulls the bones one way, bending the joint. The other pulls the other way and straightens the joint, while its partner relaxes. Even a simple movement also involves many other muscles that keep the body balanced.

MT. ST. HELENS

Mount St. Helens is a volcanic peak in the Cascade Mountains of Washington State. On May 18, 1980, a huge explosion ripped the mountain apart, releasing clouds of ash and dust (below).

Geologists knew that the volcano could erupt at any time. It had been dormant since 1857, but a series of small earthquakes during the 1970s suggested that magma was rising into the mountain. There were other warning signs too. The side of the mountain was bulging, and steam was escaping.

At 8:32 am, an earthquake broke the bulging side loose, causing the worst landslide ever recorded. Rock and lava cascaded down the mountainside and clouds of hot gases and ash plunged the valley into darkness. The eruption killed 63 people, flattened forests, and destroyed wildlife over 400 sq miles.

The volcano continued to erupt violently for days and there were smaller eruptions for several months.

Effect On Environment
After the eruption the countryside resembled a desert of ash and charred remains (below). Yet five years later, wildlife could be found once again in the area. Other, more long-term effects have resulted from the 30 million tons of ash flung into the atmosphere (right). The effect of the ash on the amount of sunlight reaching the ground may have caused changes in the weather worldwide.

THE FIRST PRIMATES

Humans, monkeys and apes belong to a group of mammals called primates. The first primates appeared in the Northern Hemisphere about 70 million years ago. They were tree-dwelling squirrellike animals that bore little resemblance to modern primate species. It took another 30 million years before the first monkeys and apes evolved. Today there are more than 180 primate species.

Film fantasy

Authors and film makers have always been fascinated by the mystery of our origins. The hugely successful film *2001, A Space Odyssey*, made in 1968, is based on a short story by Arthur C. Clark. This science fiction fantasy, explores the question of what triggered humans to make tools and thus set us apart from other animals. The scene from the film (below) shows the first human ancestor to use a bone as a tool.

Early mammals

The first mammals (above) evolved about 210 million years ago, at the time of the very first dinosaurs. They probably lived alone and were nocturnal (active at night). These early mammals are called "archaic" mammals because they are the distant relatives of living animals rather than direct ancestors.

The march through time

The first monkeys evolved 40 million years ago, and the first apes 30 million years ago. Apes and humans probably shared a common ancestor until between 10 and 6 million years ago when the line of evolution to humans and apes separated.

First monkeys
40 million years ago

First apes
30 million years ago

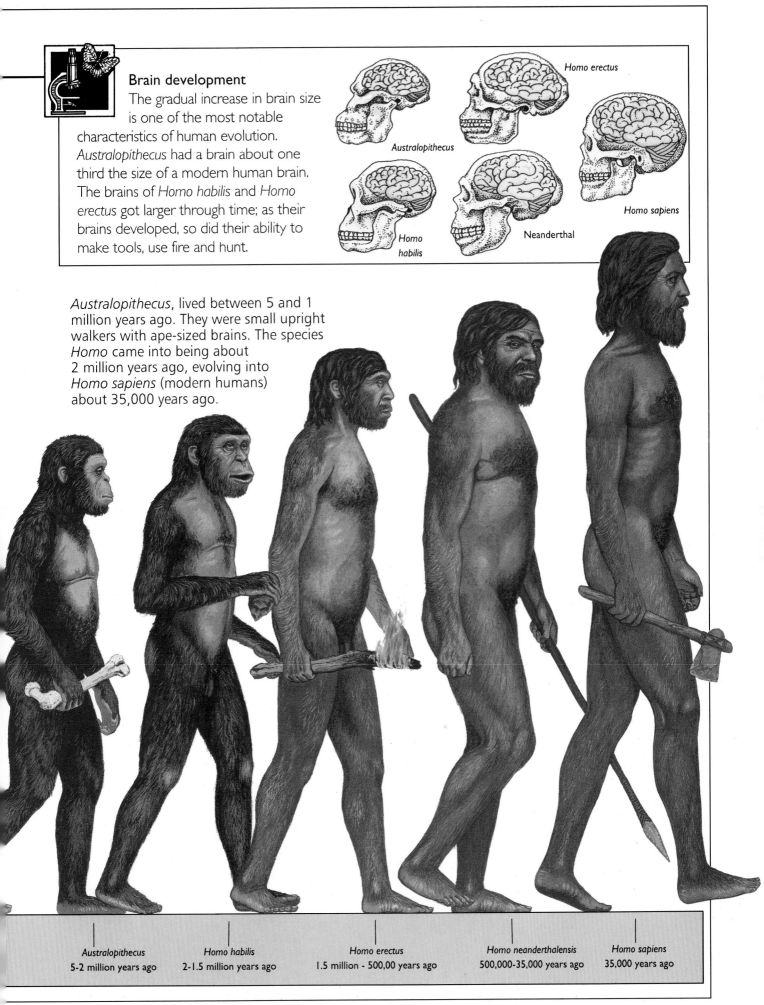

Brain development

The gradual increase in brain size is one of the most notable characteristics of human evolution. *Australopithecus* had a brain about one third the size of a modern human brain. The brains of *Homo habilis* and *Homo erectus* got larger through time; as their brains developed, so did their ability to make tools, use fire and hunt.

Australopithecus

Homo erectus

Homo habilis

Neanderthal

Homo sapiens

Australopithecus, lived between 5 and 1 million years ago. They were small upright walkers with ape-sized brains. The species *Homo* came into being about 2 million years ago, evolving into *Homo sapiens* (modern humans) about 35,000 years ago.

Australopithecus
5-2 million years ago

Homo habilis
2-1.5 million years ago

Homo erectus
1.5 million - 500,00 years ago

Homo neanderthalensis
500,000-35,000 years ago

Homo sapiens
35,000 years ago

ROMAN GODS

The Romans worshiped a great many gods and spirits – about 30,000 in all. These included the major gods and goddesses, such as Jupiter, the chief god, Neptune, god of the sea, Venus, goddess of love and beauty, and Minerva, goddess of wisdom and war. Each household also worshiped its own protective spirits – the Lares, Penates, and Manes. After Augustus's death, the emperors were considered gods, too. People all over the empire were allowed to worship their own local gods, as long as they also paid homage to the Roman gods. Large and impressive temples, often modeled on Greek examples, were built as places of worship for the state deities.

One of the household Lares; the guardian of houses.

Household gods

Every Roman house had its own shrine to the household gods (Lares), called a Lararium, where worship was carried out daily. The family offered gifts such as wine, bread, and fruit, and also gave sacrifices to the gods. Outside the home, people worshiped the Roman gods in shrines and temples (right).

Festivals

Roman festivals were regarded as holy days (holidays), during which people did not have to work.

Under Augustus there were about 130 public holidays, and this number increased under later emperors. The festivals were usually celebrated with games and races.

The Rites of Bona Dea was held in early December. The festival was for women only, and men were forbidden to attend.

Compitalia occurred in early January. Farmers built a shrine and made sacrifices to ensure the prosperity of their farms. During *Parilia*, in April, people danced around a bonfire onto which offerings were thrown.

Religious persecution

During the empire, many Romans felt the empty rituals of the state religion could no longer meet their spiritual needs. Foreign cults such as those of Mithras, Isis, and Cybele encouraged their followers to take part in ceremonies, and spread across the empire. Christianity was not tolerated by the Romans, however. Its followers refused to worship the state gods and were often cruelly persecuted.

Vestals

Vesta was the goddess of the hearth. The six Vestal virgins had to perform symbolic household duties for the state. This included tending the fire dedicated to Vesta which burned in her temple in the forum. The virgins had to remain unmarried for 30 years. Those who did not were buried alive.

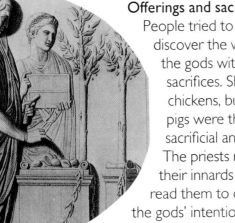

Offerings and sacrifices

People tried to discover the will of the gods with sacrifices. Sheep, chickens, bulls, and pigs were the main sacrificial animals. The priests removed their innards and read them to discover the gods' intentions.

Looking heavenward

The positions of the stars and the planets at the time of a person's birth were considered very significant by the Romans.

Mercury

Ceremonies

Special ceremonies marked important events in the lives of all Romans. A newborn baby was placed at its father's feet. The father raised the child in his arms as a sign of acceptance into the family. Funerals were very grand affairs, with professional mourners hired to wail over the body. In Republican times, death masks and mourning robes were worn. This practice was stopped during the empire.

Jupiter

Many of the stars and planets were named after Roman and Greek gods and goddesses. For example, Mercury was named after the messenger of the gods, who was also the god of trade and thieves. Venus was the goddess of love and beauty and Mars was the god of war. Jupiter was the king of the gods – the god of thunder and of lightning. Can you find out who the other planets were named after?

Roman marriages were usually arranged. The couple clasped hands (shown right) as a symbol of their marriage.

Venus

WHAT ARE BIRDS?

There are 27 groups of birds.
Biggest group: Passerines, the perching birds. This includes familiar types such as crows and sparrows (5,150 species).
Smallest group: Struthioniformes, with just one species, the ostrich.
Most common species: African quelea finch – more than 100 billion.
Rarest species: California condor – fewer than 10 in the wild.

There are about 8,500 different species or kinds of birds, making them the most numerous backboned animals living on land. They range in size from tiny hummingbirds only 2.2 inches long to the ostrich, which may be more than 7 feet tall. They are found on every continent and in all habitats from tropical forests and desert to arctic tundra and ice. But they all have in common the fact that they are warm-blooded – that is, they can keep their bodies at a constant temperature, usually about 104°F. The front limbs – legs in most reptiles and mammals – have become modified as wings, usually used for flight, and feathers provide the main body covering, with scales on the legs and toes. Feathers trap heat under them and provide large surfaces needed for flight. Birds have no teeth, but have lightweight beaks (made of horn) covering the jaws.

Flight

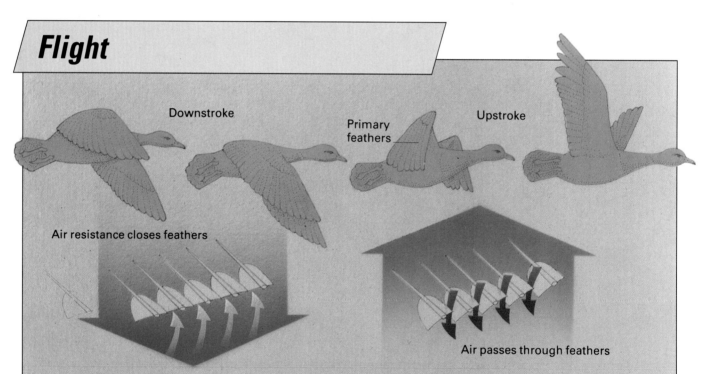

Downstroke

Primary feathers

Upstroke

Air resistance closes feathers

Air passes through feathers

The streamlined shape of a bird helps it slip easily through the air as it flies, driven through the air by its wings acting as propellers. The power to work the wings comes from large muscles on the bird's chest on each side of the breastbone. Tendons run from these to the wing bones. There is little muscle in the wings themselves, which are light and easy to swing. The inner part of the wings helps give the bird lift as it moves forward. It acts rather like the wing of an airplane. The outer part of the wings, with its long primary feathers, gives the forward push, with the primaries bending so that they help the animal forward on the upstroke as well as the downstroke. As the bird makes a downstroke the feathers are flattened against the air, making an airtight surface. On the upstroke they are turned so that air can spill between them. Flying actions and the wing shapes are adapted to the animals' needs and the type of country they inhabit.

Feathers

Feathers are very light and can be many sizes and shapes, including the large flat surfaces needed for flight.

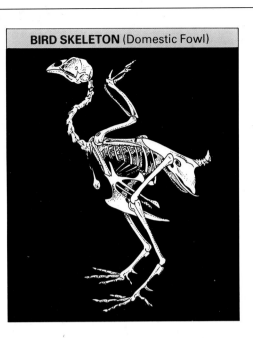

Feet

The shape of the feet varies according to the bird's environment and feeding habits.

Lungs and air sacs

Birds breathe by pumping air in and out of air sacs extending into the body beyond the lungs. Air is kept flowing through the lungs.

Nerve cord

The nerve cord transmits messages between the brain and the rest of the body, vital for flight and other complicated actions.

Brain

The large brain receives messages from sense organs and controls complex actions, although most birds show few signs of intelligent behavior.

Eggs

All birds lay eggs. Most sit on them for incubation. The strong shell protects the bird embryo, and the yolk provides food for growth. Small birds lay several eggs, whereas large ones lay only a few.

Heart

The heart has four chambers and its muscles work hard to pump blood around the body. The heart rate is nearly 500 beats a minute in a small bird such as a sparrow (compared with about 80 beats a minute in a human adult).

ROCK DOVE
Columba livia

THE ATOMIC BOMB

In a split second in 1945, the world changed forever. In the Pacific, World War II was dragging on. At 7:30 a.m. on August 6, the Allies dropped the first atomic bomb, over the Japanese city of Hiroshima. Killing and destruction were immense. In a few days, the war ended. The shadow of atomic and nuclear weapons has been with us ever since.

"Little Boy" was a metal-cased bomb about 6 feet long. Exploding over Hiroshima, it killed some 75,000 people and flattened three-fifths of the city. Thousands more died later from injuries, burns and radiation sickness.

Little Boy

How the bomb worked

"Little Boy" had gigantic destructive power because it turned matter into energy. The matter was in the form of the radioactive substance uranium-235.

At the critical moment, two pieces of uranium-235 crashed together in the bomb. Some of the uranium atoms split, in a process called nuclear fission. The resulting atomic fragments weighed less than the original atoms, because parts of them were converted to energy – in the form of light, heat, and radioactivity. The fission also made more fast-moving atomic fragments, which collided with other uranium atoms, splitting them too, and so on, in a split-second chain reaction.

Energy

NUCLEAR FISSION

Nuclear weapons today

After the war, enough atomic bombs were made to blast the whole world to pieces many times.

Then came hydrogen bombs, which were even more powerful. Their energy was released when atomic bits of hydrogen joined together, in atomic fusion. Different types of hydrogen bombs form the bulk of today's nuclear weapons.

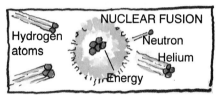

NUCLEAR FUSION
Hydrogen atoms
Neutron
Helium
Energy

Power to destroy

• One of the most powerful chemical high-explosives is TNT.

• An atomic bomb or A-bomb is a million times more powerful than a TNT bomb of the same size.

• A hydrogen bomb or H-bomb is a thousand times more powerful than an A-bomb of the same size.

FUSION POWER – *HALF AN INVENTION?*

A safe, cheap, reliable source of energy, that won't pollute the world or run out. Sounds like a dream? It has been. But in the 1990s, scientists are trying to make the dream real. Fusion power could not only change the world, but save it, too.

The hydrogen bombs described opposite work by nuclear fusion. But their energy is released all at once, in a massive BANG. Could the process be controlled in a fusion reactor? Experiments in the past few years show – hopefully, yes.

A TYPICAL NUCLEAR FISSION POWER STATION

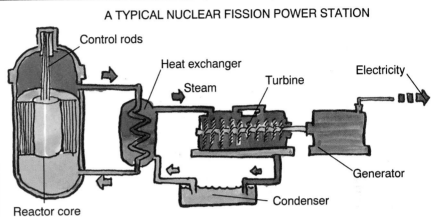

Control rods · Heat exchanger · Steam · Turbine · Electricity · Generator · Condenser · Reactor core

Plasma-filled donut

A fusion reactor will be shaped like a donut, and called a torus. Inside, two forms of hydrogen called deuterium and tritium must be heated to an incredible 1,800,000,000°F, as they whirl around. At this temperature they are not solid, liquid or gas. They are another form of matter, plasma.

Some of the atomic bits in the plasma of deuterium and tritium join together, or fuse. They produce atomic bits of another substance, helium, and also give out vast amounts of heat and other energy. The heat could power electricity generators, as in a normal power station.

Copying the Sun

Today's nuclear power stations use fission reactors which split atoms, like the atomic bomb (opposite). In theory, fusion power could be cleaner, less dangerous and less polluting. But it will take many years and experiments before fusion power changes the world.

Even so, we already rely on it! Bits of hydrogen atoms fuse to form helium, creating light and heat and other energy – in the Sun.

Cold fusion fails

• In the early 1990s there was a great argument about "cold fusion," where fusion power might be made at ordinary temperatures. A few scientists claimed they'd got it to work. Others repeated the experiments, but they didn't work. No one has proved "cold fusion" since.

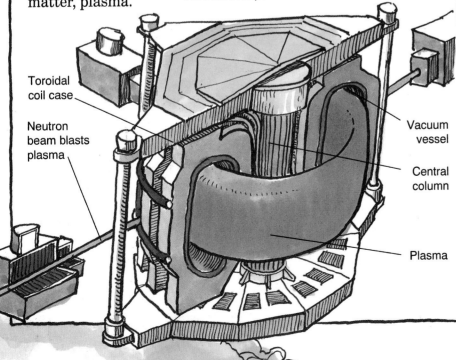

TOKAMAK experimental fusion reactor

Toroidal coil case · Neutron beam blasts plasma · Vacuum vessel · Central column · Plasma

DRAWING THE HUMAN FIGURE

When the American space program launched the rocket *Pioneer 10* into outer space, they attached a plaque to inform extraterrestrials about the planet earth. The plaque featured a drawing of two figures – a man and a woman. It's strange to think that other beings might look very different to us. Imagine that you've been given the task of showing aliens what humans look like. For an accurate picture you will need to show the body in proportion.

Getting things in proportion

Proportion is about comparing the size of one thing to another. For the artist, it is about showing different sizes correctly on paper. The drawings on the right show the proportions of the human figure. The length of the body is often measured in relation to the head. The average adult, whether male or female, is seven heads tall. The torso is three heads long from the chin to the top of the legs, and divides into thirds at the nipple line and navel. The distance from the top of the legs to the soles of the feet also measures three heads. Children's heads are larger in proportion to the rest of their bodies. Adult or child, with your arms stretched out sideways, the distance between your fingertips measures the same as your height – try it!

Foreshortening

Here the story gets more complicated; these proportions appear to change as we move about. Parts of the body appear larger or smaller, depending on whether they are near or far from the person looking at them. We found out about this in the project on perspective.

If someone's leg or arm is pointing directly at you, part of its length will be hidden. This is known as *foreshortening*. You can see it on the right in the drawings of the figures sitting and crouching, and also in the sketches at the bottom of the opposite page.

Practicing foreshortening

Foreshortening takes a more dramatic turn when you look at the figure from an unusual angle. As shown in the drawings left and middle opposite, a person with his arm outstretched toward you, or lying down, will seem to have an enormous hand or enormous feet. Have a go at drawing someone in these positions. It takes a lot of practice to get these things to look right, but you can have fun on the way as long as you don't mind making mistakes. The third picture is a sketch of the artist looking down at his own body and drawing himself at work. Try it. If you shut one eye, you can even see your nose, and include it in the picture, as he did.

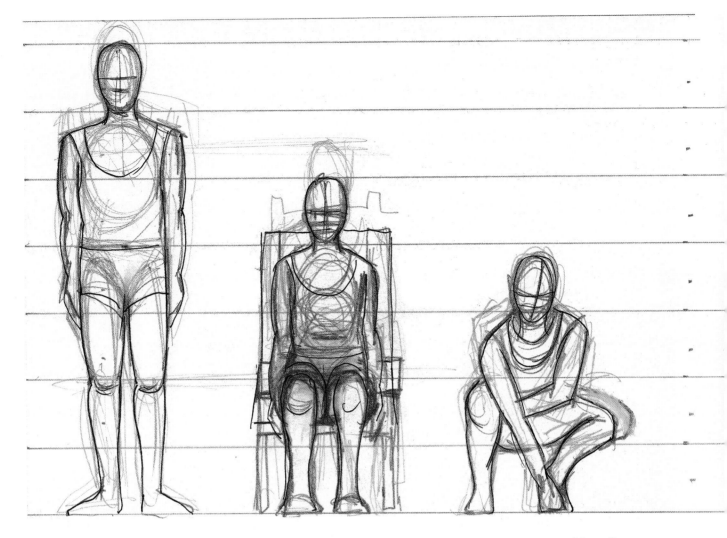

△ "Above I have drawn the proportions of the standing figure. You might want to copy this first. Try it again from memory, and then check the measurements against a real person."

△ "The seated figure shows how two heads have been 'lost' from the height; the space from hips to knees has become foreshortened. Again, check this against the real thing."

△ "The crouching figure is more complicated, as the top half is also foreshortened as it leans toward you. The legs are foreshortened differently. Can you see how?"

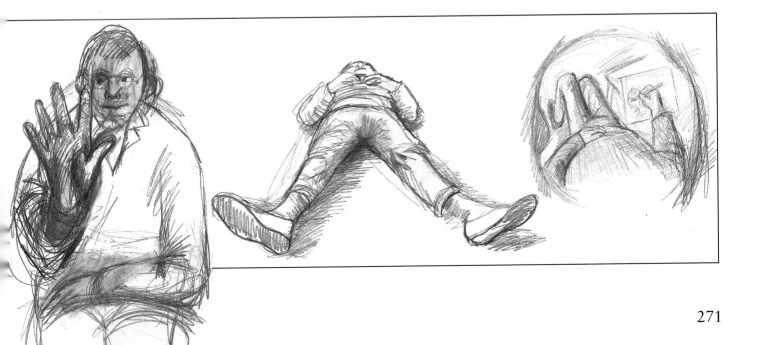

THE MILKY WAY

It is important for an astronomer to know what lies both in and outside our galaxy. Although the stars in the sky seem to be so far away that they are separate from us, the sun and almost all of the stars that we can see actually belong to a single star system called the Milky Way galaxy. The Milky Way contains about 300 trillion stars mingled with clouds of gas and dust. Its shape is similar to a pair of plates placed rim to rim, forming a flattened disk. If we could see it from above, it would look like a vast spiral of light slowly spinning through space. It is so big that even if we could travel at the speed of light, it would take 100,000 years to cross from one side to the other.

WHAT YOU CAN SEE
In some directions, the sky is dense with stars. This is because we are looking through the disk of stars that make up the Milky Way. In other directions, there are few stars against the black backdrop of space. This is the view out of the galaxy, either above it or below the disk of the Milky Way, where there are fewer visible stars.

The arrow shows a spot chosen at random within the galaxy.

The night sky there would appear like this.

HOW TO SEE IT

The Milky Way forms a hazy band of light across the sky. In the northern sky, it passes through Auriga, Cassiopeia, and Cygnus. In the southern sky, it passes through Vela, Crux, and Sagittarius. It shows up at its best on a cloudless, moonless night, away from city lights.

THE GALAXY'S CENTER

The center of the galaxy is 30,000 light years away in the direction of the constellation Sagittarius. It appears as a dense group of stars in the photo below.

WHERE WE ARE

The solar system (see box below) is situated in one of the spiral arms of the galaxy about two-thirds of the way out from the center. As you can see in this side view, most of the stars lie within the disk shape.

Our solar system

CENTER OF GALAXY

273

Underwater HUNTS

Many people dream of finding sunken treasure...but few have succeeded. Time, money, and equipment are needed to do so. However, finding treasure has been made much easier with modern technology. Once treasure is found, it is possible to go back to an exact spot in the sea using a Global Positioning System. This takes readings from satellites in space and is accurate to within a few yards.

Not all treasure is made of gold – 24,000 valuable plates were raised from a wreck called the *Diana* in 1994. The ship sank near Singapore in 1817 in only 106 feet (32 m) of water, but was quickly buried in sand.

RAISING THE PAST
The flagship of King Henry VIII of England, the Mary Rose, *was raised from the English seabed in 1982. It sank in 1545, and has told historians a lot about life in Tudor times. It was pulled up by the* Tor Mog, *the biggest lifting barge in existence.*

Liquid riches
Oil is known as the sea's "black gold." Countries like Saudi Arabia and Brunei have become rich by collecting oil from beneath their seas. Most oil rigs can work only in less than 660 feet (200 m) of water. Now special drilling ships are finding oil in much deeper places. Computers keep the ship in the right spot while it drills through the seabed.

SEARCHING FOR WRECKS

Many wrecks are found by sonar equipment (left). Waves of sound are sent to the seabed. When they bounce back, the pattern they make shows up lumps and bumps.

What is the oldest shipwreck?
The oldest known wreck dates from the 14th century B.C., and still lies off the coast of Turkey.
Do the oceans contain any other natural treasures?
Sea water contains tiny amounts of gold, but not enough to be extracted (unfortunately!). Other valuable elements, such as magnesium and bromine, can be taken from the water.

A TERRIBLE DISASTER

In 1912, the biggest ocean liner ever, the Titanic, collided with an iceberg. Over 1,500 people died as the ship sank to the seabed, 2.4 miles (4 km) below. It was found in 1985 (below), using hi-tech equipment. Submersibles have since taken scientists to see the sad remains.

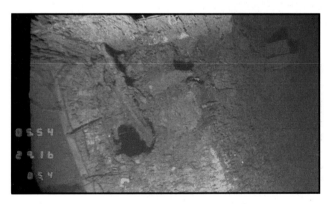

TREASURE!

In 1994, salvage expert Bob Hudson raised a haul of silver coins using a remote-controlled grab. They came from the John Barry, a ship sunk by a torpedo in the Arabian Sea in 1944. Other recent finds have included gold bars and valuable pottery.

NATURE'S GIFTS

Manganese nodules are found on the seabed below about 2.5 miles (4 km). They contain valuable metals such as copper and nickel and take millions of years to form. Specialized mining systems are being developed to collect them.

COWBOYS AND INDIANS

Cowboy hostility toward Native Americans – popularly known in the movies as Indians – is another myth of the Wild West. The myth arose because many of the best stories set good against evil, and cowboy films were no exception. The heroes were the cowboys. Searching for villains, film directors and organizers of Wild West shows often selected Indians because their appearance and tactics were good entertainment. The truth was quite different. America's westward expansion was marked by frequent fighting between immigrant and Native Americans, but cowboys were rarely involved.

The Indian Wars that began in 1864 were generally fought between Native groups and the U.S. Army. Real cowboys had little reason to dislike the Indians. In fact, many cowboys *were* Native Americans. Excellent horsemanship, good local knowledge and the ability to survive in tough conditions made them ideal cattlemen. No drover taking cattle through Indian territory wanted to make his difficult job still harder by stirring up trouble with the local people.

CUSTER'S LAST STAND

No Native group resented the arrival of the White Man into its territory more than the Sioux. Things came to a head in 1874, when gold was discovered on Sioux territory in Dakota. Miners came in the thousands, ignoring the rights of the locals. The Sioux attacked, destroying the settlers' camps. One of the U.S. army officers given the task of settling the disturbance was Colonel George Armstrong Custer. On June 25 1876, Custer led his troop of 215 men right into a Sioux ambush. They were wiped out in under an hour (*above*).

WHITEWASH. Another cowboy myth is that all cattlemen were descended from white Europeans. Mexicans and Native and African Americans all joined the cowboy ranks, and the cowboy language was not English but Spanish. Almost one in seven cowboys was black. Nat Love, for example, won many rodeo competitions for his skill with the rope and revolver. John Ware, another African American cowboy, had the reputation of being the best bronco tamer in the West.

Indian Territory
Anyone taking cattle across an Indian reservation had to pay them a dollar per head of cattle. The trail boss often employed Native Americans (left) to negotiate the fee.

Friendly Trade
Real-life cowboys much preferred talking with Native Americans to fighting them. While on the trail, they often depended on Indian traders for fresh food and other essential supplies (above).

THE LONE RANGER was one of the most popular TV cowboys of the 1950s. The masked figure on a white horse helped folk in their fight against lawlessness. He was accompanied by an Indian, Tonto. The white hero and his loyal Native American servant was typical of the way Hollywood depicted the Native Americans. It helped perpetuate the lie of white supremacy so resented by non-white Americans.

Spiders

Spiders are arachnids a large group of arthropods, or animals with segmented bodies and jointed appendages, that live on land. Arachnids, like all arthropods, have an external skeleton. Spiders have eight legs, several eyes (which see very little), and they can produce silk from glands in their abdomen. Spiders use this silk in many ways, but mainly to trap their prey – insects and other small invertebrates.

Spiders also use camouflage to catch their prey. The dull colors of many garden spiders, and their stillness, allow them to trap unwary victims. The *Myrmecium* spider even looks so much like the ants on which it feeds, that it can live in the nest.

Crab spiders are adapted to the flowers they live on.

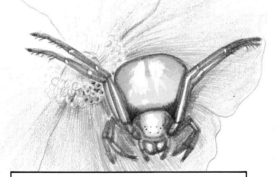

Myrmecium spiders wave their front pair of legs about to look like an insect's antennae. They fool their prey and so can get close enough to attack them.

Ant-mimic spider

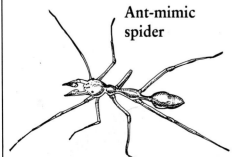

278

GEARS

Today's cyclists have a much easier time than the men and women who rode the very first bicycles over 100 years ago. The draisienne was a popular bicycle in 1820 – but it was a heavy thing without pedals; you had to free-wheel along, like you would on a scooter! About 1885, J.K. Starley produced the first commercially successful safety bicycle with pedals that used a chain to drive the rear wheel, leaving the front wheel free for steering. The bicycle continued to improve, and today modern machines make climbing steep hills and traveling at high speeds possible by the clever use of special, toothed wheels, called gears.

BRIGHT IDEAS

☀ Turn your bicycle upside down and turn the pedals slowly to make the wheels turn. Be careful not to trap your fingers. By pushing a piece of paper into the spokes when the wheel is still, you will be able to count how many times the wheel turns for each full turn of the pedals. In which gear is it easiest to go fast?

6. When both feet are attached to the bike, one leg should be up when the other is down. The left foot should be fixed to the keyhole shaped cam, not directly to the pedal wheel. The front wheel can also be fixed with a fastener.

6

PEDAL POWER

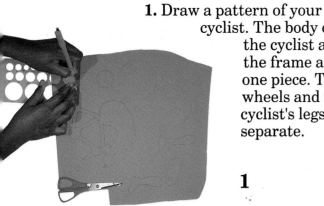

1. Draw a pattern of your cyclist. The body of the cyclist and the frame are one piece. The wheels and the cyclist's legs are separate.

1

2. Paint your pieces realistically. The back wheel is made up of 3 separate disks of thick cardboard, held with a paper fastener. The smallest 2 are your gear wheels.

2

WHY IT WORKS

As we turn the pedals on a bike, the large pedal gear turns the smaller gear wheel on the back wheel by means of the chain. In the bottom picture, if the pedal gear has 50 teeth and the rear gear has 10 teeth then the wheel will turn five times for every turn of the pedals. This is called a high gear and would be best for going fast on flat ground. In the top picture, if the rear gear also has 50 teeth, it will only turn once for every turn of the pedals. This is a low gear and would be good for climbing hills.

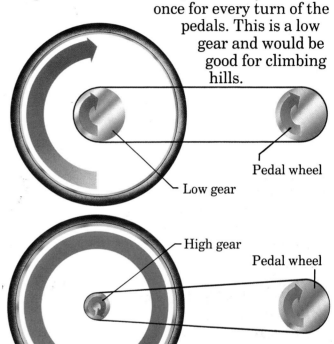

Pedal wheel

Low gear

High gear

Pedal wheel

3

3. Join the legs of the cyclist at the knee and the hip. Cut out a thick piece of cardboard, 1in across. It should be thick enough to support a rubber band. The cyclist's foot will pedal this around.

5

4.

4. Attach the disk to the bike with a piece of stick, so it turns. A small cam (the blue keyhole shape) is attached to the straw on the other side, and then to the other foot with a fastener.

5. Attach a rubber band from the back wheel to the pedal wheel. As the back wheel turns, the cyclist's legs will begin to pedal. If the rubber band is moved to the smaller gear, the cyclist will pedal faster.

PERCUSSION INSTRUMENTS

The percussion section is a very important part of any band or orchestra. It is helpful in creating the complete musical sound desired, by providing the beat and aiding with the rhythm of a musical piece. Some common percussion instruments are the bass and snare drums, cymbals, the triangle, and the tambourine. A percussion instrument can be an exciting accompaniment to any woodwind, string, keyboard, and/or brass instrument.

Japanese bamboo flute

Percussion instruments produce sound when they are hit, scraped or shaken with the correct amount of force.

Wind instruments make a sound when air is blown into them. Woodwind instruments have holes which can be covered to change notes.

Chinese mandoline

Chinese wind gong

Junk orchestra

Even if you do not have access to many instruments, it is still possible to make your own band with things you find around the home. Invite some friends over and look around for materials you can use to make music. Be creative!

Stick tacks into a wood block at lengths as shown. Stretch rubber bands between pairs of tacks and pluck away.

Turn some empty cans bottom up and hit them with something that serves as a drumstick.

Bind two lids from jars together with tape to make your own castanets.

Counting time

Music is a sequence of melodic sounds built around a rhythm, or pattern of beats. In a piece of music, the rhythms are organized into groups of beats, called bars. Musical notes have different values which stand for varying lengths of time.

o Whole note

♩ Quarter note

♩ Half note

♪ Eighth note

These values are given below. The notes in each bar of 4/4 time (below) add up to the value of four quarter notes. Try writing some more bars of four beats using the notes provided.

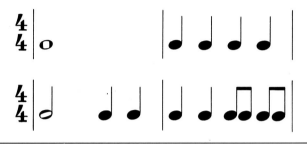

In a brass instrument, musicians vibrate their lips to make the air in the pipes move. The notes are changed by altering the length of the pipe.

Trumpet

Stringed instruments contain stretched strings which are plucked or scraped to produce musical notes. Shorter strings, tighter strings, or lighter strings have a higher pitch.

Keyboard instruments have a series of keys which activate small hammers to strike or pluck the strings. Pipe organ keys activate columns of air.

Piano

The story so far...

We can roughly date the beginnings of the musical styles we listen to today. Some folk music dates back hundreds of years. Classical music began during the 18th century and jazz sprung out of the American South in the early 1900's with blues developing from spirituals around the same time. Rock music dates from the 1950's, with its offspring soul arising in the 1960's. Reggae developed in the West Indies during the 1970's, and in the 1980's rap became popular worldwide. Popular music often influences dance styles.

Jazz

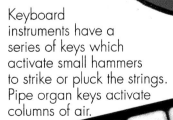

283

HOW A TREE GROWS

Each year a tree grows thicker, taller, and in some cases, bushier. Its girth increases as a new layer of wood is added to its trunk. This makes the trunk stronger so that it can support the weight of new branches. These grow longer as cells at the branch tips multiply. The tree's roots spread further underground to anchor the tree firmly. The tree also grows new leaves.

Cambium
The cambium produces a new ring of sapwood each year. It makes the trunk and branches thicker and stronger.

Sapwood
Sapwood is made mainly of living cells. It contains tiny tubes that carry water and sap around the tree.

SCOTS PINE

Heartwood
Heartwood is the hard, darker colored dead wood in the middle of the trunk. It supports the tree.

A tree's main areas of growth are at the tips of its branches, around its trunk, and at its root tips. Deciduous trees grow new leaves every year. Evergreen trees may replace their leaves or needles gradually every two or three years.

Tree records
The tallest tree species on Earth is the redwood of California. It has been known for a redwood to grow to 370 feet (113 m) tall. The fastest growing tree is the acacia tree of Malaysia, which can grow 36 feet (11 m) in three months. A bristlecone pine in California is the oldest tree – 4,600 years old.

Acacia

Redwood

1939
On September 3, World War II breaks out after Hitler's Germany invades Poland.

1969
American astronaut Neil Armstrong becomes the first man to step on the moon.

1885
Two German inventors, Daimler and Benz, pioneer the automobile.

1990
What important events happened during this year?

Annual growth rings

Each year, the layer of cambium inside the tree's trunk produces a ring of new wood. This pushes the cambium outward and makes the trunk thicker. These annual rings can be counted to find out how old a tree is. They are also a record of past weather conditions. Wide rings grow in years with plenty of rain. In dry years, the rings are narrow and close together.

There are no annual rings inside a palm tree trunk. Palm trunks contain a mass of unorganized fibers. They do not contain cambium to make new wood, so the trunk never gets wider, only taller.

Rays
Rays carry food and water sideways through the sapwood.

Making a bonsai tree

Bonsais are dwarf trees that are planted in Japanese and Chinese ornamental gardens. Although real bonsais are skillfully sculpted, you can use this shortcut to make your own. You will need to get a dwarf conifer, a shallow tray, compost, scissors, wire, and clippers. Trim the roots of the tree. Then wind wire around the roots to restrict root growth. Plant the tree in the tray and trim the branches to the shape you want. Ensure the tree gets water and light.

3 Snip out branches

2 Bind the root ball with wire

1 Trim the roots

285

CLOUDS

Clouds are made up of millions of droplets of water or ice, which are so small and light they can float in the air. Clouds form when warm air rises. This happens when air is heated by the Sun or if it has to rise up over mountains or when cold air pushes it up from underneath. High in the sky, invisible water vapor in the air cools and turns into droplets of liquid water which gather together to make clouds. The shape, color, and height of clouds helps people to predict changes in the weather. Fog or mist are clouds that form down at ground level.

Cold front

Warm front

Cold air pushes warm air up.

Warm air slides up over cold air.

cumulonimbus – storm clouds. May rise to great heights while the bases are near the ground.

Warm and cold fronts

Clouds often form where warm air meets cold air – this is called a weather front. The cold air may push up under the warm air, forcing it to rise rapidly. This is a cold front. The passing of the front brings colder weather behind. Or the warm air may slide slowly up over the cold air, forming a warm front. Warmer weather would follow this front. In both warm and cold fronts, warm air rises, cools and may form clouds. A weather front is a sign of change in the weather, with rain and sometimes storms as a result.

cumulus – heaped-up piles of fair-weather clouds.

Heavens above

If someone asked you where heaven is, you'd probably point upward toward the sky. Throughout history, heaven has been portrayed as a spiritual place above the clouds. This illustration by Gustave Dore (1832-1883) depicts a typical heavenly scene with winged angels supported by cotton- wool clouds. Films too, such as *Matter of Life and Death* (1946) show heaven as a timeless place with expansive floors of cloud.

cirrus – high ice clouds, often first to form along a weather front.

altocumulus – sometimes referred to as a mackerel sky – sign of unsettled weather to come.

stratocumulus - not as even in thickness as a stratus.

Clouds in my coffee

When you look at the clouds, do they make you feel dreamy or sad or happy or hopeful? Clouds are quite often used to convey emotions in poetry and songs. Listen to the lyrics (words) of songs. How many can you think of that mention clouds, storms, or rain?

stratus – rain or drizzle blanket clouds

Recycling the clouds

One of the ways clouds form is when the Sun heats water on the surface of the Earth. Some of the liquid water turns to water vapor and is absorbed into the air. This change from liquid water to water vapor is called evaporation. As the warm air, which is now full of moisture, rises up into the sky, it cools down. This makes the moisture turn back, or condense, into liquid water again, forming clouds. This is called the water cycle.

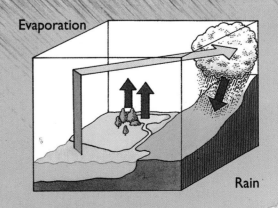

Evaporation

Rain

DINOSAUR HABITATS

A great deal is known about the lands in which the dinosaurs lived. Dinosaur fossils are found in rocks, and these rocks can give us some idea of what their world was like: how hot it was, whether it rained or not, how far the land was from the sea, what the plants were like, and what other kinds of animals lived at the same time. These clues come from the study of the *geology* of dinosaur sites; that is, everything that can be learned from the rocks. A geologist who finds fossil mud cracks near a dinosaur skeleton will know that there must once have been pools of water drying out. If a geologist finds some fossil leaves or small shells or fish mixed up with the dinosaur bones, these plants and animals must have been living at the same time, perhaps in a pond where the dinosaur died while drinking.

How fossils formed

Fossils are the remains of plants or animals that once lived on the earth. Dinosaur fossils are usually odd bones or whole skeletons. After a dinosaur dies (1), the flesh rots or is eaten away. Only the hard bones are left, and mud and sand may be washed around the skeleton, covering it over. Then, after millions of years, the mud and sand may turn into rock, and the spaces in the bone become filled with heavy minerals (2). Later, the fossil bones may be found buried deep in the rock or exposed at the surface.

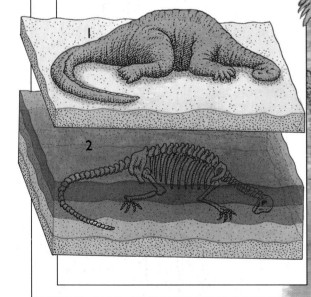

Continental drift

The continents have not always been where they are now. In fact, all of the continents were joined together during the Age of Dinosaurs. This meant that plants and animals could move all over their world without having to cross great oceans. It was about 100 million years ago that the Atlantic Ocean began to open up.

Present-day

100 million years ago

200 million years ago

50 million years ago

The Jurassic period was a time of high rainfall and lush, tropical conditions. Plant groups of all kinds spread, and huge forests of conifers were established. This climate and vegetation were favorable to dinosaurs, and it was during this time that the gigantic sauropods first appeared.

Collecting fossils

Everyone can collect fossils. Find out from your local museum or library where your nearest fossil sites are. These may be coastlines where there are rocks on the beach, or old quarries. Fossils are found in sandstone, mudstone, or limestone. Be sure to check whether you may go on to the land. Also, take grown-ups with you, since many old quarries and cliffs are very dangerous.

BUFFALO BILL

William Frederick Cody (1846–1917) did more than any other individual to create the fiction of the exciting "Wild West." Born in Iowa, he had first-hand knowledge of the West, having been a pony express rider, buffalo hunter, and scout in the Indian Wars. He had, though, never been a cowboy.

He didn't let this worry him, and when he noticed a growing public interest in the American West in the early 1880s, "Buffalo Bill" decided to cash in. In 1883 he organized Buffalo Bill's Wild West Show (*below*).

The three-hour entertainment was largely myth, but it was what the audiences wanted, and all over America and Europe they flocked to see it. Cowboys and Indians, dressed in spotless costume, enacted battles and hold-ups. Artists gave daring demonstrations of riding, roping, and marksmanship.

Real life stars were taken on, such as Sitting Bull, Calamity Jane, and the sureshot Annie Oakley. The show eventually lost popularity to the movies, and Bill died heavily in debt. But by then the myth of the Wild West was established.

BUFFALO BILL'S INDIANS

Buffalo Bill had fought against the Indians and had great admiration for their courage and skills. But his show demanded colorful villains to set off against his mythical cowboys. Indians fitted the bill perfectly.

However, the image of them that was burned into the audience's mind did the Native American peoples a great injustice.

Dime Novels
In the early 20th century, thousands of simple adventure stories featured the reinvented cowboy, no longer a cattleman but a noble fighter.

BUCK TAYLOR
William Levi "Buck" Taylor (*right*) was the star of the Wild West Show. A real Texas cowboy who worked at Cody's ranch, he was a fine horseman who knew a trick or two with the rope.

Buck set the trend for "authentic" cowboy dress – the Stetson, spurs, checkered shirt, bright neckerchief, jeans, and elaborately tooled boots.

Nice Shooting!
Annie Oakley could slice a card in two with a single bullet. Even more amazing was her ability to shoot through the pips of cards thrown into the air (left). Her life was turned into the musical Annie Get Your Gun.

MISSIE MAKES A HIT
Phoebe Ann Oakley Mozee was born in Ohio in 1860. At fifteen she won her first major shooting contest, and in 1886 she entered Buffalo Bill's Wild West Show as "Little Missie" or "The Peerless Wing and Rifle Shot." Annie was the darling of audiences the world over. She shot cigarettes from her husband's mouth and coins from between his fingers. One trick involved releasing two clay pigeons, leaping on a table, picking up a gun, and shooting them before they hit the ground!

WHAT IF SHARKS STOPPED SWIMMING?

They would sink to the bottom and stay there. Most fish have an inner body part like an adjustable gas bag, called a swim bladder. The fish adjusts the amount of gas in the bladder to float up or down. Sharks and other cartilaginous fish lack swim bladders and can only stay up by swimming, using their rigid fins like a plane's wings.

Sharks cannot pump water over their gills, like other fish. They need to swim to get oxygen from the water into their blood. If they were to stop they would need a current of water to stay alive.

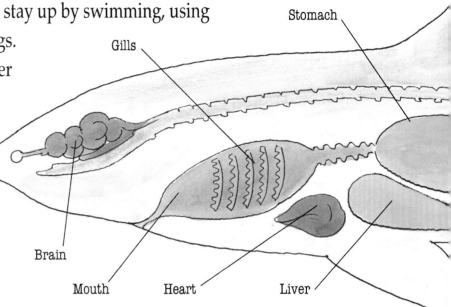

Gills

Stomach

Brain

Mouth

Heart

Liver

Which fish have wings but cannot fly?

Rays and skates are flattened cartilaginous fish. Their bodies have developed into a squashed, wing-shaped form. This is perfect for their bottom-dwelling lifestyle, where they scavenge or eat seabed creatures. While skates have a tail they can use to swim like other fish, a ray cannot swish its body from side to side, so it flaps its wings up and down to "fly" through the water.

The largest ray is the Pacific manta or devilfish. It has a "wingspan" of more than 20 feet (6 m) – about the same as a hang-glider – and weighs almost two tons. Stingrays have a sharp spine sticking out of the tail, which they can jab into enemies to inject terrible stinging poison.

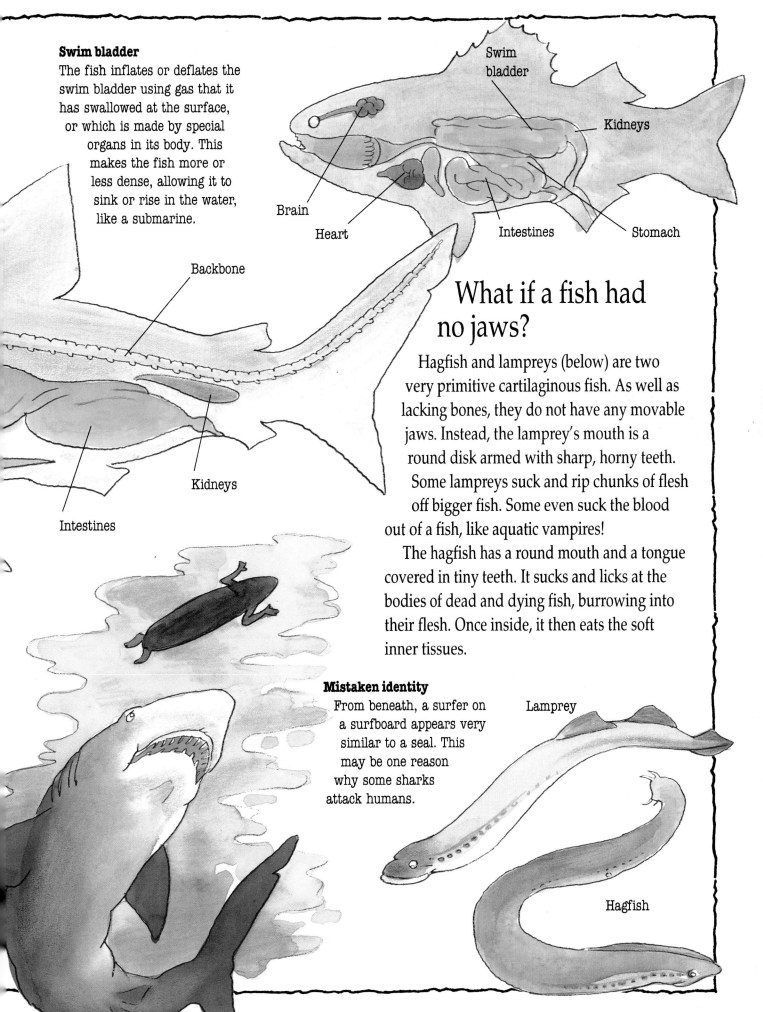

Swim bladder

The fish inflates or deflates the swim bladder using gas that it has swallowed at the surface, or which is made by special organs in its body. This makes the fish more or less dense, allowing it to sink or rise in the water, like a submarine.

Swim bladder

Kidneys

Brain

Heart

Intestines

Stomach

Backbone

Kidneys

Intestines

What if a fish had no jaws?

Hagfish and lampreys (below) are two very primitive cartilaginous fish. As well as lacking bones, they do not have any movable jaws. Instead, the lamprey's mouth is a round disk armed with sharp, horny teeth. Some lampreys suck and rip chunks of flesh off bigger fish. Some even suck the blood out of a fish, like aquatic vampires!

The hagfish has a round mouth and a tongue covered in tiny teeth. It sucks and licks at the bodies of dead and dying fish, burrowing into their flesh. Once inside, it then eats the soft inner tissues.

Mistaken identity

From beneath, a surfer on a surfboard appears very similar to a seal. This may be one reason why some sharks attack humans.

Lamprey

Hagfish

293

ROCKET ENGINE

A rocket is not propelled forwards by the explosive gases rushing from its engine pushing against the surrounding air. For a start, there is no air in space. Three centuries ago the great English scientist Isaac Newton explained it this way: "For every action, there is an equal and opposite reaction." If a shot-putter wearing ice skates throws the shot forward, he moves backward because of the momentum he has created, not because of the shot pushing against the air. Action-and-reaction is the principle of the rocket engine.

A working rocket engine is a "controlled explosion." It burns fuel in an oxidizer (usually oxygen), in a combustion chamber. This creates hot gases under enormous pressure. The gases accelerate out of the back of the chamber. Engineers found that by making a small exit, or throat, from the chamber, the gases accelerate even more, giving extra thrust. They then added a conical nozzle to the throat. This restricts the gases and accelerates them still more, and also helps with guiding the rocket.

Liquid hydrogen tank

The propellant (fuel and oxidizer) tanks are made of specially developed aluminum alloys. They are shaped like giant aerosol cans since they are designed to do the same job – withstand high pressure from within. As the propellants are consumed and the tanks gradually empty, sloshing about of their contents has to be overcome.

THE ENGINE SYSTEMS

The principle of a rocket engine is simple, but there are many practical problems. Engineers have designed various systems to overcome these. In the Space Shuttle main engine, oxygen oxidizer and hydrogen fuel are first pressurized, mixed and preburned, to form hot gases. These gases are then introduced together in an exact mixture in the combustion chamber. The ultracold fuel circulates in a heat-exchanger, to warm itself before preburning and to cool the chamber and nozzle.

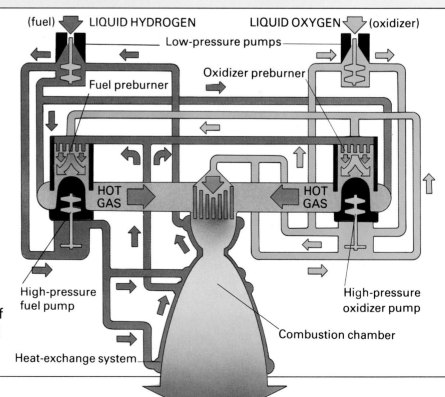

(fuel) LIQUID HYDROGEN   LIQUID OXYGEN (oxidizer)

Low-pressure pumps

Oxidizer preburner

Fuel preburner

HOT GAS   HOT GAS

High-pressure fuel pump

High-pressure oxidizer pump

Combustion chamber

Heat-exchange system

Apollo, the United States' moon program, was launched by the Saturn V rocket. This had a third stage fueled by liquid hydrogen and oxygen. These liquids were fed at high pressure and carefully-controlled rates into the combustion chamber.

Liquid oxygen tank

In this rocket stage, the liquid oxygen tank is contained within the liquid hydrogen tank. The design saves space and weight. Although the liquid oxygen tank is smaller, the weight of its contents is greater than that of liquid hydrogen. A specially adapted Saturn V third stage formed the orbiting space laboratory Skylab in 1973.

Fuel line

Gimbal engine mountings

Oxidizer preburner

Fuel preburner

Heat exchanger

Fuel pump

The engine

The third stage of the Saturn V was powered by one Rocketdyne J-2 engine. This was shielded by a "skirt" until about eight minutes after lift-off, when the second stage separated and fell away. Then the J-2 ignited and burned for about three minutes to take the vehicle into "parking orbit" around the Earth. Several orbits later it fired again for six minutes, to boost the vehicle free of Earth's gravity and towards the mission'

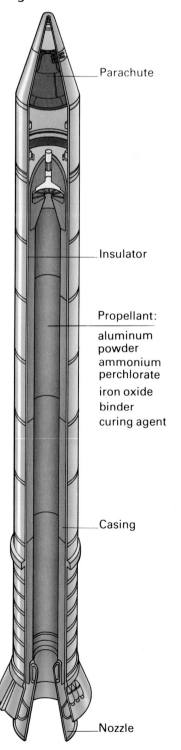

SOLID-FUEL ROCKET

The solid-fuel rocket engine does not burn gunpowder, like a toy firework, but a specially mixed propellant. But once ignited it cannot be turned off. It is used mainly as a booster, strapped to the main engine.

Parachute

Insulator

Propellant:
aluminum powder
ammonium perchlorate
iron oxide
binder
curing agent

Casing

Nozzle

UNDERSTANDING COLOR

Learning about colors is a bit like learning to speak a different language. If the first few pages of this book seem like hard work, think of them as needing to learn a new vocabulary so that you can express yourself with confidence in future.

All colors have three qualities
These qualities are brightness, tone and hue. The brightness or dullness of a color compares with a loud or soft note in music. Tone means how light or dark a color is when compared to another color. A note in music has an equivalent high or low sound. Lastly, each color also has a hue, which is equivalent to the actual note in music. The hue is the actual color you are left with when

Playing scales in color
Brightness, tone and hue are illustrated in the color charts on the right. The top one demonstrates a progression of brightness to dullness, the middle shows light to dark tones, and the bottom one is a progression of the color pink to green in the same tone and brightness, to demonstrate hue. If colors of the same tone and brightness are placed side by side, as shown below, they seem to shimmer and dance together in front of your eyes. It is difficult to get this right, but if you learn to recognize when it *is* right you are beginning to get some real control with color-mixing.

differences in tone and brightness have been removed.

Seeing hue

The idea of this project is to make a picture in which all the colors are the same tone and as much as possible the same brightness. What you will then see is their hue. Choose some colors; experiment with mixing them and painting them in simple patches. The patches below have been made into buildings. First mix your colors. Look at them on the palette and change them around until they are all the same tone before you start painting. Use black to darken or quiet colors if they look too light or too bright. Try to keep the colors clean and flat.

◁ *"To keep colors on separate brushes clean, I stand the brushes bristles up in a can with holes punched in the lid. Alternatively, you could use a container filled with scrunched-up chicken wire."*

Black is introduced here as a way of making colors darker in tone and less bright. It can also be used as a color in its own right. Like white, it may appear to be affected by colors that surround it. Sometimes painters use lines of black to separate the colors in their pictures, as panes of colored glass are separated. This can have the effect of bringing order to a chaotic image.

Changing Views of
THE UNIVERSE

The first challenge to Ptolemy's Earth-centered universe came from Nicolaus Copernicus, in 1543. He realized that the movement of the planets was explained more easily if the Sun, not the Earth, lay at the center. But he did not dare publish his theories until the year of his death. Like Ptolemy, he believed that the planets moved in circles, but Johannes Kepler (1571-1630) showed that their orbits were elliptical (oval-shaped). To explain this, Isaac Newton (1643-1727) discovered the laws of gravity (the force which attracts objects toward each other). In the twentieth century, Albert Einstein's theories linked gravity, space, and time to explain the shape of the universe.

How big is the universe? The universe is so big that light, which travels at 186,000 miles (300,000 km) per second, would take billions of years to reach us from its furthest edges.

REDRAWING THE UNIVERSE
Copernicus did not support Ptolemy's idea that all the stars circled the Earth once a day. He also realized that it could not explain all the movements of the Sun, Moon, and planets. His own theory declared the Earth an ordinary planet instead of the center of the universe.

THE PULL OF THE EARTH
Isaac Newton's theory of gravity applies equally to an apple falling from a tree and to the movement of the planets. He said that all objects are pulled together by a force based on their mass (the matter they contain) and their distance apart. This is why planets' orbits are elliptical.

EARLY OBSERVATIONS

Galileo used his telescope to confirm that Copernicus had been right to put the Sun at the center of the universe. The telescope was invented in 1608 by a Dutch

eyeglass-maker, Hans Lippershey, who called it a "looker." He found that two lenses in a tube could magnify distant objects. When Galileo heard of this, he quickly built his own telescope, which he used to make many amazing discoveries.

SEEING INTO SPACE

Tycho Brahe (1546–1601) was a Danish astronomer who built an observatory and kept precise records of the stars and planets.

His assistant, Johannes Kepler (1571–1630), later used these records to show that the planets moved in elliptical (oval-shaped) orbits, rather than in circles.

A MODERN GENIUS

Albert Einstein (1879–1955) was one of the greatest physicists of the twentieth century. His theory combines space and time so that objects are given a position in time as well as in space. Gravity works by bending this space-time, making objects follow a curved path.

Fact or fiction?

Some of the most fantastic predictions of science fiction have come true. But so far we have not met aliens, or discovered a "warp drive" to travel at the speed of light. If Einstein was right, such speeds are impossible, so most of the universe will always be out of our reach.

OUR ENVIRONMENT

A picture of the earth taken from space (photo left) shows land and sea, and swirling clouds. It gives clues about the climate on different parts of the earth, which in turn determines the different habitats below. The temperature and the amount of rain affect what kind of plants will grow. If the right balance of sunlight, warmth, and moisture exists, plants will grow. Where rainfall is high and temperatures constant, as around the equator, great rainforests grow. Where it is too dry for trees, grasslands may still thrive. If it is very dry, as in the desert, little grows.

About 11 percent of the earth's land can be cultivated. By the year 2000 about half of this land will be farmed.

The natural habitats of the world are very varied. Some, like the rainforests, have been destroyed by humans. In other cases, humans have altered landscapes and created artificial habitats which have much in common with natural habitats.

About two fifths of the land should be forest, but much has been cut down.

Farmland now takes up much of the world's grassland.

The oceans cover nearly three quarters of the world.

Grassland is the natural vegetation of about one fifth of the land.

Artificial pond

Deserts are harsh environments where few plants and animals have adapted to survive.

Rivers and lakes provide freshwater habitats.

Conifers grow high on mountain slopes. Mountain tops are cold. Little grows in their arctic conditions.

To wildlife, a city is like a desert.

Garden

Some gardens are like woodland edges.

People have exploited Africa's vast grasslands, or savannas. They are now a shrinking wildlife habitat.

ANCIENT GREEK LAW

By 700 B.C., Greece was divided into small, independent city states. Greek society was made up of citizens (men who were born in the city state) and non-citizens (women, foreigners, and slaves). Most city states were governed by an oligarchy – a small group of rich noblemen, called aristocrats. Resentment of their power led to revolts. Tyrants, or absolute rulers, were then appointed to restore order. In 508 B.C., however, a different system called democracy (*demos* = people; *kratos* = rule) was introduced in Athens. It gave all male citizens a say in the government. Other city states soon followed Athens' lead.

A woman's place
In Ancient Greece, women were thought of as non-citizens. Their lives were controlled by men – first their fathers, then their husbands. They could not inherit or own property, or take part in the running of the city. Greek women usually got married when they were about 15. The marriage was arranged and the husband was often much older than his bride. A woman's role in life was to look after the household, spin and weave cloth and raise the children. Spartan women had more freedom and were encouraged to take exercise so that they would have healthy, strong babies. This was frowned on by other Greek societies.

Slaves
Slaves were used as servants or laborers. Some were prisoners of war; others were bought and sold in slave markets. They had no legal rights.

Metics
Metics were people born outside the city state. They were free men, not slaves, and many were very wealthy.

Greek *gymnasia*
A *gymnasium* was a center for sport and learning. Apart from training facilities, there might also be a lecture hall. In the 4th century B.C., the philosopher Plato and his brilliant pupil, Aristotle, taught in the *gymnasia* throughout Athens. Each eventually founded his own school, which both became very famous.

Aristotle

Jury service

There were no lawyers or judges in Ancient Greece. Citizens conducted their own legal cases and trial was by a jury of about 200 citizens. A *kleroteria* used colored balls to pick the jury for the day. Each juror was given two bronze tokens — one for a "guilty" verdict, one for an "innocent" verdict.

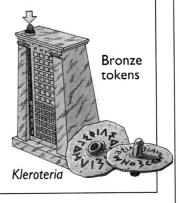

Bronze tokens

Kleroteria

Citizens

Citizens were the most privileged social class in Ancient Greece. Only citizens could take part in the government of their city state, own land, or speak in a law court. Citizens were also expected to serve in the army.

Changing fashions

Greek fashion changed over the years, although the basic dress for men and women remained a *chiton* (tunic), *himation* (cloak), and leather sandals. There were two basic styles of women's dress. The Doric chiton was wrapped around the body, while the Ionic chiton fastened at intervals across the shoulders. Hair styles also changed. Curly hair (below right) was the fashion during the Hellenistic Period.

An Ionic chiton

Education

In Athens, there were three types of schooling. A teacher called a *grammatistes* taught reading, writing, and arithmetic; a *kitharistes* taught music and poetry; a *paidotribes* taught athletics. A slave called a *paidagogos* was sometimes hired to supervise a boy's education. However, it was only the sons of wealthier citizens who could afford a higher education. Girls were taught domestic duties at home by their mothers.

303

POISONOUS SNAKES

There are nearly 2,400 species of snakes around the world. But only about one-sixth of these have venom (poison) strong enough to harm other creatures. Only a few dozen have venom powerful enough to seriously harm or kill a person. Poisonous snakes use their venom to paralyze or kill their prey. Occasionally they will bite in self-defense, for example, if a careless person treads on them. Just in case, it is best to treat all snakes with respect, and to take great care when walking in places where snakes live.

COBRA

Venom gland

Fixed front fangs

VIPER

Front fangs hinge forward to strike

Venom

BOOMSLANG

Venom gland

Grooved fangs

Venom and fangs

Snake venom is made in venom glands on either side of the head. The snake injects its venom into the victim when it bites, using its long teeth, called fangs. Back-fanged snakes such as the deadly boomslang and the twig snake have grooved fangs at the rear of the mouth. Cobras, including coral snakes, have fangs at the front. Vipers, including adders, sidewinders and rattlesnakes, have long, hinged fangs that fold back when not in use.

Snake charming

In some parts of the world people "charm" snakes by playing flute music, as the snake sways to and fro, as though dancing or hypnotized. Often poisonous snakes such as cobras are used, though they sometimes have their venom glands or fangs removed. In fact, the snake can hardly hear the flute. It may react to the rocking body of the charmer and to the vibrations from his or her tapping foot.

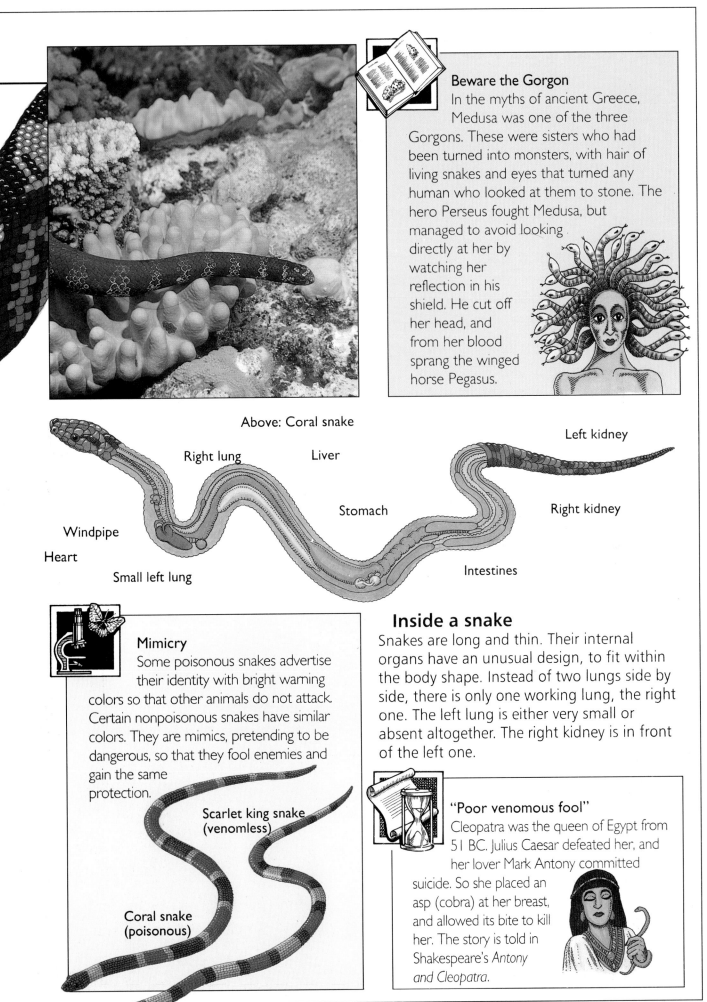

Above: Coral snake

Right lung

Liver

Left kidney

Stomach

Right kidney

Windpipe

Heart

Small left lung

Intestines

Mimicry
Some poisonous snakes advertise their identity with bright warning colors so that other animals do not attack. Certain nonpoisonous snakes have similar colors. They are mimics, pretending to be dangerous, so that they fool enemies and gain the same protection.

Scarlet king snake (venomless)

Coral snake (poisonous)

Inside a snake
Snakes are long and thin. Their internal organs have an unusual design, to fit within the body shape. Instead of two lungs side by side, there is only one working lung, the right one. The left lung is either very small or absent altogether. The right kidney is in front of the left one.

SPORTING TRUCKS

Custom trucks originated in the United States among drivers who owned their trucks. They tried to make their trucks look different from all the others on the road by painting them with startling designs and pictures. Customization may also include replacing some of the standard parts of a truck, such as the exhaust "stack" (a vertical exhaust pipe), and the fuel tank, with highly polished chromium plated parts. The demand for customized trucks is so great in the United States that many manufacturers now supply their trucks in a range of different color schemes. These serve as a starting point for the owner's unique "paint job."

Articulated truck tractors are mostly used to pull especially heavy loads along public highways at normal speeds, but the powerful tractors without their trailers are capable of traveling at very high speeds. Truck racing is one of the fastest growing motor sports in Europe.

Trucks have also taken part in ordinary car rallies including the annual Paris-Dakar race.

A truck "Superprix" race at the Brands Hatch circuit in England.

Truck racing using truck tractor units started in the United States, and then rapidly spread to Europe. There is now a European Truck Racing Championship. Every year, professional racing teams supported by many of the truck manufacturers compete for the title. The races test the trucks' top speeds and road-holding to the limit. The majority of the drivers still earn their living by driving ordinary trucks on the roads when they are not racing. Truck racing drivers do not yet receive the enormous amounts of money that Formula 1 racing drivers enjoy.

As with motor car racing, many of the improvements in ordinary truck design, engine efficiency and safety are made as a result of experimentation on the race-track.

A "funny car" with outsize wheels.

A Leyland Land train doing a "wheelie" at an exhibition event.

WORKING WITH FABRIC

You don't have to be able to sew or knit to enjoy the rich world of cloth. Fabrics open up an entirely new range of possibilities, enabling you to achieve effects you can't get any other way.

Many textures

Most households have a bag of cloth scraps tucked away. Collect as many different kinds of fabric as you can. Silk, corduroy, velvet, burlap, muslin – each material has its own unique character, a particular color, weave, texture and pattern.

▽ *"The odds and ends I collected suggested the crazy face and clothes of a clown. I chose pink nylon for the face and a background of cotton twill, and began by laying down these basic ingredients."*

Buttons, sequins, lace, yarn, and felt can all be brought in. You will also need a pair of sharp scissors, strong glue, pins or staples, and thick cardboard or cork to use as a base.

What do your scraps suggest?

Study your fragments and see what they remind you of. You could try a head like the one opposite, or an animal, landscape, or abstract pattern. Work as you have with paper, experimenting with your fragments in different positions before sticking or stapling them down.

▽ *"I chose shiny red cotton for the clown's nose, and small cotton patchwork squares for his jacket. I tried strands of yarn for the hair, but finally opted for a coarse tweed material."*

REFLECTION

When light rays hit a surface, they bounce off again, like a ball bouncing off a wall. This is called reflection. The way light behaves when it hits a reflective surface is used by people and animals to see more clearly. Cats have eyes designed to reflect as much light as possible, because they need to see in the dark. Inside high-quality periscopes on board submarines, prisms (blocks of glass) are used to bend beams of light around corners, making objects at the surface visible. Light can be made to reflect off a surface. Mirrors can also be used inside a periscope.
Make your own periscope and let nothing spoil your view!

UP PERISCOPE!

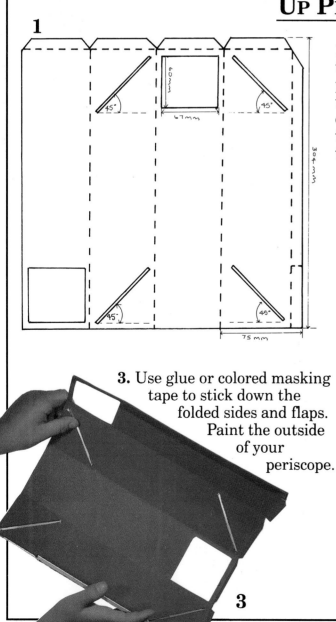

1. Use a ruler and pencil to measure and draw a plan of your periscope like the one shown here. Cut out the two windows and the four slits. Fold along the dotted lines.

2. Take two flat mirrors of the same size and put masking tape around the edges. These should be slightly wider than the periscope.

4. Slide the mirrors into the slits so that the reflecting faces are opposite each other. The edges of the mirrors will protrude from the periscope case. Make sure that they are secure. If they are not, they may slide out and break.

3. Use glue or colored masking tape to stick down the folded sides and flaps. Paint the outside of your periscope.

WHY IT WORKS

Light is reflected at the same angle as it hits an object, but in the opposite direction. The top mirror of the periscope is positioned to reflect light from the object downward to the other mirror. The bottom mirror is at the same angle as the top one and reflects the beam out of the periscope and into the eye.

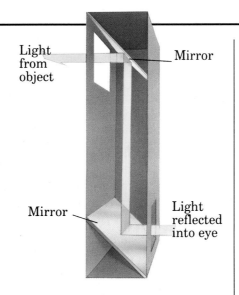

Light from object

Mirror

Mirror

Light reflected into eye

5. Use your periscope to view over an obstruction such as a fence or wall. Look into the bottom mirror to see what is hidden there. Notice what happens when you hold the periscope sideways. Try to look around corners as well.

BRIGHT IDEAS

☼ With three mirrors arranged in a triangular pattern, you can make a kaleidoscope. Cover one end with tracing paper and the other with cardboard. Make a hole in the oak tag to see through, and drop colored paper inside. Point the end toward a light source. Use materials of different colors.

☼ Write a message on paper and look at it in a mirror. You can turn a message into code by standing a mirror vertically above it and copying the image in the mirror. It can only be decoded with another mirror because it is upside down and back to front.

5

THE FIRST TOOLS

Hominids that are thought to have been our direct ancestors are placed in the genus *Homo* – the same group as ourselves. The oldest stone tools for which archaeologists can be certain about the date come from the Omo Valley in southern Ethiopia. They are 2 – 2.2 million years old.

When paleontologists find a fossil skull, they can measure its volume to discover how large the brain was. Looking at fossil skulls from Africa, they find that the brain size gradually increases as time goes by. The first noticeable increase in size comes about 2 million years ago, and the hominids with the larger brains also have slightly flatter, less ape-like faces. They are called *Homo habilis* and it is thought that they were probably the first hominids to make stone tools, because tools began to appear in the fossil record at about the same time.

Finding tools

As the hominids' brain size increased they must have shown their greater intelligence in many different ways. They may have begun to talk, share food, and cooperate more with each other. But changes of this sort do not leave any trace in the fossil record. The main evidence we can find is that they began to make stone tools.

By looking at modern Athapaskan Indians of North America, we find that although stone is important to them, they also make use of wood, animal hide, and other materials that rot away. The tools of *Homo habilis* would have been much more primitive than these, but the point is the same: most of them would not have been preserved.

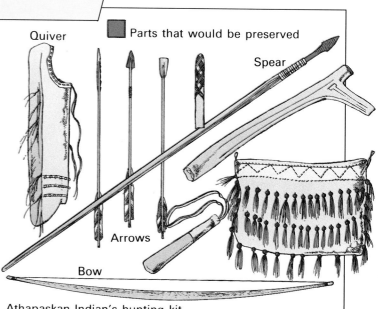

Quiver

Parts that would be preserved

Spear

Arrows

Bow

Athapaskan Indian's hunting kit

How stone tools were made

Making stone tools is not easy, and only certain types of stone will give a good result. By learning to make tools for themselves, modern archaeologists have discovered a great deal about our ancestors' skills. Having first chosen their stone, they struck it with a hammerstone at the correct angle to remove a flake. By removing more and more flakes, a chopper with a long cutting edge, as sharp as a steel knife, could be produced. The flakes themselves had sharp edges and could be held between finger and thumb and used for cutting meat or sharpening a stick.

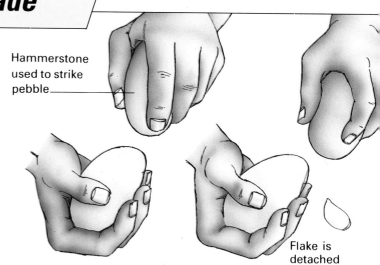

Hammerstone used to strike pebble

Flake is detached

Handyman

Homo habilis means 'handyman' or 'skillful man' and refers to this hominid's ability to make stone tools. The type of stone used for most of the early tools is lava, which does not take a 'polish' in the same way that harder stone such as flint does. So microscope studies cannot reveal what these simple tools were used for. But they are often found together with bones, often those of large animals. At one site in Kenya, stone tools have been found with the remains of a hippopotamus. It seems unlikely that a group of *Homo habilis* hunters could have killed a hippo, so they were probably scavengers rather than hunters. They would have taken meat from animals that were already dead, as vultures do.

A skull of *Homo habilis*, the tool-maker

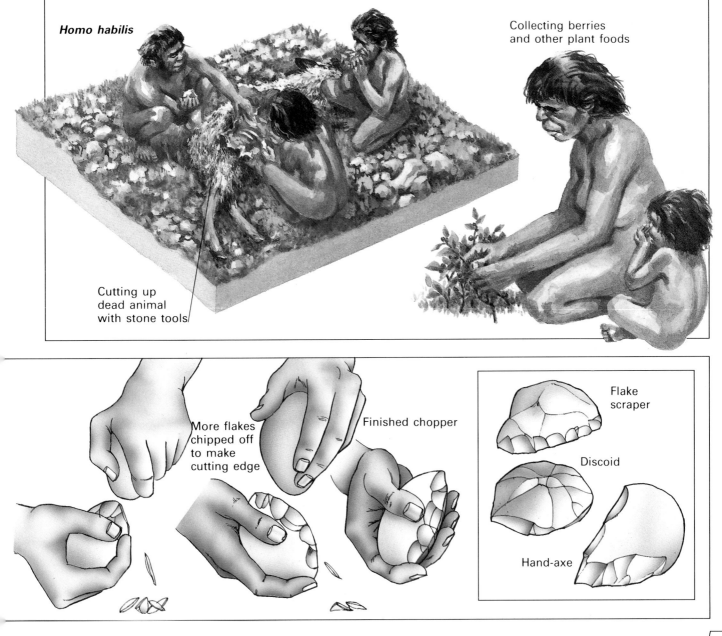

Homo habilis

Cutting up dead animal with stone tools

Collecting berries and other plant foods

More flakes chipped off to make cutting edge

Finished chopper

Flake scraper

Discoid

Hand-axe

THE SALEM WITCH TRIALS

Salem, Massachusetts, 1692. A group of girls aged between 4 and 20 sit around the fire listening to stories of a female slave, Tituba. Two of the girls become hysterical. Shortly afterward, adults complain that the girls have been bewitched.

Arrests are made (*right*) and a trial is held. Of the 150 people accused, 19 people are hanged, one is crushed to death with stones, and two die in prison. Even dogs are executed for witchcraft!

The trials went on until 1693, when local ministers helped to stop the craze. The executions were the last for witchcraft in North America, and also signaled the end of witch trials in Europe as well.

Tumbling Like Hogs (below)
Young girls from Salem on trial for witchcraft. One of the accused was said to have "tumbled about like a hog." No one is quite sure what went on. Some historians think that a local minister, Samuel Paris, used the beliefs of ignorant farmers to accuse villagers who opposed him.

314

PILGRIM FATHERS

The colony of Massachusetts was founded by religious refugees who left England in 1620. Known as the "Pilgrim Fathers" (*below*), many of them possessed a strong puritanical faith. They genuinely believed that the devil might appear at any moment. As an English colony, Massachusetts followed English law, so witchcraft was punishable by death.

Sixteen other witches had already been hanged in the region by 1692.

The Last Witch?
The Swiss woman Anna Goddi, hanged in 1782, was the last person in Europe to be executed for witchcraft.

HOLY MOTION POTION

Evil spirits can be driven from a person or place by exorcism. This is a special religious ceremony that a priest may perform only with a bishop's permission.

In earlier times, people believed evil spirits entered and left people by the body's natural openings. This led to some very odd rituals and experiences! Those possessed by a demon might be given a "holy potion" to drink, made up of oil, herbs, and sherry!

WHAT IF A LEOPARD COULD CHANGE ITS SPOTS?

A leopard's spots are designed to break up its outline and keep it hidden, especially when it's crawling through the long grass, or lying on a tree branch. Many mammals have this type of camouflage – both the hunted and the hunters, including tigers. If these animals were brightly colored, or if they had strange patterns on their fur, they would stand out, and enemies could spot them at once!

Dappled deer

Adult red deer tend to graze in open areas. But baby red deer, called fawns, hide by lying still among ferns or heather, under a bush, or in a thicket. The sunlight shining through the leaves creates light and shadow below. So the fawn's coat has similar light and dark patches to conceal it in the dappled sunlight.

What if a polar bear had no fur coat?

Its naked, pinkish body would show up clearly against the white background of snow and ice. So the polar bear would have trouble trying to sneak up on seals to eat, and it would get very hungry. It would also be extremely cold. This is another job of a mammal's hairy coat – to protect against the cold (or heat, as in the case of a camel). The polar bear's fur coat is extremely thick and warm, as well as extra white. Without it, the bear would quickly freeze to death.

Stop blubbering!

All mammals have a layer of a soft, fatty substance just under the skin, covering the muscles and other inner parts. When this is very thick, it's called *blubber*. It makes the seal's body smooth and sleek, and acts as a store of energy should food ever get scarce.

However, its major role is as a wraparound blanket of fat to help the fur keep out the cold, especially when the animal is swimming in the icy seawater. Some seals can have a layer blubber that is more than 4 in (10 cm) thick.

Fur
Skin
Blubber
Muscle

Skinny seal
A blubberless seal would not only look very thin, it would very quickly freeze to death in the cold seas that it swims through.

What if mammals had spears and armor?

Some do – the porcupine has spines and the armadillo has armor-plating. The porcupine has normal mammal fur and also very thick, sharp-tipped, spearlike hairs growing from the skin. These are quills which are only attached loosely to the skin. The porcupine can flick its tail and throw off the quills into an unwary attacker's face.

The armadillo has a covering of small bone plates embedded in horny skin, with patches of tough skin and hairs between them. The plates hang down over the creature's head, sides, legs, and tail. When threatened, the armadillo can roll up into an armor-plated ball.

CARS FOR EVERYONE

During the early 1900s, most cars became larger, more comfortable – and more costly. In America, however, entrepreneur Henry Ford was working in the other direction. Ford understood that there were only a limited number of rich people. His aim was to build small cars in huge numbers, so that they were cheap enough for the average person to buy. This would allow families to travel by car where they wanted. It was part of the freedom offered by the "American Dream," in which Ford believed so strongly. And the dream came true, with the Model T Ford.

◀ Model T, 1914

Ford production line, 1913

The Model T

Production of the "Tin Lizzie" (so-called because the body was made of thin vanadium steel) began in 1908. The car had a four cylinder, three-liter, 20-horsepower engine, and a top speed of about 40 mph (65 kph). The Model T was designed to be inexpensive and long-lasting.

Production line

Ford claimed that "the way to make automobiles is to make one automobile like another automobile, to make them all alike." At first the Model Ts were made on Ford's new invention, the production line, in his Detroit factory. In 1913 he introduced the moving assembly line, which has since been copied around the world.

Mass motoring

When the Model T ceased production in 1927, more than 15 million had been made. Cheap motoring meant more crowded roads. Without clear road markings and signs, driving was a hazardous business.

HOW MANY TUNES DOES IT PLAY, MISTER?

"How many tunes does it play, mister?"

Cars in country areas were a source of bafflement. This postcard shows how the handcrank could be mistaken for the wind-up mechanism of a barrel organ!

Car versus Horse (1904)

Total cost over five years A pair of horses, including food, stabling, vet's bills :	$4,780
Standard car, cost new:	$1,583
gas and oil:	$760
new set of tires:	$122
wages for boy to clean and maintain:	$633
repairs and spares:	$682
minus resale price:	$487
Total:	$3,293

The cost of cars

Ford set the cost trend with the Model T, and the more that were made, the cheaper they became. A basic version cost $825 when it was introduced, and $260 some years later.

Increasing choice

In the years before World War I, car manufacturers set up in most industrial countries. The home of mass production was America. European makers concentrated on the more expensive models built with hand tools, a development of the skilled tradition in building luxury horse-drawn carriages. Many famous names date from this period.

Peugeot 1905

Fiat 1914

Benz 1907

Mercedes 1914

DRAWING ANIMALS

The variety in the world of nature provides a constant source of wonder and excitement to the artist. From camels to crocodiles, from bats to bulls, animals provide a wonderful opportunity to experiment with lines and mark-making.

The texture of an animal's coat is particularly important. Let your eyes enjoy the softness of cats, the roughness of dogs, the sleekness of horses, and the prickliness of porcupines.

Back to basics
"Treat nature by means of the cylinder, sphere and cone," said the artist Paul Cézanne.

◁ *"In this example you can see how a drawing can 'evolve,' or be built up gradually. The basic shapes develop step by step into a particular horse. At each stage, more detail is added until, finally, the animal has its own special presence. Make your own version of this sequence of drawings all in one go. You might want to put the figure of a rider on the horse's back to make your drawing more interesting."*

▽ *"In the final stages, I added tone to make my horse look more solid and to complete my picture."*

The simple shapes we studied earlier are the basis for animal forms, and can be used to make your drawings look convincing. The drawings on the left show how the figure of a horse evolves from a few basic shapes. Try this out with your own drawing and then try a similar method with other animals. What basic shapes might develop into a cow, a dog or a cat?

Animals don't stay still

What all living creatures have in common is that they move and won't pose for you. As with a moving human figure, however, the combination of photographs, your imagination and, most important, your eyes, can work very well.

Field studies

Don't be afraid to draw from real life whenever possible. Even if your drawing doesn't have a textbook likeness, it may well have a special quality about it. There is nothing so exciting for the artist as confronting the real thing armed only with a pencil and pad. Use a rough sketch book; the less expensive the better, so you will not feel that what you do has to be perfect. Learn to draw quickly and directly, and your pictures will take on a life of their own.

Caught on the hop

Below you can see an example of how an animal moves. When drawing animals in motion, it is important to let your subject draw itself for you. Look at the animal and allow your pencil to follow the forms in front of you without looking at the paper.

Make a sequence of drawings as the animal moves. When it changes position, don't be frustrated. Keep the same drawing going if it is only a slight change. If your subject changes into a different pose entirely, begin another drawing. Return to the previous one when the original pose is taken up again.

BREATHING

Like any living thing, the brain needs oxygen. After a few minutes without oxygen, it would start to fade and die – and we wouldn't want that. Oxygen is an invisible gas that makes up one-fifth of the air around the body. But it cannot seep through the skull bones, straight into the brain. It must first go down the windpipe into the lungs, then into the blood, and finally to the brain.

HIC, PUFF, PANT

Sometimes the smooth in-out movements of breathing are interrupted. Hiccups are uncontrolled in-breaths, usually when the main breathing muscle, the diaphragm, gets stretched by a too-full stomach just below it. When the body is very active, its muscles need more oxygen, so the breathing gets faster and we pant.

TUBE-CLEANING

Tiny hairs, cilia, and slimy mucus line the breathing tubes. The mucus traps dust and germs; the cilia wave to sweep it upward, to be swallowed.

Rib breathing muscles

SPIES ON YOUR INSIDES

Modern X-ray machines can do wondrous things, especially when helped by computers. In the bronchoscopy, the breathing tubes are lined with a special fluid that shows up on the X-ray picture. A computer can color the picture to make it easier to see the details.

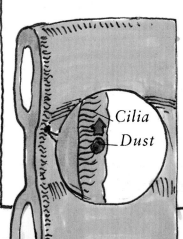

Cilia
Dust

RIBS
These long, springy bones form a protective cage for the delicate heart and lungs. They are hinged so that they move up and down when breathing.

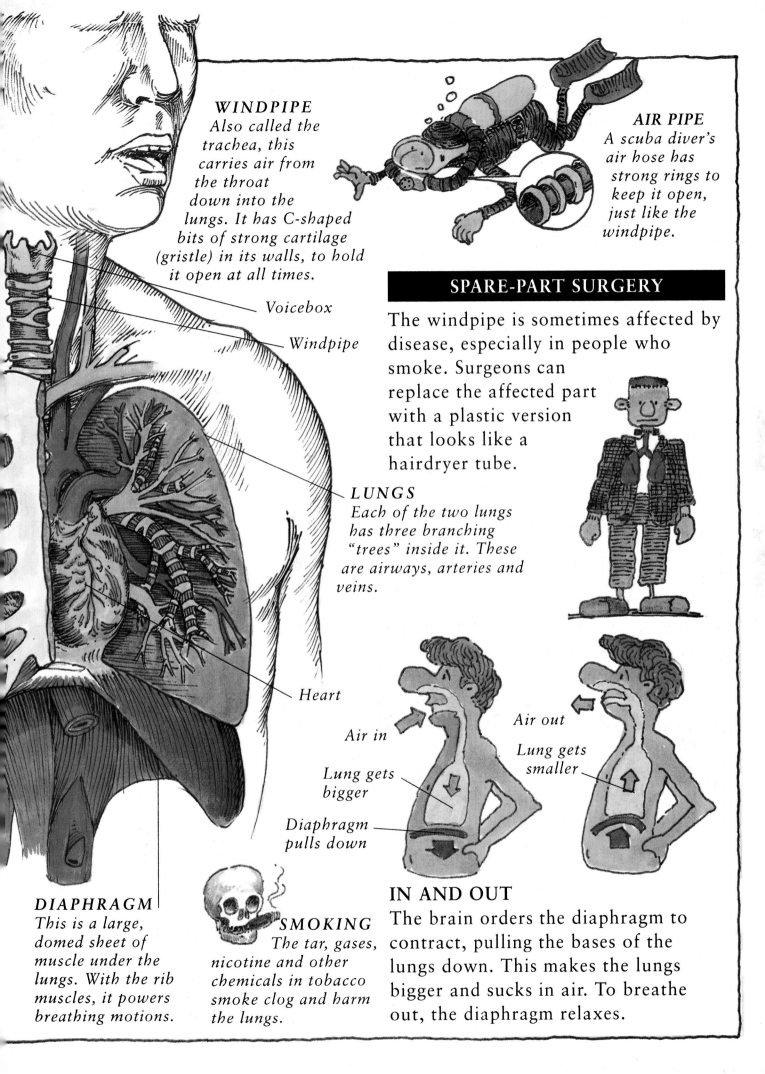

WINDPIPE
Also called the trachea, this carries air from the throat down into the lungs. It has C-shaped bits of strong cartilage (gristle) in its walls, to hold it open at all times.

Voicebox

Windpipe

AIR PIPE
A scuba diver's air hose has strong rings to keep it open, just like the windpipe.

SPARE-PART SURGERY

The windpipe is sometimes affected by disease, especially in people who smoke. Surgeons can replace the affected part with a plastic version that looks like a hairdryer tube.

LUNGS
Each of the two lungs has three branching "trees" inside it. These are airways, arteries and veins.

Heart

Air in

Lung gets bigger

Diaphragm pulls down

Air out

Lung gets smaller

DIAPHRAGM
This is a large, domed sheet of muscle under the lungs. With the rib muscles, it powers breathing motions.

SMOKING
The tar, gases, nicotine and other chemicals in tobacco smoke clog and harm the lungs.

IN AND OUT
The brain orders the diaphragm to contract, pulling the bases of the lungs down. This makes the lungs bigger and sucks in air. To breathe out, the diaphragm relaxes.

WHEN A VOLCANO ERUPTS

Volcanoes are in a sense the safety valves in the earth's crust, releasing the buildup of pressure caused by gases beneath the earth's surface.

The strength of a volcanic eruption depends on the type of magma and the amount of gases trapped in it. The magma formed when plates pull apart is very fluid. The gases in it have time to escape and there is no violent eruption. When plates collide, however, the magma formed is much thicker and stickier. Gases become trapped in it and escape explosively in a huge cloud of steam and dust thousands of feet high.

Surges of red-hot lava flood out of the volcano's crater at speeds of up to 600 ft per second. Lava will flow from the volcano as long as there is enough pressure to force it to the surface. After such violent eruptions, the entire volcano often collapses into its empty magma chamber, forming a steep-sided depression. This is called a caldera.

The explosion
When a volcano erupts, the gases dissolved in the magma are released. If the vent is blocked by a plug of hardened lava, the trapped gases escape with a deafening explosion.

A volcano may be quiet for many years before it erupts again. Often its slopes are covered with grass and trees, like an ordinary mountain. A thin wisp of vapor rising from the crater may be the only sign that it is a still-active volcano.

The buildup
There are often signs that a volcano is going to erupt. The ground starts to shake. The sides of the cone bulge out as magma collects inside it. There is a smell of sulfur as gases escape through cracks in the rocks.

▲ A fountain of molten lava erupts from a fissure on Hawaii's Kilauea volcano in 1983. Molten lava can reach temperatures of over 1,800°F.

▼ A plastic skin often forms over fast-flowing, runny lava. The skin is dragged into picturesque folds by the still-liquid lava running beneath it.

Afterwards

As well as lava and ash, the volcano belches out clouds of steam which condense into water. If there is a lot of steam, it falls as rain and mixes with the ash to form a thick mud. This may pour downhill, burying towns and villages.

ANCIENT EGYPTAIN BURIAL CUSTOMS

The Ancient Egyptians were firm believers in life after death. They went to great lengths to prepare themselves for death, burial, and the life to come. They believed that a dead person's soul traveled into an underworld called Duat. Here it had to pass through many trials and ordeals before it could reach the next world, the Kingdom of the West. There, it could lead a life very like the one it had known in Egypt, but free from trouble. The Ancient Egyptians believed that a person had three souls — the *ka*, the *ba,* and the *akh*. They could only survive in the next world if the body was preserved and not left to rot. This led to bodies being mummified.

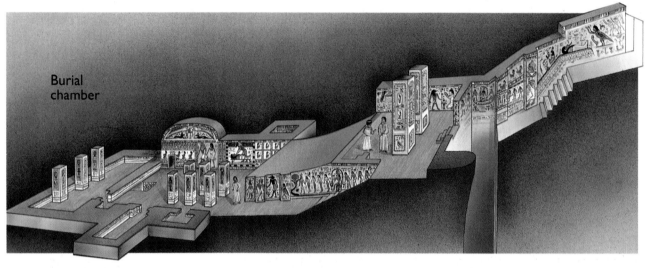

Burial chamber

The tombs of the New Kingdom kings were cut deep into the rocks of a valley at Thebes. They consist of a central tunnel with rooms leading off to the burial chamber (see above). Many Middle Kingdom tombs contain tomb models. Nonroyal tombs from all periods show activities from everyday life, such as grinding corn or plowing the fields. Hundreds of magical statues of servants, called *shabti*, have been found in the tombs of wealthy Egyptians. If Osiris ordered you to work in the fields or do some other menial task in the underworld, you could get the *shabti* to do it for you.

Model of woman grinding corn

The Egyptians filled their tombs with objects which they might need in the afterlife. These included clothes, food and furniture. Tomb walls were painted with scenes from daily life. Osiris, the Ruler of the Dead, was supposed to bring these to life.

Shabti figure of Amenhotep II

Poor burials
Very few Egyptians could afford splendid tombs or grand coffins. Poor people were often buried in simple holes in the hot sand or in a small tomb cut into the ground. However, all Egyptians, whether rich or poor, believed that if they had led a good, virtuous life, Osiris would reward them with a happy eternal life.

Wooden model of a funerary boat

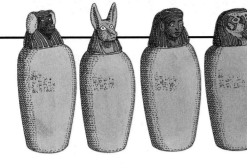

Canopic jars

Mummification

Bodies were mummified to keep them from rotting. The process was so successful that many have survived, remarkably intact, to the present day. There were different degrees of

mummification, depending on how rich a person was. In general, though, the first step was to remove the brain, liver, lungs, and intestines. These were stored in special jars, called canopic jars (shown above). The heart was left in place (see below). Then the body was packed in crystals of natron salt to dry it out. The body was padded with cloth to make it look fleshier, then oiled and wrapped in strips of linen before being placed in its coffin. The process took about 70 days.

Mummified head

Funerary texts

Passages of prayers, spells, and hymns were carved on tomb walls. These were intended to guide the dead person through the afterlife, to protect them from evil and provide for their future needs. The texts were later written down on papyrus scrolls and became known as The Book of the Dead. The texts and spells were often accompanied by colorful illustrations, such as the one shown below.

In the Judgement Hall, the dead person would stand trial before the god, Osiris. The engraving, right, shows Anubis (the figure on the left with the head of a jackal) preparing to weigh the dead person's heart against a feather, the symbol of truth. If he had led a sinful life, his heart would tip the scales and he would be punished. If he had led a good life, his heart and the feather would balance and he could go on to join his ancestors. The verdict is recorded by Thoth, god of wisdom.

RODENTS AND RABBITS

Within the order Rodentia there are 3 main groups: Squirrel group, with kangaroo rats, marmots and beavers (377 species). Porcupine group, with African mole-rats and, from South America, guinea pigs, chinchillas (188). Mouse group, with rats, hamsters and jerboas (over 1,137). The order Lagomorpha includes rabbits, hares and pikas (58 species).

Rodents, a group that includes mice, rats and rabbits, are extremely successful mammals, found in nearly all habitats except the sea. Most live on the ground, although there are many – such as squirrels – that are good at climbing or living in trees. Others, like beavers and some voles, live in and around fresh water. Many use burrows for shelters and homes, but mole-rats and other species are adapted to a life burrowing underground and almost never come to the surface. The secrets of their success include their feeding methods and their ability to reproduce fast. Hares, rabbits and the similar pikas share some of the same adaptations but are not so varied.

Teeth and jaws

Rodents have a pair of large incisor teeth at the top and bottom of the front of the mouth. These grow continuously, and are used for gnawing into tough plant food, a process that wears the teeth down as fast as they grow. The enamel on the front of the incisors is hardest, so the teeth wear into a chisel shape. Along the side of the jaws are flattened chewing teeth. Rabbits have two pairs of chisel-shaped incisor teeth. They make good use of food by passing it through the gut twice, eating the feces produced the first time.

A porcupine shows its long front incisors.

Breeding

Many rodents produce great numbers of offspring. This is not so much because their litters are large – while some species produce as many as 17 young at a time, a more typical number is 4 – but because the young themselves become able to breed at an early age. In species such as mice, pregnancy lasts just a few weeks and those less than a year old may start to produce litters. In favorable conditions populations build up fast. Rabbits, too, breed fast. With no deaths, the offspring of a single pair could reach 33 million in 3 years.

House mice produce litters several times a year.

Homes

Rodents make their homes in a variety of places. Many climbing species rest in tree holes. Others make a ball nest from sticks, as do some squirrels, or from grasses or bark, as do harvest mice and dormice. Most rodent homes are not elaborate, but wood rats and stick-nest rats build large mounds of twigs to serve as weatherproof houses. These may have several compartments, including a place to store food and a latrine. The most elaborate aboveground structures are made by beavers, which make dams of sticks and mud to control water levels around the 'lodge' containing the family. Many rodents seek refuge down burrows. Some construct complex systems of tunnels with escape holes, nest chambers, storage places and latrines. Prairie dogs build a raised lip of soil around the entrance to keep out floodwater. The longest tunnels are those of mole-rats – more than 400m (440yd) long. The homes of rabbits are similar but less varied.

A beaver's dam and lodge in Alaska

Squirrels sometimes nest in holes in trees.

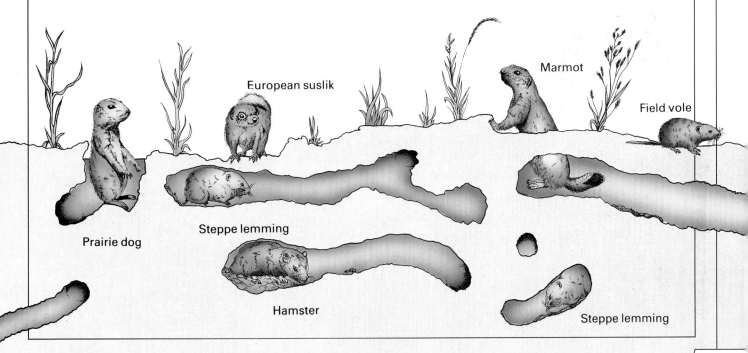

Prairie dog

European suslik

Marmot

Field vole

Steppe lemming

Hamster

Steppe lemming

SATELLITES
SPACE COMMUNICATION

Communications satellites (comsats) are capable of relaying computer data, radio, telephone, and TV signals across the world in seconds.

Today, there are hundreds of comsats in orbit around the Earth. Now there are plans to build a satellite network far bigger than any of the present systems. Made up of 840 satellites, the network would provide communications services even to the remotest parts of the world. The network would provide a global information network, linking computers in homes and offices.

Consisting of 18 satellites 11,000 miles above the Earth, GPS works out the position of the ship or plane by calculating the time the satellite's signal takes to reach the receiver on earth.

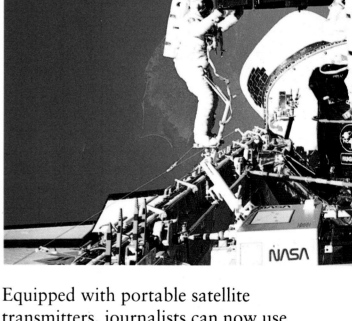

SATELLITES
HOW THEY ARE LAUNCHED

Comsats are launched into orbit by rockets (above) or carried into space by space shuttles. Satellites are equipped with booster engines that guide them into orbit and help to keep them there. Earth stations receive telephone, TV, or radio signals and send them to the satellite. The satellite amplifies the signals and retransmits them to earth using a device called a transponder.

Equipped with portable satellite transmitters, journalists can now use comsats to send live broadcasts home without having to rely on the facilities of local TV stations. Aircraft and shipping use a satellite navigation system called the American Global Positioning System (GPS). Portable receivers, such as the Sony Pyxis, make GPS more widely available.

Equipped with portable satellite transmitters (right), newspaper and TV correspondents no longer have to relay live broadcasts via a local TV station with access to a satellite, neither do they have to rely on telephone links.

The Gulf War of 1991 provided an excellent opportunity to test the portable satellite transmitters in action (below). Reporting a war is difficult as well as dangerous, because normal communications are often disrupted. Portable transmitters could transform the coverage of wars and events in remote places.

SONY

PYXIS

GLOBAL POSITIONING SYSTEM

The Global Positioning System was originally designed for military purposes, but it can also be used by sailors, climbers, explorers, and scientists. The small Sony receiver, called Pyxis (left) after the Pyxis or Compass constellation has opened up GPS to many more people. GPS allows users to know their position anywhere on earth within 30 ft, their speed to within inches per second, and the time to within fractions of a second. With the aid of GPS, scientists in Cumbria, England, have tracked the movements of individual sheep to see why some are still picking up radioactivity from the 1986 Chernobyl disaster.

Astronauts maneuver a satellite into orbit from the space shuttle (above). Other spacecraft can launch satellites but only the space shuttle can be reused. Space shuttles have made it possible to retrieve satellites so they can be serviced in space. Those that need repairs can be brought back to Earth.

SONY

POS   NAV   TRACK   EDIT   SET   MARK

EXTENSION

CLEAR   RECALL   ⇐   ⇒   ENTER

GLOBAL POSITIONING SYSTEM   IPS-360

331

FUN WITH SOUND

Some of the most difficult instruments to play in the orchestra are the reed instruments, for example an oboe or a bassoon. The reed is held to the musician's mouth and blown to make the reed vibrate. An inexperienced player, though, can blow and blow without getting a sound from the reed! Organs, too, create their sounds by blowing through reeds, though in this case, the air is pumped through by bellows. Originally, reeds were made from the reeds that commonly grow by the edge of water.

WHY IT WORKS

When you blow, the tips of the reed vibrate. This sets the air inside the straw vibrating too, which transmits sound waves to our ears. Inside the tube there is a column of air that also vibrates in response to the vibrating of the reed. You can vary the length of the column of air depending on where you place your fingers. The larger the column of air, the slower the vibrations and the lower the pitch of the note becomes.

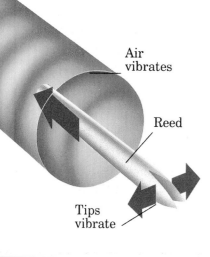

Air vibrates

Reed

Tips vibrate

REED SOUNDS

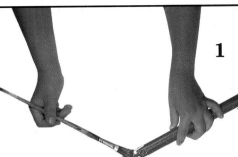

1

3

1. Begin by finding (or making) a tube of cardboard or oak tag. It needs to be about 20 in long and 1 inch in diameter. Paint your tube and leave it to dry.

3. Next, make the reed – you will need a 4 inch length of plastic drinking straw or art straw for this. Squash the straw flat at one end and cut a 0.5 inch piece from the center outward toward the edge. Repeat on the other side.

4. Place a cork or stopper in the end of the tube that has the finger holes. Next, practice blowing the reed. Place the squashed end into your mouth so that the cut parts are just inside your lips. Hold it lightly and blow gently.

4

2. When dry, carefully mark out the position of the finger holes of your reed instrument. Start with the first hole about 6 inches from one end and continue along the length of the tube. Make the hole with a sharp pencil.

2

BRIGHT IDEAS

Make more reeds. Change the length of the reeds and find out whether longer reeds played on their own make notes with a lower pitch. Make a cone of oak tag and place it on the end of your reed. It will act as an amplifier, making the sound louder.

Put the end of a hollow tube into a bowl of water and blow across the top. Move the tube up and down, so changing the amount of air inside it; what do you notice about the pitch of the sound?

You can turn your reed pipe into a flute! Make another, larger hole 4 in from the end. Make the first finger hole, 2 in from this, larger too. Now hold the pipe sideways underneath your mouth and blow across the first hole to create a flutelike sound.

5. If at first your reed makes no sound, carefully open out the cut flaps so that they are just a millimeter or two apart. Try again. By making very fine adjustments to this gap, your reed will eventually work. When it does, put the end of the reed into the tube and change notes by covering different holes.

Hi-Tech SPOOKS

Modern science is developing at a breathtaking speed. New technology enables us to explore and understand more about our world and our universe. Scientific techniques, like radiocarbon dating, help historians and archaeologists to unravel the mysteries of the past. Space laboratories, radiotelescopes, and space probes are constantly investigating the mysteries of the skies at close quarters. Satellites give scientists information about the atmosphere and the weather. As technology advances, we may discover new explanations for phenomena that we now consider supernatural.

Are the mind and the brain the same? Although many people believe that our thoughts and feelings can be explained scientifically, there do seem to be differences between the mind and the brain. When we dream, for example, our minds are not linked to our bodies and brains as closely as when we are awake.

PROBING THE MIND

Some scientists believe that our thoughts are due to electrical and chemical charges in the brain, which they can monitor with an electroencephalograph (EEG) machine. This shows changes in brain activity at various times.

ALIEN CROP RAIDERS?

In the 1980s, strange circles began to appear in cornfields all over England. They were almost perfectly circular and the crops had been flattened without harm to the stalks. People said they were made by aliens or caused by the weather. High-tech gadgets have been used in attempts to recreate such circles, but without success.

PHOTOGRAPHING THE BEAST

Infrared film has been used in the tracking of several ferocious creatures which have terrorized sheep on British moors since the 1980s. Some witnesses describe huge black dogs. Others say there must be a new breed of wild cat or that big cats have escaped from wildlife parks. There are still many different theories about the strange beasts' identities.

LIVING COLORS

In 1939, the Soviet scientists Semyon and Valentina Kirlian invented a method of photography which showed an aura, or halo, around living objects. They said that live cells give off colored electrical energy which alters according to mood, but many scientists dismiss their theory.

SCANNING THE SKIES

Scientists use radiotelescopes to search for alien messages. The Parkes radiotelescope (right), in Australia, monitors radio waves from space to check for signals which could be messages. In 1995, U.S. scientists set up Project BETA, to scan the nearest 1,000 stars for possible life.

The modern miracles

Hi-tech equipment has revealed the truth of the Turin Shroud (below). Believed for centuries to be the death wrappings of Christ, the shroud is in fact a medieval fake. But its mystery continues to puzzle scientists – no one is sure how the startling image of Christ was produced.

In 1995, thousands of people reported seeing Hindu statues drinking milk. Some said this was a miracle, but others said that the statues were made of porous stone or full of absorbent material.

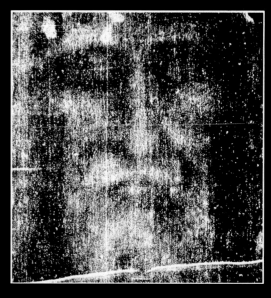

INTO SPACE

Space probes are constantly exploring the mysteries of the skies. In 1986, Giotto (below) flew through Halley's Comet, seen for centuries as a bad omen. Pioneer 10 and 11 carry greetings to any life-forms they may encounter in space.

AVALANCHES

When an avalanche strikes, more than 130 million cubic yards of snow and ice blast down a mountainside. As the ice mass falls, it collects large amounts of debris such as rocks and tree stumps on its way. In a populated mountain area, whole villages are crushed, hundreds of people and animals are buried alive, power and water supplies are cut off, and roads and railroad lines disappear – all in a matter of minutes.

The world's greatest single avalanche disaster occurred in 1962 in Peru. More than 3,500 people died and eight villages and towns were destroyed in just 7 minutes. When the avalanche finally came to rest, after a journey of almost 10 miles, the pile of snow and ice was over 60 feet deep.

Trapped under the hard, packed snow, an avalanche victim can barely move and is unlikely to survive for more than a couple of hours. Victims die from the cold, from a lack of oxygen, or from the injuries that occurred when they were first struck. Only about 5 percent of all avalanche victims are rescued alive.

6:18 p.m.
The deadly torrent of ice and rocks misses Yungay, but crushes the village of Ranrahirca, killing 2,700 people.

◄ **In the mountain village shown left, a path has been cut through the wall of snow and debris caused by a recent avalanche.**

Melting snow plunges down from the north-facing summit of the 22,205 feet high Nevado Huascarán mountain.

6:13 p.m.
The falling snow loosens millions of tons of ice from Glacier 511.

6:15 p.m.
The avalanche flattens Yanamachico and nearby villages, leaving 800 dead and only 8 survivors.

The 1962 avalanche disaster in Peru occurred when a huge chunk of ice and snow broke off the country's tallest mountain, Nevado Huascarán. The avalanche roared downhill at speeds of up to 60 mph, demolishing nearby villages with a deluge of mud and ice over 80 ft thick.

337

ALI BABA AND THE FORTY THIEVES

One day, Ali Baba came across forty thieves in the desert (*left*). Following them, he watched them open a cave by saying: "Open, Sesame!" After they had left, Ali entered the cave, and found it full of treasure. He went home a rich man.

Ali's brother Cassim was not as lucky. He forgot the password, became trapped in the cave, and was cut to pieces by the bandits! Realizing that Ali knew their password, the thieves now decided to kill him, too.

But Ali's servant, Morgiana, was more than a match for them. When they sneaked into Ali's house hidden in jars (*right*), she killed them with boiling oil!

Written in Arabic c.1500, this fine bandit story first appeared in Europe in the early 1700s in a French translation by Antoine Galland.

Aladdin meets the genie of the lamp.

ALI BABA AND THE FORTY THIEVES was translated as part of a collection of Arab, Indian, and Persian stories known as *The Thousand and One Nights, or Arabian Nights' Entertainments*. In fact, the Ali Baba tale was not part of the original Arabic work, though the more famous Aladdin (*above*) and Voyages of Sindbad stories were.

All the original stories are supposed to have been told by Scheherazade to her bloodthirsty husband, to stop him from killing her. She always left her tale unfinished, so he would have to let her live another night to hear the ending.

DESERT DANGER!

For thousands of years, Arabia was notorious for its banditry. There were no proper roads, and travelers ventured into the barren interior at their own risk. Because trade was limited largely to the coastal regions and the harsh climate made agriculture almost impossible, many Arabs had to steal to survive. Gangs of bandits would mount camels, and swoop down on unsuspecting merchants or pilgrims, and ride off into the desert again.

SAFER TIMES

The expansion of the Ottoman Empire into Arabia in the mid-1500s ended the rule of the nomadic tribes, and brought a degree of law and order to the western part of the peninsula. But it was only with the formation of the kingdom of Saudi Arabia in the 20th century that Arabia finally lost its reputation as the land of the bandit.

The Ship of the Desert
Bandits sometimes rode camels (above) only until they got close to their victims, then changed to ponies for their speed and agility.

Kali, the Hindu goddess of destruction.

THE THUGS

The original Thugs (*right*) were not really bandits, although to their victims they certainly behaved like them! They were a strange Hindu sect devoted to Kali (*above*). They showed their devotion by waylaying travelers, strangling them, and chopping them up.

The Thugs carried out murders (called *Thuggee*) following a strict code; no women, blind people, or carpenters could be killed. The group was disbanded in the 1830s.

FISH OF SHORES & REEFS

The shallow waters along the seashore provide a wide range of fish habitats, from tidal mudflats to sandbanks and rocky coasts. In tropical areas, coral reefs can support a great variety of life. Nutrients are plentiful, and the bright sun provides lots of light, so many seaweeds and other plants can grow. These plants are the basic food for all the forms of animal life, including myriad worms, crabs, starfish and shellfish, which thrive in the warm, shallow waters. They, in turn, provide food for a dazzling array of fish. In contrast, the shoreline of a wide beach is much emptier of fish.

Nooks and crannies
The blenny and rock goby use rocks and boulders to shelter from predators and ambush prey. The clingfish can stick to overhanging rocks with its suckerlike fins.

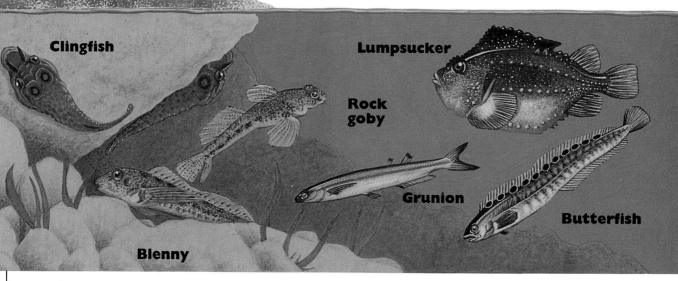

Clingfish

Lumpsucker

Rock goby

Grunion

Butterfish

Blenny

Tropical paradise
Many people dream of "getting away from it all" on a deserted tropical island. In 1719 the English writer Daniel Defoe based his adventure story *Robinson Crusoe* on the experiences of a real sailor named Alexander Selkirk. The book tells of a lonely castaway struggling to survive on a small island, beset by lack of food, water and shelter, and plagued by insect pests, pirates and islanders. Not such a paradise?

Traditional fishing
Around the world's coastlines, people use various traditional fishing methods to catch what they need from the sea. The Inuit people of northern North America fish from the shore or along coastal rivers, using nets, and spears, harpoons and hooks carved from natural materials such as walrus tusks or whalebone. However, these traditional ways of life are becoming ever more difficult to preserve.

The perils of the tide

Shores and reefs can be treacherous places for fish, because of the tides. As the tide falls, it can leave fish marooned in pools. The butterfish is named from its tough, slippery, slimy skin. This enables it to wriggle from under rolling pebbles, and prevents it from drying out as it flaps over the rocks from one pool to another. Shore fish such as gobies and blennies can withstand great variations in temperature and salinity (salt concentration), as well as buffeting by waves and rolling boulders.

Partners in life

Certain fish team up with quite different animals, in relationships beneficial to both. Clownfish swim among the stinging tentacles of anemones. Their bodies are covered in mucus that provides a barrier to the stings. The clownfish are safe from attack while the anemone consumes the food they drop. This partnership is called symbiosis.

Porcupinefish

Blue-banded Angelfish

Clownfish

Butterflyfish

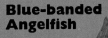

Regal tang

Coral Trout

Warm and shallow

Coral reefs are rich environments for fish and other sea life, but they form only in certain places around the world. The water must be very clean, and warm – preferably around 75°F all year – with a salt concentration of between 25 and 40 parts per thousand. The basis of the reef is the coral polyp, a tiny animal like a miniature jellyfish. Polyps grow in their millions and build hard, chalky cup-shaped skeletons around their bodies, for protection. As they die, more polyps grow on top. Over hundreds of years, billions of coral skeletons accumulate, and the rocky reef grows. The corals are food for hundreds of fish.

THE TANK

The battle tank is the main weapon of modern land combat. Its job is to disable or destroy enemy tanks. Every tank is also therefore itself the target of another tank. It may also be attacked by a range of lethal weapons carried by soldiers and aircraft. To survive so that it can do the job it was designed for, it must be able to protect itself from these attacks.

The design of every tank is a combination of three important factors – mobility, protection and firepower. A powerful engine driving a pair of metal tracks gives it mobility. It is protected by

hull. The hull must be large enough to hold the engine, fuel, weapon systems, ammunition and the tank's electronic systems, with enough space left over for the tank's crew of three or four.

A tank's electronic systems include fire control and radio communications. Fire control is a computerized system that helps the gunner to aim the main gun accurately. The tank may also be equipped with specialized instruments

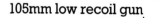

105mm low recoil gun

Wing mirror

a thick covering of heavy armor plate. Firepower may be provided by any of a variety of weapons, but by far the most important is the tank's main gun. This is mounted in a rotating compartment called a turret.

Some tanks are designed for very high speed and mobility. To save weight, they may carry less armor. Others are designed for maximum firepower and protection. The extra weight they have to carry reduces their mobility. This is why tanks come in many different shapes and sizes. Tank designers balance the three basic requirements in different ways.

The structure of the tank has two main components, the turret and the body, or

Engine dials

Driver's controls

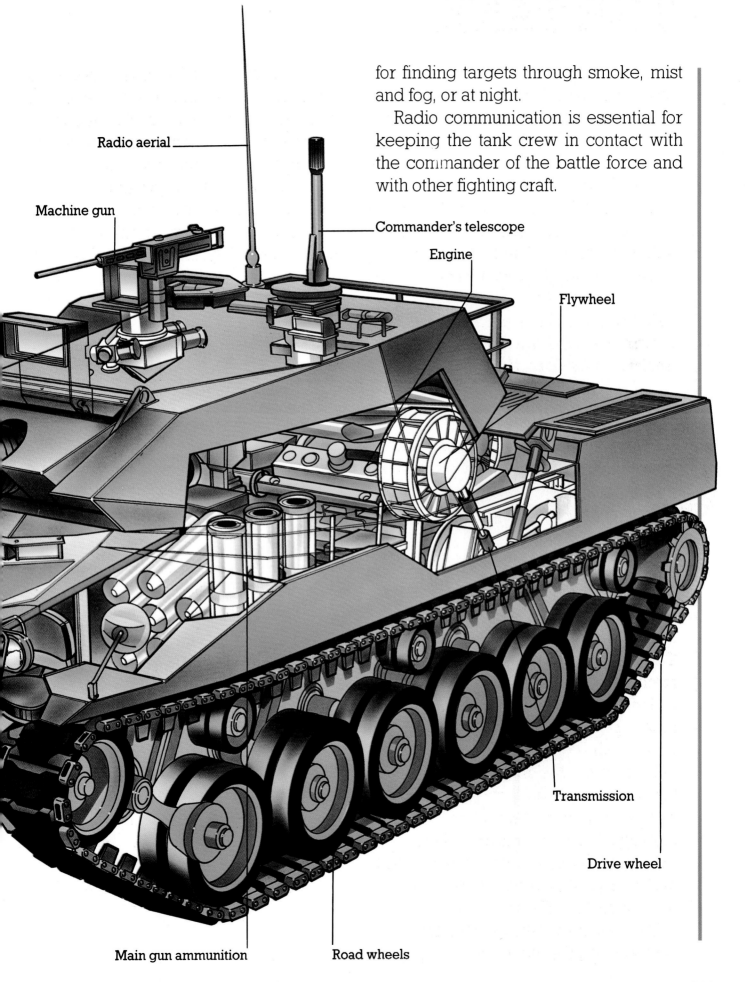

Radio aerial

Machine gun

for finding targets through smoke, mist and fog, or at night.

Radio communication is essential for keeping the tank crew in contact with the commander of the battle force and with other fighting craft.

Commander's telescope

Engine

Flywheel

Transmission

Drive wheel

Main gun ammunition

Road wheels

PAINTING SELF-PORTRAITS

Painters paint self-portraits for all kinds of reasons, but the most obvious has to be that your own face is always there when you want it. Have a good look in the mirror and see what shape yours is. Ask yourself what kind of person you are and how you can show this in a painting. Are you cheerful or sad? Do you shout a lot or do you keep things bottled up? Do you like to do things quickly, or do you take your time? Using some of the ideas from the previous projects, try to combine careful observation and the expression of feeling in a portrait of yourself.

Getting set up

Begin by getting comfortable. Place your paper or board on an easel or rest it against a wall or the back of a chair. Arrange yourself in such a way that you can look straight from the mirror to your painting without turning your head too much.

Make a pencil sketch as you did earlier, taking care to establish the particular proportions of your face. Mix your colors, and change them around until you are satisfied that they represent you.

Showing how you feel

Do several pictures of yourself in different moods and change the colors and the way you put on the paint accordingly. After the first painting, you may want to dispense with the mirror and paint your "inner self" from imagination.

△ *"These three portraits use color to convey mood. This boy in shades of pink looks gentle and thoughtful."*

Features and expressions

Here are examples of the same face with three very different expressions, looking in turn angry, frightened and perplexed. These emotions are conveyed chiefly through the shape of the mouth and eyes. Notice, however, that the eyebrows, hair, even the nose and ears can also express emotion. Lines and shapes turning upward look cheerful and full of life; turning down they look sad or fierce. To convey perplexity the lines are undecided and may turn in both directions.

△ *"I have tried to convey the scattiness and good humor of this boy through the use of bright colors and jagged strokes."*

△ *"My third sitter seemed anxious and sad. I chose gloomy colors and applied them with nervous, scratchy strokes."*

WHAT ARE ELEMENTS?

Everything in the world is made up of elements. An element is a simple chemical substance which itself is made of tiny particles called atoms. Diamonds (right) are made from the element, carbon. There are 105 elements known to man. Some, like iron or copper, were used in ancient times, while others have been made by modern scientists. Many elements can be combined to make new substances – copper and tin can be melted together to make an alloy (mixture) called bronze. The periodic table arranges all the known elements in a special way.

PERIODIC TABLE

1. Each square contains the symbol for a different element. The symbol comes from the common name or Latin name of the element; C stands for carbon and Al for aluminum. The Latin for iron is ferrum, so the symbol is Fe.

H								
Li	Be							
Na	Mg							
K	Ca	SC	Ti	V	Cr	Mn	Fe	Co
Rb	Sr	Y	Zr	Nb	Mo	Tc	Ru	Rh
Cs	Ba	La	Hf	Ta	W	Re	Os	Ir
Fr	Ra	Ac						

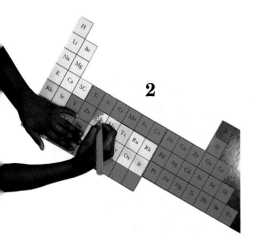

2

3. Now you can begin to search for some things which contain common elements in your own home or school. On the periodic table below, you can see some Na which stands for sodium (in salt), Mg – magnesium (in powdered milk of magnesia), Cr – chromium (used to coat car bumpers and keys), Fe – iron, Cu – copper, Zn – zinc (in a battery), Ag – silver, Sn – tin, S – sulphur (in matches), Pb – lead, Al – aluminum and Au – gold.

3

2. To construct your own periodic table you need to copy the grid below carefully. The table is always set out just as you can see it here and the position of the boxes may not be changed. To find out what all the symbols mean you could visit a library and look for more information.

					He
B	C	N	O	F	Ne
Al	Si	P	S	Cl	Ar

Ni	Cu	Z	Ga	Ge	As	Se	Br	Kr
Pd	Ag	Cd	In	Sn	Sb	Te	I	Xe
Pt	Au	Hg	Ti	Pb	Bi	Po	At	Rn

Now try to find some... C – carbon (soot, pencil lead, diamonds and charcoal are all forms of carbon), Hg – mercury (the silver stuff in thermometers), Pt – platinum (a metal used in jewelry making) and Cl – chlorine (added to drinking water to kill bacteria).

WHAT IF THE EARTH STOOD STILL?

If it were daytime, the first thing you might notice was that the Sun stopped moving across the sky. You'd wait for evening – but it would never come. It'd be daylight forever! The Earth spins around like a gigantic top on an imaginary line called its axis, that goes through the North and South Poles. It makes one complete turn every 24 hours, giving us the cycle of day and night. As your area of the surface turns, the Sun appears to move across the sky in daytime, and the stars and Moon move across at nighttime.

Direction of Earth's spin

Axis of spin

A still Earth would heat up unbearably on the daytime side.

Daytime on the side facing the Sun

On the shady side, it would be dark, cold, and soon freeze over.

A hard day's night!

If we had endless daytime, the Sun would shine without a break and you might get sunburned. You would also have to go to sleep in bright daylight. People on the other side of the Earth would be in constant cold and darkness. They would become pale and sick.

No more seasons in the Sun?

Besides spinning like a top, the Earth also goes around the Sun in a long, curved path called its *orbit*. One orbit takes one year. The Earth's spinning axis is tilted, so some parts of its surface are closer to the Sun during certain times in the orbit. On these closer parts it is warmer – and summer. If the Earth stopped orbiting and stood still, the seasons would cease, too. It would be endless summer in some areas, and everlasting winter in others!

Summer in south

Sun

Spring in north

Fall in north

Summer in north and winter in south

Winter in north

Nighttime on the side away from the Sun

How might animals react?

They'd get very confused! Their internal "body clocks" need the pattern of night and day to stay accurate. With no day or night, they wouldn't know when to eat or sleep. With no seasons, they wouldn't know if they should begin a winter's sleep (hibernation) or set off for a long fall or spring journey (migration).

What would happen to clocks and calendars?

Clocks would keep ticking, and we might continue to use them to tell time. But this would be less useful. We could no longer say things like "It gets dark at 8 o'clock." The calendar would be less useful, too. Without seasons, every month would have the same weather and you would soon get very bored!

The best place to live

A still Earth would have a very narrow strip on each side, one in constant dawn, and the other in continuous dusk. These areas would not get too bright and hot or too dark and cold. They'd be the best places to live.

TYPES OF DINOSAURS

Dinosaurs are probably the best-known form of prehistoric life. They ruled the Earth from the Late Triassic until the end of the Cretaceous, a total of 165 million years. Although we usually think of dinosaurs as one group (or order) of animal, two distinct types existed. The first were the saurischian, or lizard-hipped dinosaurs. Saurischian dinosaurs included the theropods (meat-eaters) and the giant sauropods (plant-eaters). The second group were the ornithischians, or bird-hipped dinosaurs. Most plant-eating dinosaurs were ornithischians.

The first dinosaurs
In 1842, Sir Richard Owen recognized that some large bones found years before were different from living reptiles and he grouped them together as the "Dinosauria." The first creature to be described was *Megalosaurus*, a large carnivorous dinosaur found in the Jurassic rocks of the Cotswolds in England. Two others were herbivores, and of Cretaceous age. *Hylaeosaurus* was an armored dinosaur.

The Jurassic world
By the Jurassic, dinosaurs ruled the Earth. During the early Jurassic, the most common dinosaurs were the prosauropods, ancestors of the sauropods (reptile feet); small ornithischians, for example, the fabrosaurs; and the carnivorous *Megalosaurus*. By the Middle Jurassic, the giant sauropods like *Cetiosaurus* and *Brachiosaurus* came into their own. Other herbivores included stegosaurs (plated reptiles), and a selection of ornithopods (bird feet) such as the hypsilophodonts. These animals were hunted by *Megalosaurus* and *Ornithomimius*.

Jurassic

The Triassic world
The Triassic world was dominated by many groups of large vertebrates including rhynchosaurs and thecodontians. Dinosaurs evolved from the thecodontians, and first appeared in great numbers during the Late Triassic.

Masrocnemus

Rhynchosaur

Triassic

Dinostars

One of the most successful dinosaur films is Steven Spielberg's *Jurassic Park* (right), based on the book of the same name by Michael Crichton. Jurassic Park is a dinosaur theme park created by a businessman. But things go horribly wrong! The dinosaurs were brought to life for the movie by computer graphics and model animation. It's probably the most realistic dinosaur film ever made.

Cretaceous

We know from fossils that many dinosaurs laid eggs. Some fossil eggs (below) have been found containing babies.

Cretaceous world

At the end of the Cretaceous, the reign of the dinosaurs ended. This may have been caused by a meteorite hitting the Earth. Evidence for this comes from the iridium layer (marked by the white circle below) which is a rare element found at the Cretaceous-Tertiary boundary. Other theories suggest dinosaurs died out due to a change in climate.

Hot-blooded or not?

Dinosaurs used to be thought of as large, slow, stupid reptiles. But today, even though scientists think they led more active lives, the question of their metabolism (how their bodies produced heat) has still not been decided. Some people think that dinosaurs were warm-blooded, like mammals, generating their own body heat without having to use the sun's rays to warm them up. However, most scientists agree that the large size of their bodies probably meant that a dinosaur stayed warm, even though it could not produce heat internally. This meant they could act in an almost "warm-blooded" manner.

Iridium layer

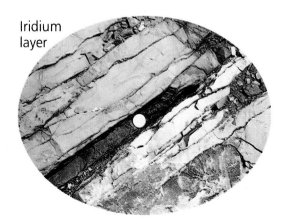

PIRATES OF THE MEDITERRANEAN

In the Mediterranean, piracy was as old as civilization itself. However, the most famous age of piracy began with the Muslim conquest of North Africa in 709 A.D. The Mediterranean became a frontier between Christians and Muslims, and shipping from either side became a fair target. Christian privateers operated out of Marseilles, Malta, and Sicily. Their Muslim counterparts, known as corsairs, were based along what we call the Barbary Coast – the seaboard of Algiers, Tunis, and Tripoli. Unlike Caribbean pirates, the corsairs used galleys, and the most prized loot was not gold, but people. Captives were held for ransom, sold as slaves, or put to work as oarsmen.

The Bagnio (right)
The bagnio was the prison complex where the corsairs held their captives. It was like an enclosed town, with its own shops and taverns.

Prisoners faced a lifetime of hard labor unless they bribed a guard to let them work in the prison shops.

CAESAR AND THE PIRATES

Even the great Roman leader Julius Caesar (*left*) was once captured by pirates. Traveling slowly by boat to Rhodes in 78 B.C., he was seized and taken prisoner. Although well treated, he promised that once ransomed he would return and take his revenge.

In due course his ransom was paid and he was released. A few weeks later he was back with four ships and 500 men. The pirates who were not killed in his attack were crucified.

Bombardment of Algiers
When the Napoleonic Wars ended in 1815, the British and Dutch bombarded Algiers to end the threat from the Barbary Coast forever. As a result, 3,000 prisoners were freed.

Prisoners of the Corsairs
Once taken prisoner by the corsairs, European captives were chained and taken to the bagnio. If they were lucky, perhaps because their native country had a treaty with the corsairs, they would be ransomed. If not, they would either work for the master of the bagnio or be sold as slaves. An alternative was to adopt the Muslim religion, or "turn Turk." This might bring some freedom, but it led to problems if ever they met Christians.

THE CAMERA

A camera is a device designed specially to record images on light-sensitive film. There are many different types of camera, but they all work in much the same way. The Single-Lens Reflex, or SLR, camera shown here is an example of one of the most popular types.

A camera is basically a lightproof box. A lens is fixed to one side and film is positioned inside the box opposite the lens. Light is prevented from entering the box by a shutter, a type of blind, behind the lens. When closed, the shutter stops light passing through a hole, the aperture, in the camera body. Light entering the lens of an SLR is reflected upward by a mirror. At the top of this camera, a specially shaped block of glass called a penta-prism reflects the light out through the viewfinder. Other types of cameras have separate viewfinder and shutter-lens systems.

When a camera user wishes to take a photograph, or "shot," almost the exact image that will be recorded on the film can be seen in the viewfinder. At the right moment, the shutter is opened by pressing a button known as the shutter release. If the camera is an SLR, the mirror flips up out of the way, allowing the light to pass through the lens and reach the film. The lens bends the rays of light so that they produce a sharp image on the film. The amount the light rays have to be bent, or refracted, depends on how far away the objects are from the camera. Refraction is adjusted by rotating the focusing ring on the lens. Some cameras use a fixed-focus lens that is suitable for photo-

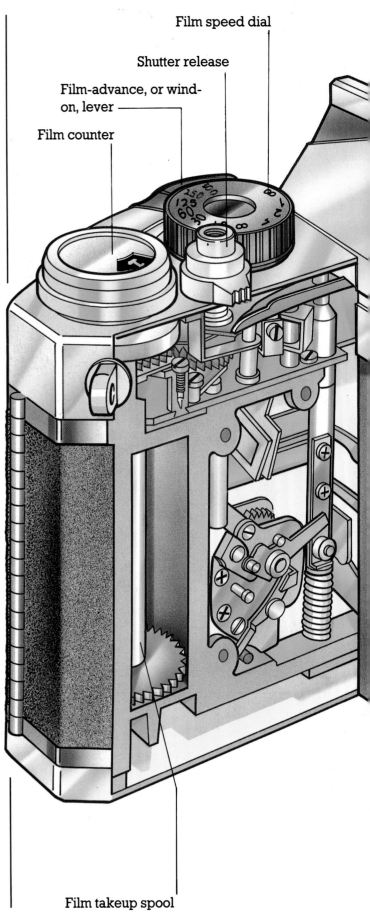

Film speed dial

Shutter release

Film-advance, or wind-on, lever

Film counter

Film takeup spool

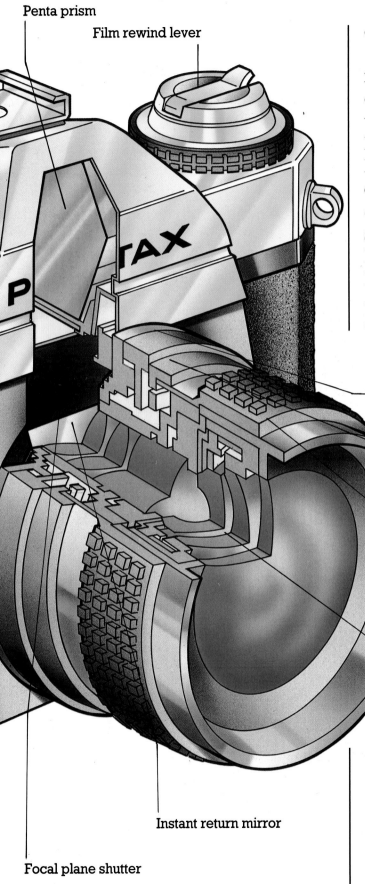

Penta prism

Film rewind lever

Aperture ring

Depth of field scale

Focusing ring

Lenses

Instant return mirror

Focal plane shutter

graphing both near and distant objects.

The amount of light falling on the film must be controlled carefully. This is done in two ways. The hole in the front of the lens, the aperture, can be made larger or smaller to vary the amount of light entering the camera. Or the length of time the shutter stays open can be controlled by changing the shutter speed. Most modern cameras have built-in light meters which measure the brightness of the scene in front of the camera. They use this to set the aperture and shutter speed automatically.

Some types of film are more sensitive to light than others. They need less light to produce a photograph. When setting the aperture and shutter speed to expose the film to the correct amount of light, the film sensitivity, or film speed, must be taken into account. High-speed film is the more sensitive.

WHAT ARE PLAGUES?

A plague is an invasion by large numbers of animals or insects. The animals often carry disease, and they eat enormous quantities of growing crops and stored grain. This can bring about a severe famine.

Some of the most destructive plagues consist of swarms of locusts. A single swarm may contain up to 50 billion insects.

Plagues of locusts have threatened several African countries in recent years. Rains in 1988 helped to relieve the drought. However, when combined with warmer weather, they provided ideal conditions for the locusts to breed. As a result, swarms of migratory locusts swept across North and Central Africa, destroying the much-needed harvest there.

Locusts

▲ Locusts can strip bare a whole field of maize in less than one hour.
▼ By June 1988, locusts were reported in every African country in a belt, stretching from Cape Verde in the west to the Sudan in the east.

▶ Locusts fly thousands of miles in search of food. Locust invasions, such as the one in Dakar, Senegal, shown right, have plagued farmers throughout the world since ancient times. Locusts will eat any kind of vegetation, and can consume more than their own body weight of food in just one day.

▼◀ A locust is a type of adult grasshopper with wings. Its body is about 3 inches long. The female locust can produce hundreds of eggs in a single breeding season. As locusts become crowded and restless, they begin to migrate in swarms to other areas. The swarms can be so large, they block out the sunlight.

Kangaroos

Animal plagues can also involve large mammals such as kangaroos and goats. More than 3 million kangaroos are killed in Australia each year. Australian farmers consider that some of the 50 different kinds of kangaroo are pests. They feed and drink in the same areas as the farmers' sheep and cattle.

Controlling the kangaroo population has proved difficult as they cannot easily be contained by fencing.

UNDERSTANDING PERSPECTIVE

Perspective, which means "looking through," is a way of creating the illusion of three-dimensional space on the flat surface of a picture. The kind of perspective that is usually most familiar is based on the idea that the painting on the wall is like a window through which we can see the real world.

Getting angles right
Everyone knows how difficult it can sometimes be to get a particular angle of a building or table exactly right, so that it looks as if it were moving toward or away from us. People who find this skill difficult to master often give up the idea of being good at art before they have discovered all the

Background

Middle ground

Foreground

other aspects of painting that are exciting and enjoyable.

Creating distance

There are at least four different ways of showing that one thing is behind or in front of another. Many pictures combine several or all four, though some use none at all.

◁ *"The sky in my picture opposite shows that a strong blue can appear to be in front of a paler, thinner blue as it fades toward the horizon. I used the brightest colors in the foreground and middle distance. I applied the paint thickly and more vigorously in those areas too."*

For the painter perhaps the most appropriate way of portraying distance is through color. As a rule, dark and dull colors tend to go back, or recede, in space. Light and bright ones tend to come forward. Think of how the rays of a yellow sun reach out from a background of blue sky.

The strongest contrasts in tone should be in the foreground. Colors in a landscape seem to get bluer and mistier the further away they are, and the same effect can be achieved in painting. Recession can also be emphasized by using thinner paint in the middle and background. Paint a landscape and test out these theories.

A sense of space

The diagrams below illustrate some of the other ways of showing perspective. The first is an example of "linear" or line perspective. Lines that would in fact run parallel in the real world, like the roadsides in the diagram, appear to meet at a point on the horizon called the "vanishing point."

The second diagram shows an example of overlapping. The hill that blocks out part of another hill must be in front of it; the human figure blocks them all out and so must be the nearest thing to you. In the third diagram the darker, stronger and "speedier" lines and tones in the foreground appear to be in front of the softer, "slower" lines.

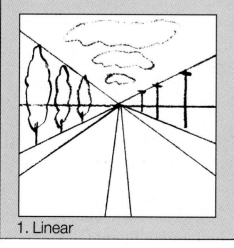

1. Linear

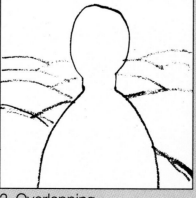

2. Overlapping

3. Tonal

WHAT IF AIRCRAFT DIDN'T HAVE WINGS?

Most of them would speed along the runway... and crash at the end, without taking off. Wings make a plane rise into the air, by providing lift. The wing shape also tells you how fast a plane goes. Slower planes, especially gliders, have very long, thin wings that stick out sideways. These wings have a very narrow chord (the distance from the front of the wing – leading edge – to the rear of the wing – trailing edge). This is the same design as the wings of gliding birds, like the albatross. Faster planes have swept-back wings, usually with a bigger chord, like fast hunting birds such as hawks.

An uplifting experience

Some aircraft don't get their lift from wings. It comes from a jet engine or propeller facing straight down, which pushes the aircraft into the air. A strange test craft from the 1950s, called the "Flying Bedstead," did this. So does the Harrier Jump Jet, which can take off straight up, and hover in mid-air. Hovercraft use lifting fans, like propellers facing downward, to create a cushion of air.

What if a plane flew upside down?

First, how does a wing work? Seen end-on, a wing has a special shape, known as the airfoil section. It is more curved on top than below. As the plane flies, air going over the wing has farther to travel than air beneath. This means the air over the top moves faster, which produces low pressure, so the wing is pushed upward – a force known as *lift* – which raises the plane. If a plane flew upside down, the wing would not give any lift. To overcome this, the plane tilts its nose up at a steep angle. Air hitting the wing then pushes it up, keeping the plane in the air.

Air moves faster

Lift

Wing

Air moves slower

Can planes fly in space?

A few can, like the X-15 rocket planes of the 1960s and the space shuttles of today. First, they need engine power to blast up there. The X-15 was carried up on a converted B-52 bomber, while today the shuttle uses massive rocket boosters. Once in space, there's no air (or anything else), so wings can't work by providing lift. The power for all maneuvers in space comes from small rocket thrusters.

How do spy planes fly so high?

Spy planes, such as the U-2 and the Blackbird, need to fly high, at 100,000 ft (30,000 m) or higher, so they are beyond detection by enemy planes or radar. However, as air is very thin at such heights, they need very special wing designs, with an extra-curved top surface, to give the greatest possible lift. With the arrival of spy satellites, the use of spy planes declined, until recently. A new generation of pilotless, remote-control spy planes, such as DarkStar, has arrived.

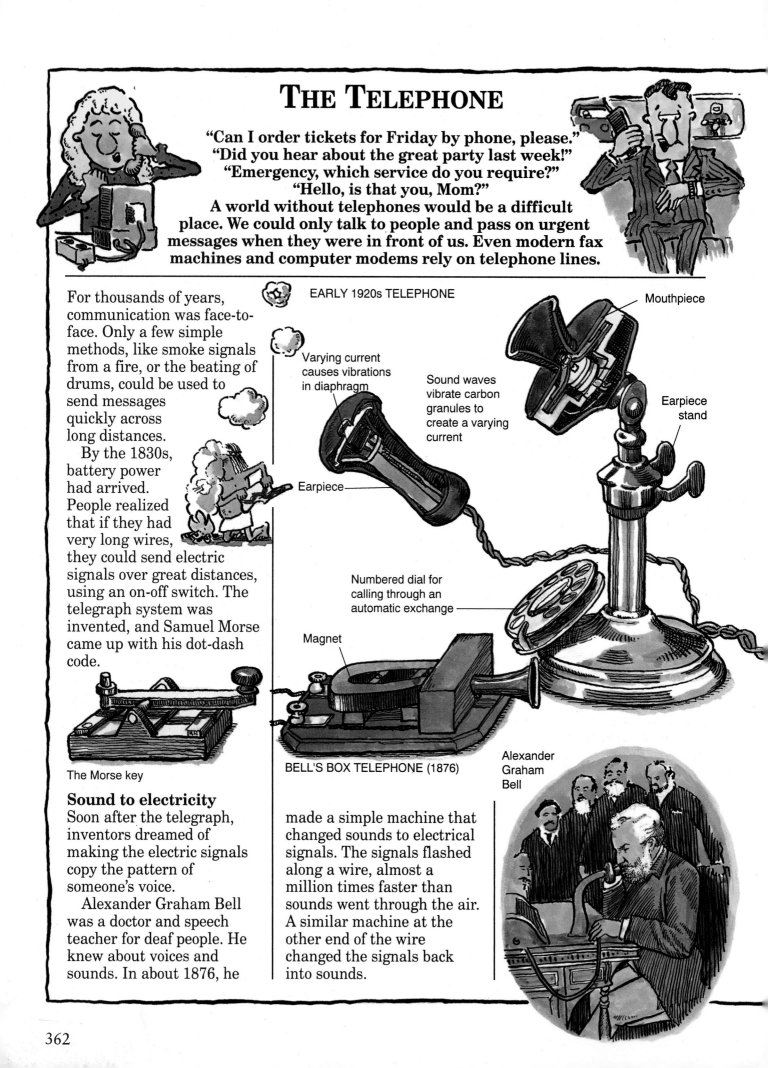

THE TELEPHONE

"Can I order tickets for Friday by phone, please."
"Did you hear about the great party last week!"
"Emergency, which service do you require?"
"Hello, is that you, Mom?"
A world without telephones would be a difficult place. We could only talk to people and pass on urgent messages when they were in front of us. Even modern fax machines and computer modems rely on telephone lines.

For thousands of years, communication was face-to-face. Only a few simple methods, like smoke signals from a fire, or the beating of drums, could be used to send messages quickly across long distances.

By the 1830s, battery power had arrived. People realized that if they had very long wires, they could send electric signals over great distances, using an on-off switch. The telegraph system was invented, and Samuel Morse came up with his dot-dash code.

The Morse key

EARLY 1920s TELEPHONE

Varying current causes vibrations in diaphragm

Sound waves vibrate carbon granules to create a varying current

Mouthpiece

Earpiece stand

Earpiece

Numbered dial for calling through an automatic exchange

Magnet

BELL'S BOX TELEPHONE (1876)

Alexander Graham Bell

Sound to electricity

Soon after the telegraph, inventors dreamed of making the electric signals copy the pattern of someone's voice.

Alexander Graham Bell was a doctor and speech teacher for deaf people. He knew about voices and sounds. In about 1876, he made a simple machine that changed sounds to electrical signals. The signals flashed along a wire, almost a million times faster than sounds went through the air. A similar machine at the other end of the wire changed the signals back into sounds.

THE TELEPHONE

Coast-to-coast phones

In 1877, Bell showed that his machine could send signals almost 20 miles, from Boston to Salem, Massachusets. Within a few years, telephones were being installed in important buildings and in the homes of rich people.

At first, when you called someone, all the connections were made by hand. Operators worked switches and plugs in the local exchange. The first automatic switches arrived in 1892. By 1915, Americans could phone coast-to-coast. Today, many phone systems use satellite links.

All the same signals

There are probably almost one billion phones in the world. We use them for shopping, passing on messages, doing business, finding out information (such as the sports scores), and simply chatting.

When you talk into a telephone, it converts your voice to electrical signals. The phone lines can carry any similar type of small signals. So they can pass on signals from computers, teletypes, radios, televisions, fax machines and many other gadgets.

How the telephone works

A telephone has two main parts. These are called the mouthpiece and the earpiece.

In the mouthpiece, sounds make a flat piece of metal vibrate. This squashes and stretches tiny pieces of carbon in a container. Electricity goes through carbon pieces more easily when they are squashed, and less when they are stretched. So sounds are converted to very fast-changing electrical pulses or signals.

The signals go along the wire to the earpiece of the other telephone. They pass through a coil of wire, called an electromagnet. The magnetism produced pulls on a nearby sheet of metal. The strength of the magnetism varies with the fast-changing signals, so the metal moves back and forth very quickly. This makes the sound waves that you hear.

MODERN TELEPHONE

Earpiece

Mouthpiece

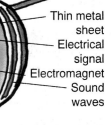

- Thin metal sheet
- Electrical signal
- Electromagnet
- Sound waves

Electrical signal

Carbon granules

Soundwaves

Whoops, a bit of trouble

- Alexander Graham Bell first spoke on the phone by accident. A test system was set up in his workroom, when he spilled some acid. He called to his assistant, Thomas Watson, "Mr Watson, come here, I want you!" In the next room, Watson heard the words over the test system. The first phone call was a plea for help!

- Many phones now have push buttons instead of a circular dial. But people still say, "Dial this number."
- Most phones have a bleeper or buzzer instead of a bell. Yet people still say, "Give me a ring."

INDEX

INDEX

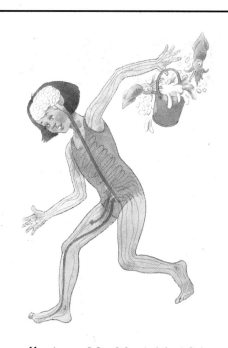

INDEX